Private Sector and Development

Annual World Bank Conference
on Development Economics—Global
2008

Private Sector and Development

Edited by
**Justin Yifu Lin and
Boris Pleskovic**

THE WORLD BANK
Washington, D.C.

ISBN: 978-0-8213-7125-1
eISBN: 978-0-8213-7126-8
DOI: 10.1596/978-0-8213-7125-1
ISSN: 1813-9477

Cataloging-in-Publication data for this title is available from the Library of Congress.

Contents

ABOUT THIS BOOK   vii

INTRODUCTION   1
Justin Yifu Lin and Boris Pleskovic

OPENING SPEECH   9
Janez Janša

OPENING SPEECH   15
Andrej Bajuk

OPENING SPEECH   17
François Bourguignon

KEYNOTE ADDRESS   19
Tarun Das

KEYNOTE ADDRESS
Privatization in Development: Some Lessons from Experience   25
François Bourguignon and Claudia Sepúlveda

KEYNOTE ADDRESS   47
Janez Potočnik

KEYNOTE ADDRESS
Informality, Productivity, and Growth in Mexico   53
Santiago Levy

KEYNOTE ADDRESS   65
Abdoulaye Sarre

Finance and Economic Opportunity   69
Asli Demirgüç-Kunt and Ross Levine

    COMMENTS
    Liliana Rojas-Suarez   89
    Victor Murinde   93

Bring Me Sunshine: Which Parts of the Business
Climate Should Public Policy Try to Fix?   99
Wendy Carlin and Paul Seabright

    COMMENTS
    Loh Wah-Sing   147
    Jan Svejnar   151

Comments on "Reforming Public Service Delivery,"
by Timothy Besley and Maitreesh Ghatak
    Jean-Paul Azam   155
    Gábor Péteri   161

About This Book

The Annual World Bank Conference on Development Economics is a forum for discussion and debate of important policy issues facing developing countries. The conferences emphasize the contribution that empirical economic research can make to understanding development processes and to formulating sound development policies. Conference papers are written by researchers in and outside the World Bank. The conference series was started in 1989. Conference papers are reviewed by the editors and are also subject to internal and external peer review. Some papers were revised after the conference, to reflect the comments made by discussants or from the floor, while most discussants' comments were not revised. As a result, discussants' comments may refer to elements of the paper that no longer exist in their original form. Participants' affiliations identified in this volume are as of the time of the conference, May 17–18, 2007.

The planning and organization of the May 2007 conference was a joint effort by the Government of Slovenia and the World Bank. We gratefully acknowledge timely and valuable contributions made by all the members of the steering committee and several anonymous reviewers. We would also like to thank, Leita Jones, Conference Coordinator, whose excellent organizational skills helped to ensure a successful conference. Finally, we thank the editorial staff for pulling this volume together, especially Mark Ingebretsen, Stuart K. Tucker, and Nora Ridolfi from the Office of the Publisher.

Introduction

JUSTIN YIFU LIN AND BORIS PLESKOVIC

The Annual World Bank Conference on Development Economics (ABCDE) is a leading forum for advanced, forward-looking research on important development issues. Each year, the ABCDE brings policy makers and politicians together with researchers from academe, international organizations, and think tanks. The diverse perspectives of the international development community mingle and coalesce through in-depth debates on important themes on the development agenda.

The 2008 ABCDE was devoted to the theme "The Private Sector and Development" and highlighted such issues as financial inclusion, key factors in the business climate, and the provision of public services by nonstate actors. The conference, cosponsored by the government of Slovenia and the World Bank, took place in Bled, Slovenia, May 17–18, 2007.

The conference began with words of welcome and opening remarks by Janez Janša, Prime Minister of Slovenia; Andrej Bajuk, Minister of Finance, Slovenia; and François Bourguignon, Chief Economist and Senior Vice President, development economics at the World Bank. Bourguignon later gave one of the keynote addresses, as did Tarun Das, Chief Mentor of the Confederation of Indian Industry; Janez Potočnik, European Commissioner for Science and Research; Santiago Levy, Senior Fellow at the Brookings Institution; and Abdoulaye Sarre, a successful entrepreneur and businessman from Senegal. The conference's three plenary sessions featured four papers presented by leading development economists. Delivering the closing remarks were Bajuk; Shigeo Katsu, World Bank Vice President for Europe and Central Asia; and Trevor Manuel, Minister of Finance, Republic of South Africa.

Justin Yifu Lin is Chief Economist and Senior Vice President for Development Economics at the World Bank. Boris Pleskovic is Research Manager for Development Economics at the World Bank.

Annual World Bank Conference on Development Economics 2008, Global
© 2009 The International Bank for Reconstruction and Development/The World Bank

Opening Addresses

In his welcoming address, **Janez Janša** emphasizes the importance of the private sector in improving standards of living and meeting other development challenges. Development economics seeks to identify the most important factors influencing economic growth and improvements in living standards. It thus stands at the crux of theory and practice, knowledge and action. Janša praises the World Bank's special role as the driving force behind progress in development economics and as a provider of financing and technical assistance to developing countries. Although poverty remains a global challenge, the World Bank's achievements in assisting poor countries in their economic development have been great. Janša then enumerates Slovenia's impressive achievements since it gained independence in 1991. At the beginning of independence, Slovenian enterprises lost 80 percent of their export markets overnight, and unemployment grew rapidly. But Slovenia took determined policy measures to improve the operating environment for the private sector, and between 1992 and 2006 the private sector's share of gross domestic product (GDP) grew from 30 to 65 percent. Now, Slovenia's economic situation has never been better. In 2004 Slovenia graduated from World Bank assistance (the first transition country to do so), became a Bank donor, and joined the European Union (EU). In January 2007 Slovenia adopted the euro, and in January 2008 it assumed the six-month presidency of the European Union. Janša states that Slovenia is proud to have joined the World Bank and other international organizations as a donor in the fight against poverty and recognizes that both the public and private sectors must play important roles.

Andrej Bajuk remarks that the ABCDE, originally held each year in Washington, DC, has become increasingly global. He observes that in 2006 it took place in the most populous country in the world, China, and in 2007 was being held in one of the smallest, Slovenia. Bajuk also notes the importance of this year's theme. He points out that the World Bank, in its first four decades, paid scant attention to the private sector, focusing instead on public sector projects. But, he adds, over the past 20 years the World Bank, along with the international community as a whole, has recognized the crucial significance of the private sector in fostering economic development and growth. The development of the private sector has been crucial to Slovenia's successful economic transition and its adoption of the euro. Bajuk reports that now that it has become a donor rather than a recipient of international aid, Slovenia is focusing on the private sector's contribution to eradicating poverty in developing countries.

François Bourguignon states that the purpose of the ABCDE is to combine diverse perspectives on development, learn from one another, and share knowledge that will improve development effectiveness. He agrees that three or four decades ago the private sector would hardly have been the theme of a major development conference, but since then a consensus has formed regarding the central role of the private sector in development. The proper task of government is now seen as the creation of a policy environment and administrative structure conducive to development of the private sector, rather than intervention in the private sector. Bourguignon praises

Slovenia's accomplishments in weathering its transition, noting that real GDP growth in 2006 amounted to 5.2 percent and reiterating that the country has joined the European Union and, within the World Bank, moved from borrower to donor status. Like all countries, Slovenia continues to face challenges, but it has become much wealthier, and its future within Europe looks bright.

Keynote Addresses

Tarun Das describes the development impacts of India's revitalized private sector. After outlining the economic history of independent India, he describes the character of the country's private sector. During the past 15 years or so—a period of liberalization and opening to the global economy—the private sector has been transformed, and a new spirit of entrepreneurship has taken root. India's private sector has developed rapidly, forming numerous geographic clusters. Das argues that the psychological turning point for the country's private sector was its success in information technology in the 1990s, which gave India faith and confidence that it could compete with world leaders in the industry. Another important psychological change has been in the way India views its population. Before the 1990s India's enormous population was regarded as a liability, but today its 1 billion people are seen as an asset. Das notes that a decade ago, business leaders in India considered development the government's problem, but today the business community sees development issues as their problem, too. The biggest development challenge facing the private sector, according to Das, is to strengthen human capacity. Already, the private sector is training millions of people, including the disadvantaged, setting up skills development centers across India, and supporting rural education. Das points out that the private sector has become deeply involved in other sectors as well, such as infrastructure, health care, microfinance, and environmental and energy issues. While the government provides leadership and the policy framework, private companies are putting resources and drive into development. The private sector's leadership in India's development has helped overcome traditional distrust of profit-making enterprises, and society's expectations of the private sector have become very high indeed.

François Bourguignon observes that it is now widely accepted that transferring ownership from the public sector to the private sector brings gains in efficiency and productivity; and as a result, privatization of state-owned enterprises has been extensively practiced in recent decades. The effects on efficiency and productivity are well understood, but researchers have not adequately examined one crucial area of privatization: its distributional effects. These effects deserve much greater attention because they directly affect public opinion and are absolutely crucial for understanding the welfare consequences and political economy of privatization. Reviewing the literature on privatization, Bourguignon observes that when evaluating the scale of privatization, researchers have generally compared privatized enterprises (assets) in a given country to the country's GDP (a flow). But what matters are the relative sizes of the private and public sectors and the changes taking place. A better comparison,

Bourguignon asserts, would be the ratio of privatized assets to total national assets. Roughly speaking, total national assets can be computed using GDP and a capital-output ratio. Applying such a measure, one can say that approximately 5 percent of assets in the transition countries of Europe and Central Asia have been privatized since 1998, and the figure is about 4 percent in Latin America. Bourguignon illustrates some of the fundamental issues of distribution that have been largely overlooked in the literature. Presenting a stylized example of water supply, he shows that transfer of ownership to a well-regulated private monopoly could be expected to yield clear efficiency gains but also important distributional effects—a range of winners and losers. The winners might be the taxpayers, the new owners, and new consumers; the losers might be certain consumers who now have to pay more, as well as laid-off employees. Privatization in a competitive environment would likely yield smaller price changes and less change in terms of distribution. In that situation, the effect of privatization would be mostly efficiency gains. Bourguignon states that more research is needed to understand privatization impacts with respect to social welfare and political economy, but his simple illustration highlights many overlooked dimensions of privatization. He goes on to review empirical evidence from several developing and transition countries, which for the most part shows the sorts of outcomes one might expect: in competitive industries, negligible price effects and clear-cut efficiency gains, and in noncompetitive industries, a large price effect with many distributional effects. Bourguignon concludes with the observation that the distributional impact of privatization is ripe for analysis.

Janez Potočnik observes that globalization is a fact of life today. New global problems, whether in health, social security and aging, climate change, energy, environment, security, or food supply, require a global response. The only context in which a sustainable future might be found is in the global movement toward a knowledge society. Potočnik states that Europe is in the middle of a difficult transition from a resource-based economy to a knowledge-based economy. In 2000 the European Union adopted the Lisbon Strategy to make the EU the most dynamic and competitive knowledge-based economy in the world by 2010. Potočnik sees current developments as a new "industrial revolution" in which the globalization of trade and knowledge will stimulate innovation, economic development, and new approaches to global problems such as climate change. He states that Europe must lead by example and that it is ready to solve global energy and environmental problems in partnership with developing countries. This can be done only with private sector involvement and leadership, including leadership by fast-growing developing countries such as India, where there is a significant research and development (R&D) base. In 2002, Potočnik notes, the European Union set a goal of investing 3 percent of GDP in science and research, with two-thirds coming from the private sector. So far, Europe is far from that target. The most important factors for attracting R&D investment are the existence of a market, a strong knowledge pool, and a high-quality public research base. Surprisingly, wage levels are not very important. EU research policy is helping developing countries build their knowledge base so that they will be better able to attract R&D investment and better positioned in the global economy. More than half of the

EU framework program budget is dedicated to cooperative research projects, including international cooperation.

Santiago Levy examines the case of Mexico and shows that policy interventions intended to protect workers in the informal sector can introduce distortions that favor the informal sector over the formal sector and lead to lower productivity and slower growth. Mexico's experience demonstrates that economic growth does not invariably lead to increasing formalization of the economy and that interventions in the labor market can have the unintended result of entrenching the informal sector and creating political pressure to maintain and expand the social protection benefits of informal workers. Levy explains that Mexican workers employed in the formal sector receive social security benefits financed by employer-paid taxes, while workers in the informal sector receive social protection benefits financed from general state revenues. Thus, Mexican employers pay salary and benefits for formal workers but only salary for informal workers. Consequently, the cost to a firm of hiring a formal worker is about 50 percent higher than the cost of hiring someone informally. From the economic point of view, the dichotomy of social security for salaried labor versus social protection programs for nonsalaried labor amounts to a tax on firms and a subsidy to informal firms. Levy's analysis of the Mexican economy demonstrates that firms in the informal sector are more profitable and thus attract more investment. Employers have a clear incentive to favor informal employment, but the analysis shows that workers also have an incentive because they do not value social security benefits at their full cost. Consequently, evasion of formal employment is massive. In fact, according to Levy, about 58 percent of Mexico's labor force is in the informal sector; only 38 percent is in the formal sector. Moreover, a large portion of those in the formal sector do not receive social security entitlements because of evasion. Levy concludes that although it is widely expected that economic growth will lead to greater labor formalization and the expansion of social security coverage, this is not always the case, as the experience of Mexico shows. In fact, in Mexico the current mechanism is enlarging and entrenching the informal sector, even under conditions of slow but sustained growth. This is a lesson that may apply to other developing countries, and Levy cautions that the challenge is not to dismantle social protections but to isolate them from the labor market.

Abdoulaye Sarre offers a private sector perspective from Africa, pointing out that the public sector plays a larger role in the economy in Africa than in other parts of the world. Sarre cites the general agreement that the private sector is more efficient and should be the driving force in the economy. He adds that the private sector also needs to have input into some areas that clearly belong to the public sector—above all, education. Education in Africa, especially at the university level, is not meeting the needs and the expectations of business. In Senegal, Sarre notes, more than a third of the state budget is invested in education. The government and society clearly value education and are making a large investment in it, but the university curriculum is too distant from the needs of the private sector, which has no real voice in what is taught. Education is not synchronized with the needs of the economy, and the training itself is often obsolete. In Senegal, for instance, 5,000 students are studying history and geography, but fewer than 200 are studying information technology. Entrepreneurs and investors are important to development in Africa, Sarre observes, but they face a number of serious problems: lower-ranking government officials are suspicious of them and do not understand the importance of the private sector; the legal environment is outdated and has not adapted to important new sectors such as service export and information technology; and the education system is not producing people with the right kinds of skills. Furthermore, the financial sector is not sufficiently developed, and interest rates and collateral requirements are too high. Poor infrastructure and utilities also hinder development. Even in cases where infrastructure is good, as in Senegal's telecommunications sector, monopoly pricing slows economic development. Sarre concludes with a discussion of areas in which the private sector would like the World Bank's assistance: improving the access of small and medium-size businesses to capital markets; encouraging lower interest rates; and financing training programs to induce entrepreneurship, productivity, and innovation.

Financial Inclusion

Asli Demirgüç-Kunt and **Ross Levine** argue that development economists need to pay more attention to assessing how formal financial sector policies affect economic opportunity and poverty. It is widely recognized that imperfections in capital markets cause a larger share of society's savings to flow to those with accumulated wealth. It is not so well understood that there is also, as the authors' research indicates, a strong negative relationship between financial development, on the one hand, and poverty, inequality, and discrimination, on the other. If the economics profession develops a better understanding of how imperfections in financial markets affect intergenerational income dynamics, returns to schooling, saving behavior, and so on, the new findings should play a prominent role in reforms aimed at improving welfare and economic opportunity. Demirgüç-Kunt and Levine observe that recent theoretical and empirical studies strongly suggest that the level of development of the formal financial sector—banks, securities markets, and other financial institutions—is an important determinant of who can exploit economic opportunities and who cannot. The financial system's level of development is not the only determinant, but it appears to be a highly significant factor in delimiting individual economic horizons. On the societal level, financial development determines the extent to which economic opportunity is open to talent and initiative or, on the contrary, depends on family wealth and social connections. In well-developed financial systems, creditworthy firms have easier access to external financing, which affects their growth and performance positively. Working with other researchers, Demirgüç-Kunt and Levine have demonstrated, in previous large-scale cross-country studies, that financial development disproportionately benefits the poor, decreases income inequality, opens new economic opportunities for the poor, reduces the financing obstacles facing small firms, and disproportionately benefits small firms. Studies of microenterprises by other researchers yield consistent results.

Which Factors Matter Most for Improvement of the Business Climate?

Wendy Carlin and **Paul Seabright** guide us through the extensive and sometimes confusing literature on the business climate and its role in economic development. The authors provide valuable guidance to policy makers struggling with the issues of which elements of the business climate make the most difference to the performance of firms, and which should have the highest priority for policy. Over the past decade or so, Carlin and Seabright observe, a consensus has emerged that the quality of a society's institutions is of critical importance to successful development; but there is no agreement on how to identify the dimensions of institutional quality that matter most. Cross-country econometric analysis has established that institutional quality partially determines living standards, but this type of analysis is not able to specify which institutions or elements of the business environment are the most important for long-term development. Using the analogy of a doctor treating a patient, the authors suggest that policy makers take information from all available sources to make their diagnosis and recommend a treatment. There are three main kinds of diagnostic evidence: subjective reports of managers of firms, which have been systematically collected in recent years in many countries; cross-country regression analyses; and regional or country case histories. Carlin and Seabright undertake a detailed examination of findings based on the three kinds of research evidence. Specific findings vary widely across countries and regions; for example, physical infrastructure (with the exception of electricity) has rarely been a constraint, except in some countries in Africa; crime and corruption vary in importance worldwide; and labor regulation is a problem only for rich countries. Although research findings vary widely, they are only rarely contradictory. Building on their analysis, the authors present a tree diagram and a checklist of questions that policy makers can use as a diagnostic protocol to help them prioritize policy measures for improving the business environment in their countries. In conclusion, the authors stress that just as the diagnosis will not be the same for each patient, so it will not be the same for every country.

Opening Speech

JANEZ JANŠA

Ladies and gentlemen, excellencies, members of the leadership of the World Bank, welcome to the Annual Bank Conference on Development Economics, being held this year to our great pleasure in Bled, Slovenia.

The role of the private sector in development is a topic that is more to the point and more relevant now than ever before. Hunger, shortage of drinking water, underdevelopment, poverty, backwardness, lack of privilege, corruption, and illiteracy are still, sadly, the cruel reality of the twenty-first century. The majority still lives in poverty. According to the available information, 2.8 billion people live on less than US$2 a day, while 1.2 billion inhabitants of our planet may spend even less than US$1 a day. Child labor remains a common practice in many parts of the world. Climate change threatens the ecological balance and calls for serious and concerted action by all of us to prevent consequences that may be fatal for the entire planet.

The question that is self-evident is, how to improve the standard of living in developing countries. Development economics is the branch of economics that tries to find an answer to this question. Since 1950, when the first model of development economics was formulated, we have seen many theories and models that have been changing, developing, and improving. Development economics has become increasingly interdisciplinary. Today it links economics, sociology, anthropology, political science, sociopsychology, medicine, geography, and other sciences.

Modern development economics seeks to determine what are the crucial elements in securing faster economic growth and improvements in living standards, in developing countries in particular. Is the key factor diet, health systems, primary and higher education, an efficient legal system, fair trade, just distribution of income, or the right economic policies and development strategies?

Janez Janša was prime minister of the Republic of Slovenia at the time of this conference. He is currently president of the Slovenian Democratic Party.

Annual World Bank Conference on Development Economics 2008, Global
© 2009 The International Bank for Reconstruction and Development/The World Bank

Michael Todaro and Stephen Smith describe development economics as the coordination of human yearning and human endeavors. The essence of development economics is to move from theory to practice, to turn words into deeds. A former president of the World Bank, Lewis Preston, said that development theory by itself has little value unless it is applied, unless it translates into results, and unless it improves people's lives. In other words, the findings of a science are successful if they help developing countries move toward more rapid progress and economic growth.

The World Bank is the driving force behind advances in development economics and, at the same time, the main source of financing and expert assistance to developing countries. Although the needs are great and assistance is almost always insufficient, the Bank's achievements since its establishment in 1944 speak for themselves. The organization, owned by its member countries, which today number 184, has contributed to a great extent to the alleviation of problems in the world. The establishment of the Bank is a project that has brought together the nations of the world. The World Bank, founded with a noble objective, provides financing to countries that have no access to international markets. It extends interest-free credit to least developed countries and low interest loans to developing countries, with a longer repayment term. It also offers expert and technical support for projects that are important for the improvement of poor living conditions and for sustainable development. In the fiscal year extending from June 2005 to July 2006, the World Bank made available almost US$23.74 billion in loans for 279 projects.

We set ourselves ambitious goals in the Millennium Declaration in 2000. We pledged to reduce poverty by half by 2015. We pledged to help member countries overcome extreme poverty and hunger, to help ensure education for children and rights for women, to reduce child mortality, to improve the health of pregnant women, and to ensure protection against lethal diseases such as HIV, malaria, and tuberculosis. We pledged to protect nature and natural resources and to develop an international partnership for development.

The Annual Bank Conference on Development Economics is an opportunity for numerous development economists to outline their views on the problems of sustainable development in today's world. The choice of Bled as the conference venue is of extraordinary symbolic significance for us, and we are delighted that by being selected to host the conference, we stand side by side with Brussels, Amsterdam, and Tokyo—capitals that have hosted this conference in the past three years.

Slovenia is a young state. It started on its course of independence and democratic change in 1991. The path that we have traveled in these 16 years has not been easy. Slovenian companies lost 80 percent of their market practically overnight. Employment dropped by 10 percent in 1992 and 1993 alone. Real imports declined sharply. These were moments of uncertainty, and the Slovenian economy had to find new opportunities in the demanding markets of the European Community. It took a great deal of hard work and courage to achieve the results that are visible today.

Exports, which are of key importance for the small Slovenian economy, rose from 51 to 69 percent between 1996 and 2006. The private sector was given a better opportunity, and between 1992 and 2006, it increased its share in gross domestic product (GDP) from 30 to 65 percent. Today, Slovenia is in the best economic situation ever in its history. We are visible in the world as a developed country. We adopted the euro as our own currency, very successfully, at the beginning of 2006, the first and only of the new European Union (EU) states to do so. This success is even greater if you consider the fact that we have succeeded in maintaining economic balance and low inflation. Other economic and public finance indicators are also very good. In 2006 economic growth was 5.2 percent, and we reached almost 84 percent of the average EU GDP, measured in purchasing power. Employment increased in 2006 by 1.3 percent, and unemployment currently amounts to less than 6 percent. Growth of value added was 5.3 percent in 2006, and labor productivity was 4 percent.

I am delighted to add that the good economic indicators have been successfully translated into the lives of people. In 2006 gross salaries in Slovenia increased in both nominal and real terms, and we reduced public debt, which is now 27.8 percent of GDP. The public deficit has been lowered as well, to 1.4 percent of GDP. It is important, also, that favorable forecasts as to growth and development have been made by foreign and domestic institutions for 2007 and 2008.

Although we are proud of our achievements, we are well aware that there is a great deal of hard work still to be done in order to realize our long-term objectives. After all, poverty and social exclusion are not problems faced only by developing countries. In the words of former World Bank president James Wolfensohn, "Our primary goal in development goal must be to reduce the disparities across and within countries—to bring more people into the economic mainstream and to promote equitable access to the fruits of development, regardless of nationality, race, or gender. . . [T]he key development challenge of our time is the challenge of inclusion."

We wish to reduce poverty, or eradicate it to the greatest possible extent in Slovenia, and recent trends in our country have been positive. One of the first documents that the government of the Republic of Slovenia adopted at the beginning was a development strategy, a program of economic and social reforms that we had to carry out to ensure Slovenia's achievement of these good economic results in the long term. We adopted tax laws as part of economic reforms that significantly lessened the excessive tax burden on the economy and encouraged employment of highly educated workers and, in general, employment that will be less costly for companies. Further privatization of companies that are still chiefly in state ownership is under way and will be carried out in such a way as to ensure the best possible effects for the growth and development of the economy. Special attention is being paid to the privatization of the banking and insurance sector, where it is our duty to ensure the stability of the financial system. We have also adopted a number of other economic and social reform measures to increase the competitiveness of Slovenia's economy. Negotiations with the social partners on labor legislation are in the final stage. There will be considerably greater flexibility of the labor market, and we will thus create conditions for higher employment. We have adopted a new municipality-financing act. Under preparation is legislation on provinces whose objective is more harmonious regional development.

In its transition from a developing to a developed country, Slovenia has enjoyed the assistance and support of developed countries. The door to the European Union and the euro zone was open for us. On January 1, 2008, we are entering the Schengen visa system, and on that date we will assume the six-month presidency of the European Union. Slovenia has also received an official invitation to join the Organisation for Economic Co-operation and Development (OECD).

We are aware of the importance of our experience and knowledge. Today, Slovenia is rightfully expected to help other countries with financing, experience, and knowledge. Slovenia was the first of the countries in transition to conclude the World Bank's graduation procedure in 2004. We undertook a commitment to cease borrowing from the World Bank and drawing on free-of-charge technical assistance and, instead, to help other countries toward faster development. Here it is necessary to mention Slovenia's long donor tradition. Immediately on gaining independence, Slovenia, as a developing country, allocated approximately 0.08 percent of its GDP to development assistance for the countries of the western Balkans.

Today, of course, much more is expected from us. Under the auspices of the World Bank, within the multilateral debt relief initiative, we are active in reducing the debts of the poorest countries of the world. We participate in the replenishments of the International Development Association (IDA) and the Global Environment Facility. We have participated in the fight to combat HIV, malaria, and tuberculosis and in the program for combating river blindness in Africa. Slovenia has contributed funds to the International Finance Corporation (IFC) for the Balkans. We are the first transitional country to contribute funds to the Western Balkans Fund of the European Bank for Reconstruction and Development, between 2007 and 2010. Slovenia helps with payments to the EU budget, and we will also be paying into the European Development Fund.

We are well aware that the needs are much greater than what is gathered in these funds. It can therefore rightfully be expected that we will devote more attention to development topics and development finance. Our objective is indeed to achieve the commitment of 0.17 percent of GDP for development assistance by 2010.

Although donorship is noble and indispensable, other forms of assistance must be also used to combat poverty. Economic, social, political, and institutional mechanisms are necessary for the sustainable development process and for rapid and extensive improvement of living conditions in developing countries. These mechanisms must include both the public and private sectors. The role of the private sector has become increasingly important in development. Here it is necessary to point out again that the private sector must respect the global rules of the United Nations by protecting human rights, by not using forced or compulsory labor or child labor, and by respecting progressive standards of environmental protection.

Ladies and gentlemen, Adam Smith said in 1776, "No society can surely be flourishing and happy, of which the far greater part of the members are poor and miserable." It is our duty and moral obligation to jointly help people who cannot live in decent conditions and to minimize poverty and finally eradicate it.

In conclusion, I wish this conference to be a resounding success and to contribute to the exchange of ideas that will yield, in the future, effective solutions for providing assistance to the poorest and to underprivileged inhabitants around the world. Words are useless if not followed by action.

I wish you every success in your work and a pleasant stay in Slovenia.

Thank you very much.

Opening Speech

ANDREJ BAJUK

Prime Minister, dear François, your excellencies, ladies and gentlemen.

I would like to begin by wishing you a warm welcome to Slovenia, and especially to Bled. It is an honor to participate in the opening of one of the World Bank's biggest and best-known international events, being held in Slovenia this year.

I am pleased about the choice of Bled because the venue lends the Annual Bank Conference on Development Economics (ABCDE) an increasingly more global character. In its early days the conference was held in Washington. Then it moved to the capitals of developed European countries, then to Japan, and this year to Slovenia. It is definitely an interesting coincidence that this year's regional ABCDE was organized in the biggest country in the world, that is, China; and the global ABCDE is being held in one of the smallest countries in the world, Slovenia. When, at the end of the ABCDE in Tokyo in May 2006, we announced in a videoconference the organization of this year's conference, we, to be honest, did not realize how extensive the preparation would be. I believe that during this year cooperation between the World Bank headquarters in Washington, the office in Paris, and Slovenia's Ministry of Finance was exemplary. I should like to take this occasion to thank the staff of the World Bank, the members of the steering committee, and my colleagues from the Ministry of Finance for well-performed work. I also express my gratitude to the speakers and discussants for their quality contributions. I hope and believe that their contributions will trigger interesting discussions that will contribute to creating more effective policies in developing countries.

The central theme of this year's conference, the private sector and development, was chosen to emphasize the important role played by the private sector in the development of economies around the world. The significance of the private sector has not been self-evident. It should be noted that even the World Bank, during its first 40 years, did not

Andrej Bajuk served as prime minister of Slovenia in 2000, then as minister of finance from 2004 to 2008.

Annual World Bank Conference on Development Economics 2008, Global
© 2009 The International Bank for Reconstruction and Development/The World Bank

devote enough attention to the private sector. In 1985 this was directly highlighted by the then-president of the World Bank, A. W. Clausen, who observed, "Over the last two to three decades, the thrust of the development effort has been directed towards public sector activities. We have been less concerned with promoting private sector growth than with assisting the development of an effective public sector. Aid agencies ought to be taking a more balanced approach." It then took seven years before the World Bank introduced a special vice president for Financial and Private Sector Development.

The situation today is completely different. There is practically not a single document or publication issued by the World Bank that does not contain a reference to the private sector. We all agree on the significance of the private sector. We rely on the private sector in fostering growth and development. Slovenia is no exception in this respect. Without a strong private sector, our transition would not have progressed so quickly, and Slovenia would not be one of the first new member states of the European Union to adopt the euro. This experience steers Slovenia's international development cooperation. Our donor activities are designed to develop private sectors that will enable people from developing countries to eradicate poverty through their own commitment and work.

During this conference we will talk about three aspects of the role of the private sector in the promotion of development, in three plenary sessions: (1) Financial Inclusion; (2) Which Factors Matter the Most for Business Climate? and (3) Provision of Public Services by Nonstate Actors. The first plenary session will focus on the extent to which reforms in the financial sector can influence the eradication of poverty and income distribution. We will be interested in how economic policy measures in the financial sector can improve the economic possibilities of the poorest inhabitants. The second session will be dedicated to the business environment. We will consider the definition of the business environment, the institutional restrictions on the operations of private companies, and what is of the utmost importance for the economic policy actors; and we will endeavor to define the related public finance priorities and legislative measures. The third plenary session will highlight the overlap of the public and private sectors. We will touch on the public goods that the private sector supports or complements and the associated economic policy measures.

A number of events, discussions, workshops, and roundtables will be organized parallel to the plenary sessions. Finally, there will be an opportunity to meet informally in this exceptional atmosphere of Bled.

I would like to conclude with a reference to the last ABCDE conference. At the closing session in Tokyo, our Japanese hosts, according to their tradition, gave us a Daruma doll with only one eye painted in. It is our duty, at the beginning of this year's conference, to paint the doll's other eye in order to bring happiness to all of us—or so we were told in Japan. I hope that the discussions on topical issues of development here in Bled will contribute to a better understanding of the relationship between the private sector and development. I also wish you every success in your work.

Opening Speech

FRANÇOIS BOURGUIGNON

Mr. Prime Minister, Minister Bajuk, ladies and gentlemen,

On behalf of the World Bank, I welcome you to this new edition of the Annual Bank Conference on Development Economics (ABCDE). As you know, the objective of this conference is to gather a part of the international development community for in-depth debates regarding important issues on the development agenda. The conference is intended to be a forum that combines diverse perspectives on development—those, for instance, of academics, policy makers, politicians, and civil society. By bringing together participants with very different backgrounds, experiences, and origins, we hope it will be possible to share fundamental knowledge about the mechanism of development and the effectiveness of development policy and to learn effectively from each other. The location for this mutually enriching, extensive, and intensive exchange of views changes every year. This year, we have been fortunate that Slovenia has agreed to host the conference and I would like to thank wholeheartedly Slovenia's prime minister and minister of finance for cosponsoring and hosting this event. Their gracious efficiency is evident in our setting today and we can quite clearly all look forward to a very productive event.

This is my first time in Slovenia and my first time in Bled and I must say that I am absolutely overwhelmed by this location. I read somewhere a very nice tale about Slovenia that, it seems to me, wonderfully fits the landscape around us and in this place where we meet. According to that story, God could not hear the Slovenians at the time he allocated land to all nations on earth. There were not enough Slovenians, and their voices were too soft. So in the end, the Slovenians had absolutely no land, and they again asked God to give them a piece of land, and finally God told them, "Look, I have this piece of land which was for me, but I agree to give it to you."

François Bourguignon is director of the Paris School of Economics. He is a past senior vice president and chief economist of the World Bank.

Annual World Bank Conference on Development Economics 2008, Global

In other words, Slovenia is a little paradise. This is the first time that the ABCDE is taking place in the paradise, and we are very grateful to our hosts for making it happen.

Three or four decades ago, I'm not sure that the topic of this conference would have seemed appropriate for such a paradisiacal location. Indeed, for some time the private sector was even considered in the field of development as rather evil, or at least as not good enough to function without massive state intervention in the development process. It is quite remarkable to see that in three or four decades things have completely changed. A consensus has emerged on the absolutely central role that the private sector plays in development and the fact that the most important task of government is to provide an adequate environment and an appropriate policy and administrative setting for the private sector to develop in a dynamic and equitable way. Various dimensions of this private sector topic will be discussed today and tomorrow. I will not repeat what Minister Bajuk has already said, and I will not repeat what is in the program. I am simply very happy that, with the steering committee, which, as Minister Bajuk said, has been working very hard on the program, it was possible to draw up such a satisfactory and exciting program for these two days. And I thank the members of the steering committee, and I thank all of you—participants, speakers, and discussants—for attending this meeting.

Let me get back for a moment to the case of Slovenia and the lessons that the international development community can learn from its development. As Prime Minister Janša said, Slovenia is poised to take over the European Union presidency in 2008, and it faces a future full of challenges and promise. But the important point is that the country seems to be well prepared for this new role, partly because of government policies that have promoted a well-governed banking sector and rapidly improving business regulations. Slovenia weathered its transition remarkably well, as the prime minister said, and it can take pride in recent achievements. In 2004 it joined the European Union and graduated from World Bank borrower status to donor status. In January 2007 it adopted the euro.

Positioned at the heart of Europe and blessed with smart, well-educated people, real gross domestic product (GDP) growth of 5.2 percent in 2006, and wealth that now surpasses that of Portugal and Greece in the European Union, this country faces a bright future in which the private sector will prosper. Slovenia looks like a perfect example for the development of countries which have not yet reached that very favorable stage in their development process.

To close, let me say that with this ABCDE conference—with all of us gathered today for a very exciting and promising and ambitious program for discussion—the World Bank stays remarkably firm in its commitment to work with the rest of the development community for the eradication of poverty in the world, which we are able to pursue today with the help of our host, Slovenia.

Let me wish you a very nice conference for these two days, and thank all of you again.

Keynote Address

TARUN DAS

It is a great privilege to be here at the World Bank meeting, especially in this terrific environment of Bled, Slovenia. I have fallen in love with the area since yesterday, when I arrived, as I am sure many of you have.

My intention is to share with you the Indian experience, because that is my experience and I thought it could be relevant to others. It has been a story of struggle to promote the private sector and the role of the private sector in development.

We got our independence in 1947. So it is 60 years, as of 2007, of independence and development with democracy. That is the framework in which we have operated, and I want to mark out some particular blocks of time so that you can see the evolution of Indian policy and of the Indian private sector.

The first block of time is 1947 to 1991, 44 years. Essentially, the economy was heavily controlled, heavily regulated, protected, not open, isolated. As a result, the private sector was not competitive, not efficient, and not comfortable with the world, not engaging with the world. Those policies went through a paradigm shift. The country was in great economic difficulty—in fact, in a crisis. And so the new paradigm of policy started in 1991.

The next time frame is the five years 1991 to 1996, a period of liberalization, deregulation, opening to foreign investment and international trade, progressive reduction of tariffs, and competition accompanied by growth. We went from 3 percent growth to five years of 6 percent growth. There was competition, but everybody was happy because of the growth.

And then came 1997. In the period 1997 to 2002, following the Southeast Asian financial crisis, India was not in financial crisis, but our growth decreased. There was pain in the economy, pain in industry in the private sector, especially in manufacturing industry, and therefore restructuring, downsizing. So, the paradigm changed from protection, to growth, to no growth and having to survive in that situation. With the

Tarun Das is chief mentor of the Confederation of Indian Industry (CII), where he was chief executive from 1974 to 2004.

Annual World Bank Conference on Development Economics 2008, Global

lower tariffs, imports were coming in from East Asia; industry was under threat; and there was a lot of difficulty at that time. But it was a good time in retrospect because that was the time of real change in the private sector.

That brings us to the period from 2003 to 2007. Industry—competitive and no longer afraid of globalization, having withstood the pain of the previous five years— is now confident and ready to engage the world, and you can see it now as we invest internationally, as we reach beyond our own shores and our own boundaries into the world beyond. In this process we went from 3 percent growth to 6 percent growth, had a dip in growth, and are now roughly at 8 to 9 percent growth, with the private sector growing in double-digit figures, at more than 10 percent.

What does the future look like? As I will explain, it looks like 10 percent gross domestic product (GDP) growth for the next 10 years, plus or minus 1 percent. Maybe 10, maybe 9.5, maybe 11.5 percent, but that's the kind of range or outlook. And that colors policy and where the private sector is.

So, this huge change happened between 1947 and 2007; change in India, change in policy frameworks, and change in the private sector. Now the private sector, traditionally, was essentially some large companies, some family businesses. Some died out during the period 1997 to 2000. Some have restructured and are globally competitive and doing well. And many new people and new entrepreneurs have entered this large business bracket. We have a respected newspaper in our country called *Business Standard,* and that paper carries out an annual survey of India's billionaires. A recent survey shows that 130 of India's billionaires are first-generation entrepreneurs, meaning, essentially, that they have been in business for the last 10 to 12 years, since the opening up of the economy in 1991. That's a transformation.

The second part of business, small and medium-size enterprises, suffered considerably from the micromanagement of the economy and were really inefficient. They have been greatly transformed, and the entrepreneurship and the enterprise of these people have come to the fore in the new environment in India. The small and medium-size enterprises grow around large companies, in 50 clusters. They are in specific geographic areas, and with the help of Japanese experts, we have worked on transforming these companies and these clusters of small industries into competitive forces. And it has been a great success story.

Now, what are the huge changes and huge challenges that we see for India and therefore for the private sector? First on the list is human resource capacity building: training and educating millions of people who are part of a competitive private sector, a globalized private sector. The Indian private sector has voluntarily undertaken an affirmative action program that is being carried out across the country, company by company. In other words, they are reaching out to the disadvantaged, training them, and then employing them or helping them to be self-employed. I'll give you another example. The private sector, under the Confederation of Indian Industry (CII), has set up a skills development initiative because, even with this growth of 9 or 10 percent that we are suddenly facing—we have millions and millions of people, but shortages of the skill sets that we require. So, the private sector is going beyond its normal responsibilities, through the government, which had earlier set up training institutes across the country. The government has 5,000 of these institutes. The private sector has found that many of the products of these government institutions are not really as good as required. So, the private sector is setting up skills development centers across the country to supplement the government's work.

In addition, private sector companies have established foundations that are taking primary education to the villages and rural areas of India. The best known is the Azim Premji Foundation. Another, Pratham, was set up by the ICICI Bank. And we at the CII have set up something called Shiksha, which is information technology–enabled education. We prepare content in different languages (India has 25 languages) and deliver it to schools so that the children can benefit. In particular, this approach can help in distance education. The CII has also set up training centers across the country so that the training delivery system is strengthened and, again, people become empowered through the process.

The second challenge is infrastructure development and investment. For almost 50 years, the government owned, controlled, and managed the infrastructure. That has changed. The government has reached out to the private sector. It was a difficult transition because the expectation that had grown in India was that infrastructure was free. It came from the government; why do we have to pay for it? The private sector has to borrow, has to raise equity, has to earn money from infrastructure services, has to pay back its shareholders. So this new paradigm that has emerged has brought about new guidelines, independent regulators, and all that. In the past 10 years the private sector has become deeply involved in infrastructure, for the first time in the 60 years of independent India.

The third is environment and energy. We are addressing these issues very actively in India, and the government is providing the leadership and the appropriate policies. For example, all buses and public transport in Delhi run on compressed natural gas (CNG), which has helped enormously in reducing pollution. The CII has set up a green development center in Hyderabad, staffed by engineers—men and women trained in the United States—who are advising and helping companies and architects and designers to build a green society. This is very practical. We have a green building program; in fact, the building itself in Hyderabad has a platinum rating, the highest rating under the U.S. green building code and the only one of its kind, as far as I know, outside the United States. The United States itself only has two or three. We are driving a movement for conserving energy, cutting energy use, and building a better and safer environment; and the private sector is doing this, putting resources into this work.

The fourth area of change is health care. The private sector health care industry is supplementing the government system, growing rapidly, and providing not only commercial health care services but also a great deal of subsidized, free health care services for people who can't afford world-class health care facilities. You will now find in remote districts of India private sector–supported hospitals run by nongovernmental organizations (NGOs). And that is a new dimension; NGOs and the private sector are gradually getting over their old mistrust and are able to work together in building up capabilities, especially on the social infrastructure side.

My final example is microfinance. Ten years ago CII established, with private sector funding, a program for helping people set up small enterprises. From that fund, we would give a small loan, and because of our credibility, we would persuade the banks to give an additional amount. But the most important point was that every case had a mentor, a volunteer from a private sector company. That means the borrower is getting help from a professional, free of charge, to help run a business. Repayment rates are amazingly high. We are delighted. And by the way, more than 50 percent of the people who have benefited from this program are women. The first women who took loans from us in the 1990s are now millionaires. They are employing other people. They don't speak English. They are from remote communities. But it is a terrific success, as indeed the microfinance program has been in Bangladesh and elsewhere. Lately, because the prime minister, Manmohan Singh, has been wanting us to get engaged in rural development programs, we have started working with the corporate sector and the district administration at the local level to set up rural business hubs and develop employment opportunities in industry in rural areas, using local resources and local people. It is very challenging, very tough for the private sector, but companies are coming forward to partner and sponsor similar programs and to buy products made in these rural areas.

We have struggled for change in India. It has not been an easy story. Ten or 12 years ago, when I would go to my board and talk about these issues, they would say, "This is not my problem; this is the government's problem. Or maybe it is the World Bank's problem to deal with these developmental issues." But today there has been a transformation. Of course, it is a work in progress but the private sector is looking beyond profitability and shareholder satisfaction, at least in India.

The private sector issued its own code for corporate governance before the government came into this area in the 1990s. And that later became the model for the government's code and the government's laws. The private sector has also taken the initiative to engage with development issues and go beyond just itself. But at the end of the day, the private sector has to be efficient, has to be competitive, and has to generate resources to do all these things.

The good news out of India today is that more and more private sector companies are competitive, and competitive in the sense of not worrying—that is, not worrying about Chinese imports coming into India, for example. In 1999 China-India trade was US$1 billion, and Indian companies clearly were afraid and were very worried, and there was an imbalance of trade. Today, trade between China and India is over US$20 billion and is rising like a rocket. Very soon China will be our major trading partner, but trade is, by and large, balanced, plus or minus 5 to 7 percent—no big deal. So, Indian companies are able to compete and to enter the Chinese market. Indian information technology (IT) companies, pharmaceutical companies, and auto component companies have invested all around Shanghai and have set up manufacturing or software development facilities. One Indian company is training 1,000 Chinese in software development, and that is the emphasis in Bangalore. The whole scenario for the private sector has changed enormously as a result of this new competitiveness, and therefore more resources are being poured into technology development, new products, new processes, and so on.

This is not the end of the road. I think we have a long haul ahead. I will just highlight two things. What was the turning point for the private sector? The turning point was the success in information technology in the 1990s. No question about it. It gave us faith. It gave us confidence. It gave us self-belief that we could be among the best in the world. We didn't have to sit in a corner somewhere; we could come near center stage. So the IT change was a huge thing. And the second was the whole understanding of how we looked at people. Until the 1990s, we looked at India's population as a liability. And this was constant; our population was huge—700 million, 800 million people, however many. Today, with the assistance and with the help of technology and especially IT, we now see our 1 billion people as an asset. And therefore all this talk about affirmative action or talk about skills development is because we are looking at these people and saying, "They can make a difference." If you empower them, and if you help them, they can make a difference for India. So these are two big things that have happened.

The prime minister has accepted my request to engage in a dialogue with the private sector. And the dialogue is that we need inclusive growth, inclusive development, in India. That means tackling the issue of disparities, the issue of 700 million people today living in rural areas, 500 million people under age 30; how do we integrate them into the mainstream of economic life, into the mainstream of our society? And what can the private sector do toward this? So, in a daylong session, chief executives, the prime minister, the finance minister, and others will meet later this month to discuss just one issue: inclusive growth and what more the private sector can do as we go forward and as we strive for 10 percent growth, globalization, and so on. What can the private sector do to multiply its efforts in this issue of inclusive growth?

Now, there are huge expectations of the private sector in India. We have come from a situation in which the private sector was mistrusted and profit was a dirty word to one in which, suddenly, everybody is looking at the private sector and saying, "Do something." Why is this happening?

I think what we are seeing is, first, the desire to harness our growing competitiveness and our managerial and organizational capabilities for development. And the private sector is responding.

The second consideration is the financial resources of the private sector. Profits are at all-time highs. Dividends are at all-time highs. Plowback is at an all-time high. So, can the private sector give more and more money out of its resources for development issues? This is happening, and it needs to happen much more. Of course, the government's tax policies are helpful because our tax rates, both personal and corporate, are around 33 percent and, I think, generally heading downward to around 30 percent and below, which is generating more and more confidence within the private sector.

The third is the needs of the country. When I talk to business associations in France or London or the United States, the reaction is, "Why are you doing all of this? Why are you employing 800 people in the CII?" Well, out of the 800 people, 250 are working on development issues of different kinds: environment, energy, corporate social responsibility, rural development, and so on. This is not needed in other countries, perhaps, but it is needed in India. Our institution has the responsibility of being a partner to the government in development.

Fourth, the public-private partnership (PPP) model is evolving. We are learning every day. We are making mistakes. We are falling down and getting up and going forward, but it is something that has come to stay. And we see this as new guidelines are being developed jointly, and new frameworks are being developed for public-private partnership in India. It is working and will surely work better with time.

Fifth is the evolving trust in the private sector. This is a huge change. You know, you get very motivated when the prime minister or the finance minister reaches out to you, and this is happening across all political parties. We have 18 parties in the coalition and 25 parties in the opposition, but everybody is reaching out to the private sector. And this growing trust is motivating the private sector to behave better than perhaps it would have behaved otherwise.

Finally, there is the explosion of entrepreneurship and enterprise in India arising from the opportunities and the space which is being given by government policies. Government is moving back, and industry is moving ahead and is being given the space to get going.

So, that's the story of the past 60 years, and it looks good for the future: huge challenges, huge problems—but a good feeling that together, we can make it.

Keynote Address
Privatization in Development: Some Lessons from Experience

FRANÇOIS BOURGUIGNON AND CLAUDIA SEPÚLVEDA

The role of the private sector in development, which is the theme of this conference, cannot be addressed fully without discussing privatization—the process whereby an activity is shifted from the state, mainly state-owned enterprises (SOEs), to the private sector.[1] The conventional wisdom is that privatization should increase the efficiency of the economy because private firms are effective cost minimizers and profit maximizers, whereas SOEs often face soft budget constraints and engage in objectives other than cost minimization, such as implementing the state's social welfare policies.

The efficiency argument for privatization is voiced at times with exceeding forcefulness by some economists. Not a long time ago, a Nobel laureate in economics attending a conference on growth and development concluded his presentation on growth strategies with this simple recommendation: "In order to grow, in order to develop, you need to do three things: liberalize, stabilize, and privatize."

In this paper we briefly review what is known about privatization in developing countries (including transition economies) in order to draw some lessons for policy and to offer some suggestions on how to assess privatization, at least in countries where there is still scope for it. We will show that the prescription for achieving growth and development is not as simple as the recommendation of the Nobel laureate.

It is true that our understanding of the efficiency gains of privatization has increased significantly in recent years, but there is an important area about which we know little: the distributional effects of privatization. Whether we are arguing from the standpoint of welfare economics or of political economy, distributional effects are critical to the outcome, or the perceived outcome, of privatization. Indeed, it is

François Bourguignon is director of the Paris School of Economics and is a past senior vice president and chief economist of the World Bank. Claudia Sepúlveda is a senior economist in the Office of the Chief Economist, World Bank. The authors are grateful for the excellent research assistance provided by Shilpa Phadke and Bruno Vincent.

Annual World Bank Conference on Development Economics 2008, Global

FIGURE 1.
Negative Views of Privatization in Latin America, 1998 and 2005

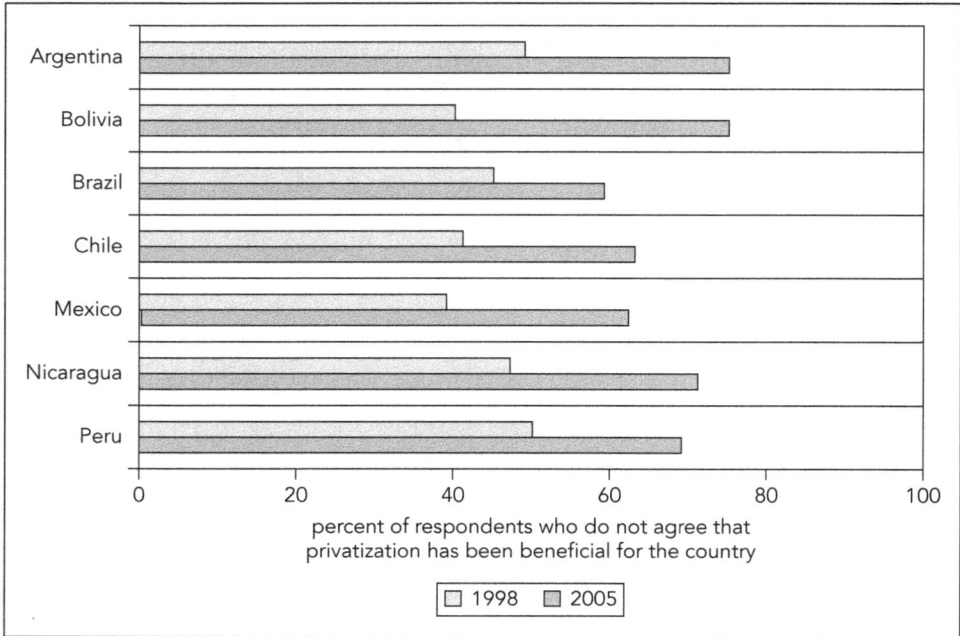

Source: Latinobarómetro.

possible that much of the attitude of the public toward privatization might be linked to distributional effects that are not being well captured in our current analysis.

Figure 1 shows indexes of dissatisfaction with privatization in Latin America for the years 1998 and 2005 as reported by Latinobarómetro, an annual public opinion survey carried out in 18 countries in the region. The poll asked the public in several Latin American countries whether privatization had been beneficial for the country. As early as 1998, negative opinions about privatization averaged 40 percent, and seven years after privatization had peaked in the region, more than 60 percent of respondents in all reporting countries expressed negative views.[2]

If we believe that the efficiency argument is so strong, why are there such high levels of negative opinion about the benefits of privatization? That is the central question of this paper.

In what follows, we first describe the trends in privatization in developing countries and the indicators used to measure the extent of privatization. Next, we briefly discuss the economic theory behind privatization. We do not attempt a comprehensive review; there are many good and exhaustive books on this topic, chief among them those by the distinguished late Jean-Jacques Laffont and his colleague Jean Tirole. Rather, we simply illustrate a few basic points concerning the economics of privatization. We then present empirical evidence on the main effects of privatization and, finally, draw conclusions.

Trends in Privatization in Developing Countries

Since the 1984 privatization of British Telecom, developed and developing countries have adopted privatization programs to different extents. To date, almost every developing country has divested some SOEs to the private sector; cumulative proceeds raised by privatizations during the period 1988–2005 approach US$530 billion in constant 2000 U.S. dollars.

Considering first the two most widely used indicators, proceeds and number of deals, we see that privatization started slowly in the 1980s, with fewer than 89 transactions per year and proceeds of less than US$4.0 billion. Two decades after the privatization of British Telecom, however, proceeds approached US$56 billion per year, and the number of transactions had increased to about 200 per year. During those two decades, developing countries witnessed various waves of privatization. From the standpoint of proceeds from privatization, three waves can be identified: from 1990 to 1994, from 1996 to 2002, and starting in 2003 (figure 2, top panel). But when the focus is on the number of deals (transactions), the situation is different. There was only one big wave, in the mid-1990s, and it was driven mostly by the privatization process in Europe and Central Asia (figure 2, bottom panel). A comparison of the proceeds from privatization and the numbers of deals shows that the average size of privatization operations has increased substantially over the years. In 1995 the average size of a privatization was rather small, at US$40 million, but by 2005 the average was US$290 million.

Proceeds from privatization and the number of deals are neither sufficient nor informative enough as indicators of the extent of privatization. For a better and more complete picture, indicators that relate privatization to the size of the economy, as measured by gross domestic product (GDP), aggregate capital stock, or the importance of public enterprises in the economy, would be more valuable. Figure 3 shows the proceeds from privatization as a share of GDP in three world regions. In Latin America and the Caribbean two waves of comparable importance are evident, in the early 1990s and in the late 1990s. Among the countries responsible for those big waves are Mexico, where the proceeds from privatization represented 3.6 percent of GDP in 1991, and Brazil, with 4.1 percent of GDP in 1998. Thus, the privatization process in Latin America and the Caribbean during the 1990s was rather sizable.

The Europe and Central Asia region exhibits more peaks and troughs than other regions in proceeds as a share of GDP, and until recently, the size of the proceeds was below Latin American levels. But the 2000s have witnessed a radical change in the latter indicator, with accumulated proceeds during the period 1988–2005 approaching US$150 billion in constant 2000 US dollars, against US$223 billion for Latin America and the Caribbean. Finally, in East Asia and the Pacific proceeds from privatization have been generally low as a share of GDP.

In assessing the potential role of privatization, what matters most is the relative sizes of the private and public sectors and the structural change attributable to privatization. Accordingly, it is useful to analyze not only the annual flows of

FIGURE 2.
Privatization in Developing Countries, 1988–2005

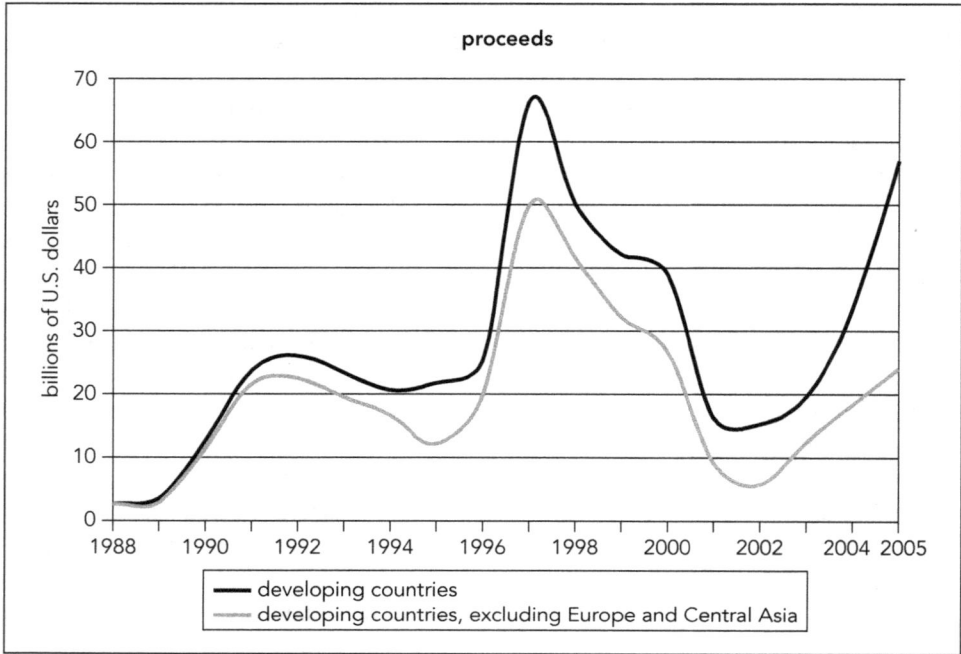

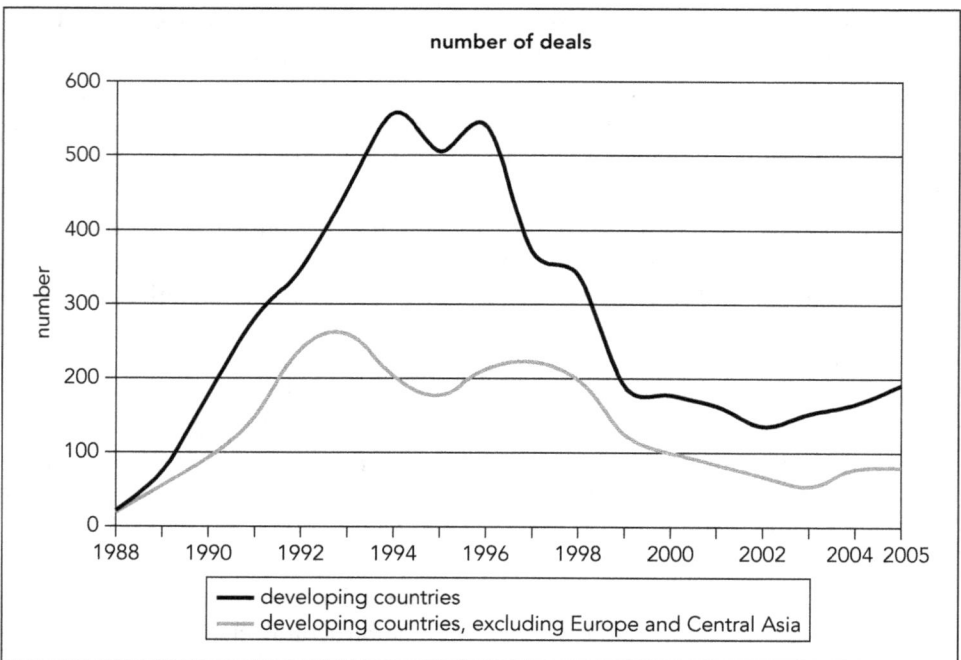

proceeds

developing countries
developing countries, excluding Europe and Central Asia

number of deals

developing countries
developing countries, excluding Europe and Central Asia

Source: World Bank Privatization Database, http://rru.worldbank.org/Privatization/.

FIGURE 3.
Privatization Proceeds as Share of Regional GDP, by Region, 1988–2005

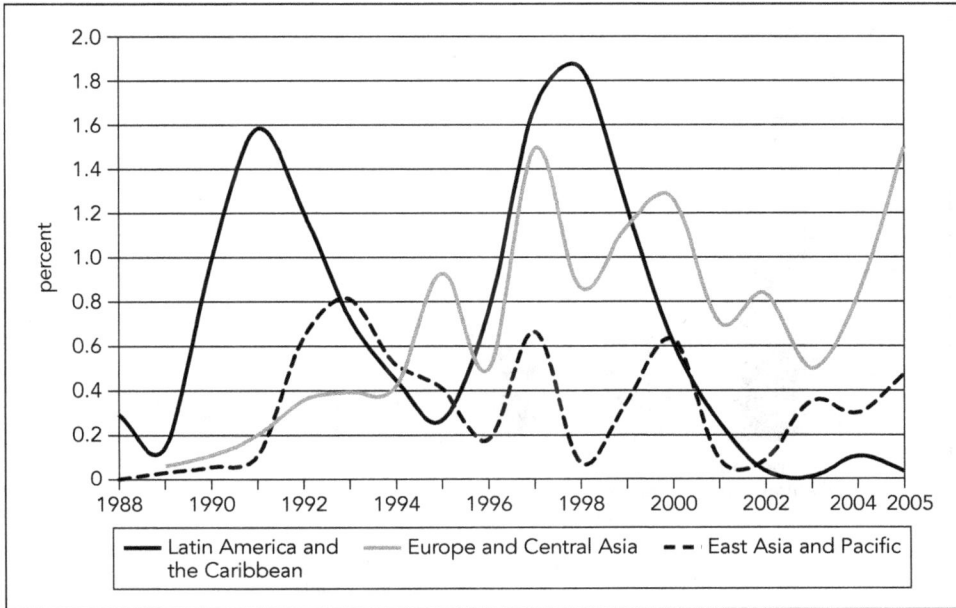

Source: World Bank Privatization Database; *World Development Indicators.*

Note: GDP, gross domestic product.

privatization proceeds but also the cumulative flows, as illustrated by figure 4. The accumulated proceeds from privatization in Europe and Central Asia for the period 1988 to 2005 came to about 16 percent of 2000 GDP, equivalent to around 5 percent of productive assets in those countries (assuming a capital-output ratio of about 3). In Latin America and the Caribbean the accumulated proceeds amounted to about 11 percent of 2000 GDP, or close to 4 percent of productive assets. Keeping in mind that privately operated assets are more productive than publicly operated assets, the contribution of the privatization process to GDP growth, in static terms, has been substantial. For instance, on the assumption that the productivity of assets is twice as high when they are privately operated than when they are publicly managed, privatization in Latin America and the Caribbean contributed about a quarter of a percentage point annually to growth, which is not negligible. In East Asia, South Asia, and Sub-Saharan Africa the intensity of privatization has been much less and may have contributed, at most, 0.1 percent of growth during this period.

The dominant sectors for privatization during the period 1988-were infrastructure, finance, and energy. This is important because later we argue that these sectors are probably less competitive than the manufacturing sectors, with important implications for the impact of privatization.

FIGURE 4.
Accumulated Proceeds as Share of 2000 GDP, by Region and Sector, 1988–2005

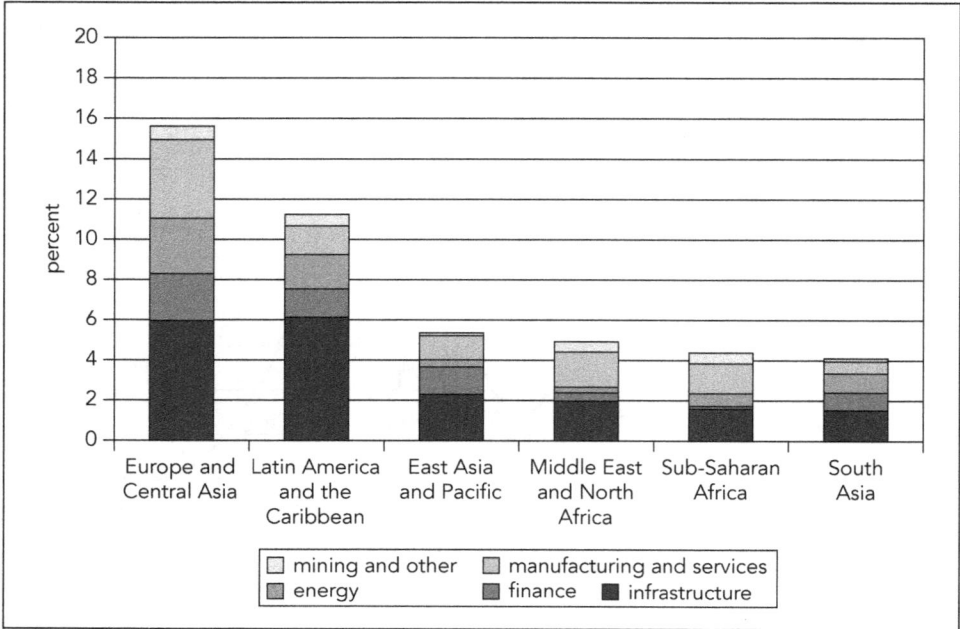

Source: World Bank Privatization Database; *World Development Indicators.*
Note: GDP, gross domestic product.

Although we do not have reliable information on the size of the public sector at each point of time, we do have some data gathered by the World Bank in the mid-1990s on the share of SOE activity in GDP and the share of SOEs' investment in gross domestic investment (GDI). These data, combined with the figures on accumulated proceeds as a share of GDP, provide a more complete picture of the extent of privatization in a sample of countries over the last 15 years. In Argentina, for instance, SOE activity was about 3 percent of GDP in 1990, as shown in figure 5, and the accumulated proceeds from privatization for the period 1988–2005 were about 14 percent of 2000 GDP. Using a capital-output ratio of roughly 3, one can conjecture that in a country such as Argentina, privatization of the economy has basically been completed. In India, by contrast, the assets that have been privatized are small in comparison with the share of SOEs in GDP in 1993, and so the scope for privatization there is still rather large. The same can be said of China and many African countries, such as Côte d'Ivoire.[3] So, privatization is not an issue that belongs to the past and it is all the most important to understand how best to privatize in countries where there is still scope for it.

FIGURE 5.
Privatization Proceeds and the Size of State-Owned Enterprises (SOEs), Selected Countries, 1990s

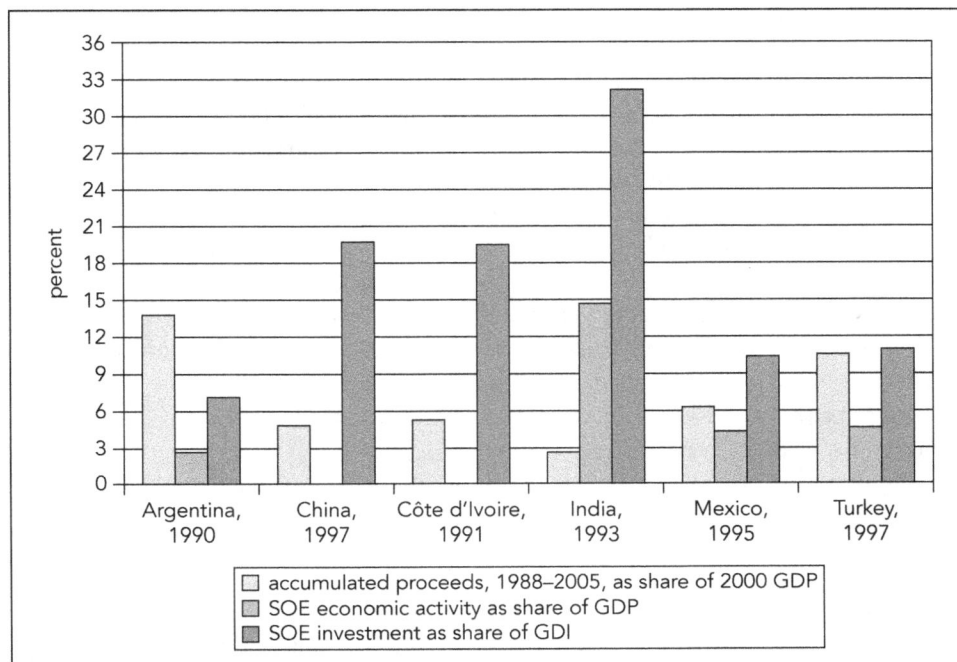

Source: World Development Indicators 2000.

Note: GDI, gross domestic investment; GDP, gross domestic product.

The Simple Economics of Privatization

We begin this section with a brief review of the main theories of state versus private ownership. Next, a simple example is presented to illustrate the trade-offs that policy makers face when considering privatization, in particular with respect to distributional issues. The main conclusion of this discussion is that theory alone is unlikely to yield a definitive answer about the merits (or shortcomings) of privatization. The type of private ownership to emerge after privatization, the characteristics of the product market (competitive or noncompetitive), the method of privatization, and other considerations will determine the overall outcome of privatization.

There is a huge theoretical literature on public versus private ownership and management. For the most part, the debate concerning the role of SOEs has been framed according to three views. The *social view* sees SOEs as institutions created by a social welfare–maximizing government to resolve actual or perceived market failures; whereas private firms maximize profits, SOEs maximize broader social objectives (Atkinson and Stiglitz 1980). The *agency view* also assumes that governments seek to maximize social welfare but focuses on the discrepancy between the objectives of managers (the agents) and of owners (the principals) within the two ownership regimes. SOE managers, confronted with weak incentives compared with those facing private firms, will channel resources to socially profitable activities but will expend less effort (or divert more resources) than their private counterparts.[4] This view concludes that, given the differences in incentives associated with public or private ownership, overall social welfare should depend on the trade-off between internal economic efficiency (under private ownership) and allocative efficiency (under public ownership); see Alchian (1965); Vickers and Yarrow (1988, 1991); Shapiro and Willig (1990); Laffont and Tirole (1993). Finally, the *political-economy view* suggests that SOEs represent a mechanism for pursuing the individual goals of politicians, such as maximizing employment or financing favored enterprises. Accordingly, SOEs are inefficient because of the deliberate policy of transferring resources to their supporters (Shleifer and Vishny 1994; Shleifer 1998).

A textbook example will help illustrate these issues, as well as others that are intrinsic to the privatization process. Consider the case of a municipality that intends to privatize the provision of clean water. The market for water provision has the characteristics described next.

The quantity, q, of water demanded depends on the price, p, at which it is sold, according to the following demand schedule:

$$q = 100 - 0.1p \tag{1}$$

The cost, C, of distributing water comprises a fixed cost equal to 1,000 monetary units ($) and the cost of labor. Employment (E) to distribute q units of water is given by:

$$E = q/\lambda \tag{2}$$

where λ is a productivity parameter. Under these conditions, the total cost of water is:

$$C = 1,000 + wq/\lambda \tag{3}$$

where w is the unit cost of labor; w is initially set at $10 and λ at 0.1.

In response to the large fixed cost, significant economies of scale, inelastic demand, and externalities (not taken into account here) involved in the provision of water, it is assumed that water is provided by a SOE that is subsidized by the government. As the first column of table 1 shows, the subsidy allows the SOE to sell water at a price of $80 (below its marginal cost of $100), but only 85 units of water are provided. The low price and the relatively small quantity imply that some consumers are rationed; at the price of $80, consumers would like to consume 92 units instead of the 85 units offered by the SOE. In this simple example, it is assumed that because of lack of monitoring incentives at the managerial level, workers in the SOE produce only 80 percent of what they would produce otherwise. To produce 85 units of water, the SOE thus employs 1,062.5 labor units instead of 850. At a wage rate of $10, the total wage bill is $10,625. The total amount of government subsidy to the SOE is $4,825 (including fixed costs), and that figure is equal to the SOE loss. The cost for consumers, at least for those who have access to water, is $6,800.

TABLE 1. From a State-Owned Enterprise (SOE) to a Regulated Private Monopoly: A Stylized Example of Privatization
(*$, except as specified*)

Indicator	Subsidized SOE	Private monopoly (no subsidy; price cap)
Price	80	120
Subsidy, including fixed costs	4,825	0
Quantity supplied (units)	85	88
Quantity demanded (units)	92	88
Employment (labor units)	1,062.5	880
Sales	6,800	10,560
Wage bill	10,625	8,800
Profit (+) or loss (−)	−3,825	1,760
Total profit or loss, including fixed costs	−4,825	760
Implicit demand price	150	120
Consumer surplus	42,075	38,720

Source: Authors' calculations.

The consumer surplus is a measure of the overall welfare of consumers. It is equal to the price they would be willing to pay for each successive unit of water they consume, up to their actual consumption, 85 units, minus the actual amount they pay, or $6,800. In this particular case, it is equal to $42,075.[5]

Assume now that the government decides to privatize water provision. There are many ways to privatize; consider as a starting point a private monopoly that is regulated so that the private company has a cap on the price that it can charge. Assume that the price is set at $120, with the company having the contractual obligation to provide universal service and to distribute all the water that is demanded at the set price. Finally, it is assumed that the private monopoly receives no subsidy for its operation (that is, it has a hard budget constraint). What are the implications of this type of privatization?

The first consequence, as shown in the second column of table 1, is that the quantity of water supplied increases from 85 to 88 units. Second, at the higher price, the quantity demanded decreases, and there is no rationing, in accordance with the terms of the contract under which the monopoly is regulated. Third, managerial incentives are such that workers devote more effort, and they work now at full productivity. Consequently, employment decreases from 1,062.5 labor units to 880 units, even though output is now larger.[6] Fourth, the government subsidy is zero. Fifth, total expenditures by consumers increase from $6,800 to $10,560. As a consequence, consumer welfare falls to $38,720.

If we compare the two situations, a subsidized SOE and a regulated private monopoly, we find, in the first place, an efficiency gain; the monopoly produces more output with fewer workers (table 2). The explanation is that the private monopoly is monitoring labor in a more efficient way. There are changes in the distribution of welfare; this outcome is crucial from our viewpoint, as is discussed below, but it has

TABLE 2. Efficiency and Distributional Impact of Privatization, with State-Owned Enterprises (SOEs) as Reference
($, except as specified)

Impact	Change
Efficiency gains	
Production (units)	3
Employment (labor units)	−182.5
Distributional effects	
Taxpayers	4,825
Consumers	−3,355
Access	—[a]
Employees	−1,825
Business owners	760
Total distributional effect	
(excluding valuation of access)	405

Source: Authors' calculations.

a. The valuation of access depends on the rationing scheme.

received little attention in the theoretical and empirical literature. Consider the distribution of costs and benefits among agents in this example.

First, the taxpayer gains from the privatization process. The government had been subsidizing the SOE in the amount of $4,825, and now there are no more subsidies. The taxpayer thus gains back the $4,825. (Alternatively, the government can allocate that money to other objectives thought to be valuable to taxpayers.) Second, consumers lose because the price has increased. But the story actually is slightly more complicated; consumers are worse off because of the price increase, but access to water has increased. The disappearance of rationing should contribute positively to consumer welfare, but it is difficult to measure that effect without getting into the details of the rationing scheme. This, again, is an important distributional issue.[7] Third, employees are worse off, in two ways: fewer workers are employed, and workers have to expend more effort working for the private monopoly than when they were working for the subsidized SOE. (This effect is not taken into account in table 2.) Fourth, business owners, who were not making money in the SOE, are now making a profit of $760. The total gain for the economy from this privatization is thus $405. The important point is that the privatization generates both losers and winners.

To go further we would need to understand better who are the "agents" listed in table 2. Who are the taxpayers? Are they the same individuals as the consumers? Who are the employees? Are they taxpayers? Are they consumers? Who are the business owners? Are the business owners the taxpayers? And within each group, we would like to know whether the individuals affected by the privatization are poor, members of the middle class, or rich. Who will be protesting in the streets tomorrow against privatization, and who will lobby the government for the privatization to go on? That depends on the answer to all these questions. This is the sort of analysis that is needed in order to evaluate the social welfare impact of privatization while taking its distributional effects fully into account.

In the preceding example, privatization entails a private monopoly with universal service, a price cap, and no subsidy. But privatization can also involve a monopoly that charges a price equal to the marginal cost and receives a subsidy for the amount of the fixed cost. Then the profit of the operator would be zero, and the distributional effects would be completely different. We can also think about unbundling the SOE, with an agent managing the fixed-cost part of the operation and competitive firms sharing the variable cost of the industry. Again, this will lead to different distributional implications.

Thus, theory alone is unlikely to be conclusive about the trade-offs between government and private ownership. All the dimensions discussed above are important, and they should be taken into account when thinking about privatization. Realistically, what do we know about these factors? In view of the simple example above, there clearly are at least two criteria that should be considered when evaluating privatization: productive efficiency and distributional impact. In the next section, we review some empirical evidence along both dimensions.

Empirical Evidence

It is surprising that when most of the privatization programs started in the mid-1980s, there were few empirical studies on the impact of privatization on firm performance and welfare distribution, and the existing studies were far from conclusive. Since then, the number of empirical studies has increased and includes privatization programs in different settings—competitive and noncompetitive markets, developed and developing countries, and so on. Yet, as will be seen below, many of these studies still have conceptual and methodological shortcomings.

Conceptual and Methodological Issues

Beyond the usual data and sample size difficulties, assessment of the impact of privatization is plagued with conceptual and methodological issues. First, to assess the impact of a policy change such as privatization, we need a counterfactual; that is, we need to imagine what would have happened in the absence of privatization. This is inevitably problematic. The problems are more pervasive in the case of utilities, where privatization can generate a host of general equilibrium effects, including relative price changes in output markets (tariff rebalancing) and input markets, as well as spillovers to other sectors of the economy. Second, causality is an important issue in assessing the impact of privatization. For example, performance may change because of other events or circumstances contemporaneous with privatization, such as shifts in the macroeconomic environment, regulatory changes, or promotion of competition. This issue is of particular relevance in the assessment of privatization in transition economies. Third, the potential selection bias in the SOEs to be privatized—the endogeneity problem—is important. If the allocation of firms for privatization is nonrandom, studies that do not adequately control for endogeneity will be biased.[8]

This section reviews the empirical evidence concerning the impact of privatization on efficiency and welfare distribution and illustrates some of the issues mentioned above with examples drawn from existing empirical studies.

Firm Performance

In the last few years, three excellent surveys reviewing the empirical evidence of privatization on firm performance have been published: Megginson and Netter (2001), Djankov and Murrell (2002), and Estrin et al. (2007). From our perspective, the strength of these surveys in comparison with similar papers is that they review the evidence while giving unique consideration to the methodological problems discussed above.[9]

Megginson and Netter review 38 studies that examine the impact of privatization on the operating efficiency, ownership structure, or financial performance of former SOEs in developed and developing countries (including transition economies), as well as in competitive and noncompetitive markets, mostly utilities. They find that almost all studies of nontransition economies that examine postprivatization changes in output, efficiency, capital investment spending, and profitability document significant increases in these variables and significant decreases in leverage. The studies, however, are less unanimous with respect to the impact of privatization on employment. Some studies find significant increases; others, significant decreases; and still others, insignificant changes in employment following privatization.[10]

A first example to illustrate the empirical evidence concerning the impact of privatization on efficiency is drawn from the wave of privatization of nonfinancial firms in Mexico during the period 1983–91 (La Porta and López-de-Silanes 1999). The authors include in their sample both SOEs and a control group of privately owned firms spanning a wide variety of industries and firm sizes, to control for potential biases.

Figure 6 presents four indicators of firm performance: sales per employee, employment, sales, and prices. These indicators are documented for the industry overall and for the competitive and noncompetitive parts of the industry.[11] For all industries, as well as for the competitive and noncompetitive subsectors, privatization has a significant efficiency effect in this sample of Mexican firms. Sales and productivity increase, whereas employment drops. On a different register, prices increase slightly. In agreement with theory, there is almost no price effect for privatized firms in competitive subsectors, but there is a large price effect for privatized firms in noncompetitive sectors. This example illustrates clearly the difference that a competitive environment makes for the effects of privatization.

In their review of the empirical evidence for transition economies, Megginson and Netter distinguish between Central and Eastern Europe and the former Soviet Union (FSU). In Central and Eastern Europe the evidence suggests that private ownership is associated with better firm-level performance and that foreign ownership, where allowed, is associated with greater performance improvement than purely domestic ownership. Majority ownership by outsider (nonemployee) investors is associated

FIGURE 6.
Change in Median Efficiency Performance in Competitive and Noncompetitive
Industries before and after Privatization, Mexico, 1983–91

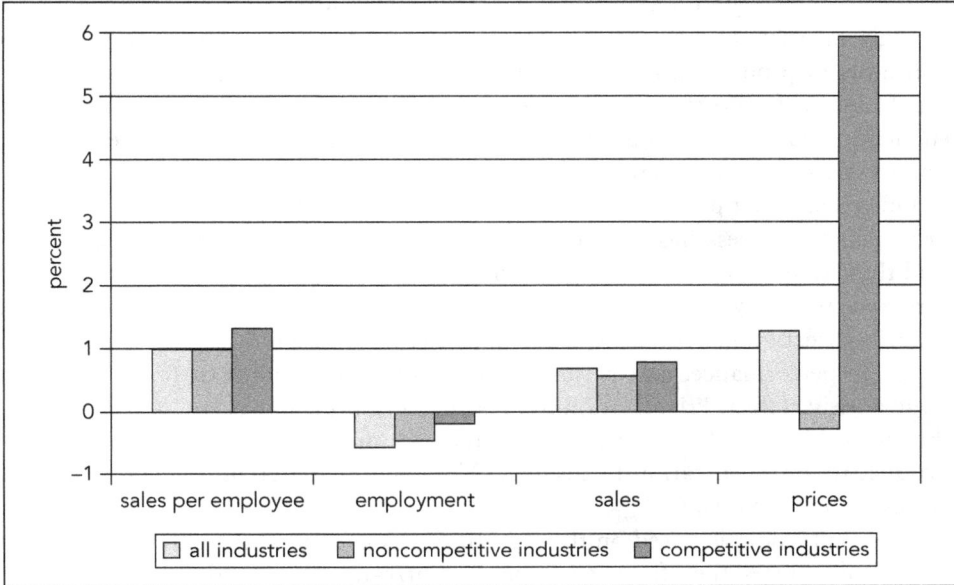

Source: La Porta and López-de-Silanes 1999.

with significantly greater improvement than any form of insider control. The key
advantage of outside control is the restructuring that takes place at the firm level. The
impact of privatization on employment is ambiguous, mainly because employment
decreased for almost all firms in transition economies after wide-ranging reforms
were initiated.

The authors note that assessing the impact of privatization in the FSU is much
more difficult because these republics were under communist control the longest and
the transition from a planned economy coincided with the disorders created by the
dissolution of the Soviet Union. In addition, at the time of the survey the contraction
of output that occurred after 1991 was far greater than anywhere in Eastern Europe,
with no upturn in sight. Thus, according to the authors, there is no empirical study
of the impact of privatization on performance that is truly persuasive from a methodological point of view. That being said, an important result of all the studies is that
insider privatization has not been a success in the FSU.

Djankov and Murrell (2002) review the empirical evidence on the effects of privatization on firm performance (productivity, sales, profits, etc.) and on qualitative indicators (wage arrears, creation of new products, and so on) in transition economies.[12]
In contrast to Megginson and Netter (2001), they use formal meta-analysis to synthe-
size the evidence of more than 100 empirical studies instead of relying on a verbal
description or an interpretative summary of the studies. From our perspective, one of
the most interesting characteristics of this survey is that the methodology can explicitly

address the issue of differences in the quality of studies, thereby showing to what extent the conclusions change if greater weight is given to studies that appear methodologically sound. Even so, the meta-analysis echoes in some respects the initial results presented by Megginson and Netter. Djankov and Murrell find that privatization is strongly associated with better performance and with improvements in qualitative indicators of production restructuring. These findings, however, are not statistically significant for firm performance in the countries of the Commonwealth of Independent States (CIS). The results are robust to the use of weights that reflect different attention to selection bias or to the quality of the analysis.

One reason that privatization may have varying effects across regions is that the privatization process has led to different mixes of owners. Djankov and Murrell find that state ownership within traditional state firms has less effect on firm performance than any other ownership regime except worker ownership, which has a negative effect on performance.[13] Privatization to diffuse individual owners has no effect on performance, and privatization to investment funds or foreigners has a large positive effect. Privatization to investment funds is five times as productive as that to insiders, and privatization to foreigners or blockholders is three times as productive as privatization to insiders. The effect of different ownership regimes varies among regions.

A second example based on the privatization experience of Central and Eastern Europe illustrates the efficiency impact of privatization. Frydman et al. (1999) draw on firm data from the Czech Republic, Hungary, and Poland for the period 1990–93 and seek to disentangle the efficiency effect of privatization according to type of ownership. Their study is also interesting because it includes a control group (a counterfactual) consisting of firms that were SOEs at the beginning of the period and remained SOEs at the end of the period. The only shortcoming of this work is that no correction has been made for the selectivity of the privatization process. Privatized firms in the sampled countries were not selected randomly. In the countries covered by Frydman et al., privatization improved efficiency when the firms were acquired by outsiders (figure 7). Revenue increased, and employment did not change, leading to sizable productivity gains. Interestingly, when privatization entailed the transfer of ownership to firm insiders (either the managers or employees working in the SOE before privatization), the impact on efficiency was radically different. Revenue decreased in comparison with the control group, and employment increased, leading to a drop in productivity. A possible explanation is that managers and workers of a privatized SOE try to extract more rent from the firm when they are in command.

Finally, the survey by Estrin et al. (2007) addresses more rigorously the issue of selection bias or endogeneity that arises when better firms may have been privatized first in transition economies. The authors present some new results, as they can draw on recent studies in transition economies that employ better methodology, as well as studies for China that were barely reviewed in the two surveys cited above. Broadly, Estrin et al. find that privatization to foreign owners increases efficiency in relation to SOEs, although this result is less clear for China. Domestic private ownership has

FIGURE 7.
Impact of Ownership on Performance, with State-Owned Enterprises as Reference, Fixed-Effects Coefficients, Czech Republic, Hungary, and Poland, 1990–93

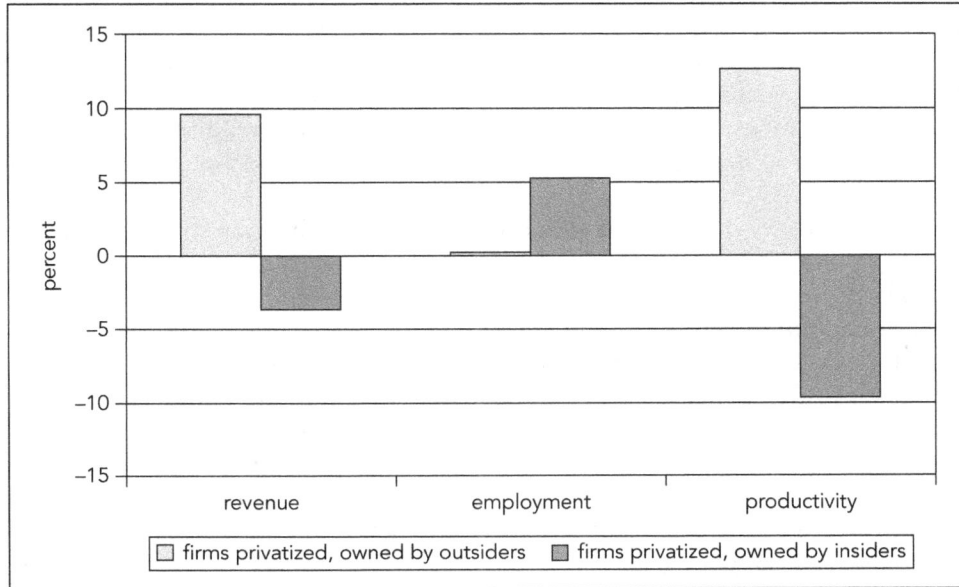

Source: Frydman et al. 1999.

Note: The fixed-effects coefficients are estimated controlling for year and country. The coefficients for privatizations owned by outsiders are statistically significant at 1 percent for revenue and productivity.

a positive effect on efficiency in Central and Eastern Europe, but the effect is smaller than that of foreign ownership. Russia seems to be different in that domestic private ownership and mixed ownership have a negative or insignificant effect on efficiency. Worker ownership in Central and Eastern Europe and the CIS, and collective ownership in China, do not seem to have a negative effect relative to other forms of private ownership, unlike the findings in the Djankov and Murrell study. Finally, data from Central and Eastern Europe and the CIS suggest that new firms appear to be as productive as or more productive than firms privatized to domestic owners and that foreign start-ups appear to be more efficient than domestic start-ups. Studies of employment find that privatizations in Central and Eastern Europe, the CIS, and China are not associated with reductions in employment.

Finally, it is important to emphasize that the empirical evidence accumulated regarding firm performance is mainly based on data from member countries of the Organisation for Economic Co-operation and Development (OECD), Latin American countries, and economies in transition. The empirical evidence on the effects of privatization in Africa is not as deep and robust as the evidence discussed above. Thus, caution is necessary in generalizing the results presented above to low-income countries.

Distributional Impact

In contrast to the huge number of studies on the impact of privatization on firm performance, relatively few studies analyze the impact on social welfare and its distribution. Moreover, these studies mostly cover OECD and Latin American countries; they focus mainly on the impact of privatization on consumer welfare in the utility sector; and they are less successful in controlling for potential biases. Birdsall and Nellis (2003) review some of this literature. As is outlined here, our knowledge falls short of what is desirable for adequately assessing the impact of privatization on social welfare.

Galal et al (1994) is the most persuasive of the studies. Its main strength is the construction of a clear counterfactual that allows for the measurement of the financial as well as the welfare impacts of privatization. The authors analyze 12 privatized companies (mostly airlines and regulated utilities) in Chile, Malaysia, Mexico, and the United Kingdom to determine whether the transfer to private ownership increased efficiency and, if so, how the costs and benefits of the adjustment were allocated to government, foreign and domestic buyers, competitors, consumers, and employees. Galal et al. document welfare gains in 11 of the 12 cases analyzed. In no case were workers worse off after privatization, and in three instances they were better off. Although this study is rigorous, it examines only a small number of firms in four countries and does not cover the wider range of aspects described earlier in this paper.

Another study that attempt to shed some light on the implications of privatization for welfare is Ugaz and Waddams Price (2003). In contrast to Galal et al. (1994), this study focuses only on consumer welfare, using household surveys before and after privatization. The seven cases analyzed correspond to utilities in Latin America, Spain, and the United Kingdom and present a mixed picture. They show that prices have often risen as a result of the rebalancing of tariffs after privatization, and this has affected low-income groups more than others. But the study also shows that most companies have extended their coverage (access) so that the poor in developing countries, who initially enjoyed the least coverage, are benefiting the most from this aspect of privatization.

Similar research was carried out for Latin America by the Inter-American Development Bank. The case study presented here is about the privatization of water distribution in two provinces of Bolivia, La Paz–El Alto, and Cochabamba (Barja, McKenzie, and Urquiola 2005). As was seen above, when discussing the simple economics of privatization, the two main determinants of the impact of privatization on consumer welfare are price and access. In the case of Bolivia, the 1997 privatization of water distribution in La Paz and El Alto produced only a slight increase in prices (figure 8), but in Cochabamba, where privatization took place in 1999, prices increased enormously months later.

To evaluate the welfare impact of privatization on consumers, access needs to be taken into account. Figure 9 shows the impact of privatization on households in La Paz and El Alto according to their initial access to water. The welfare of those households that enjoyed access before privatization did not change much, as prices did not

FIGURE 8.
Real Water Prices in Two Provinces of Bolivia, 1992–2000

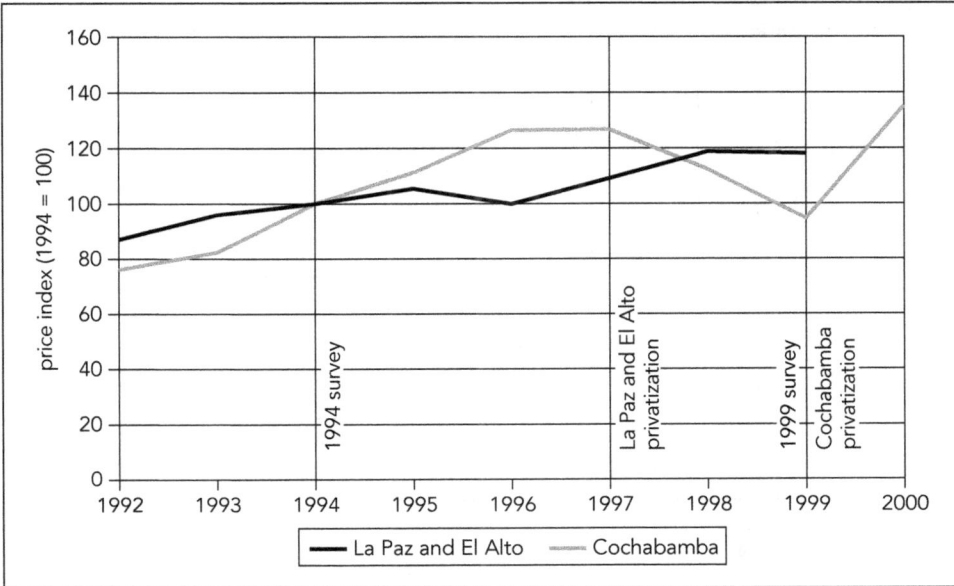

Source: Barja, McKenzie, and Urquiola 2005.

FIGURE 9.
Change in Welfare after 1997 Water Privatization, by Income Group, La Paz and El Alto Province, Bolivia

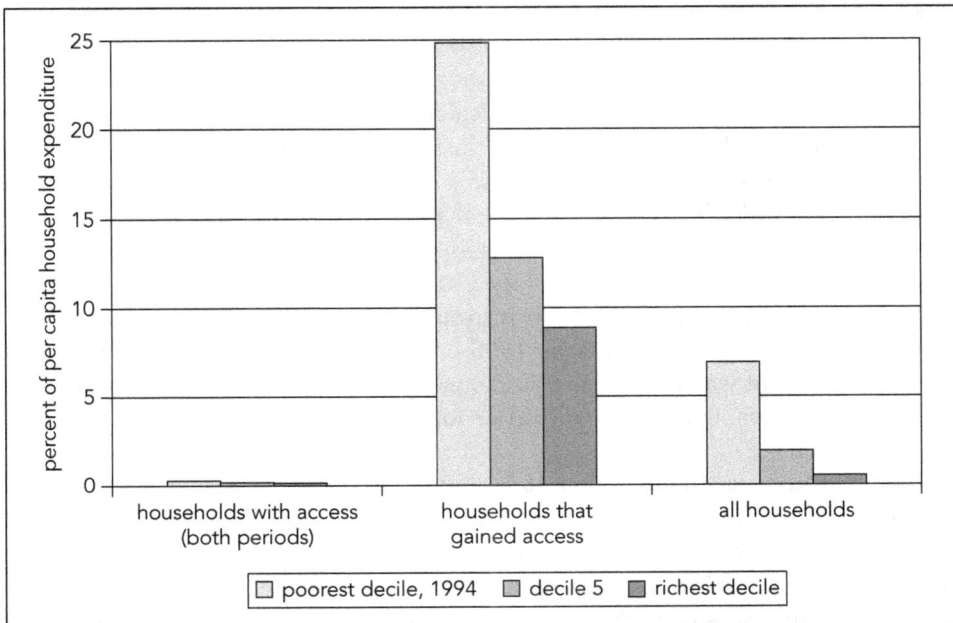

Source: Barja, McKenzie, and Urquiola 2005.

FIGURE 10.
Change in Welfare after 1999 Water Privatization, by Income Group, Cochabamba Province, Bolivia

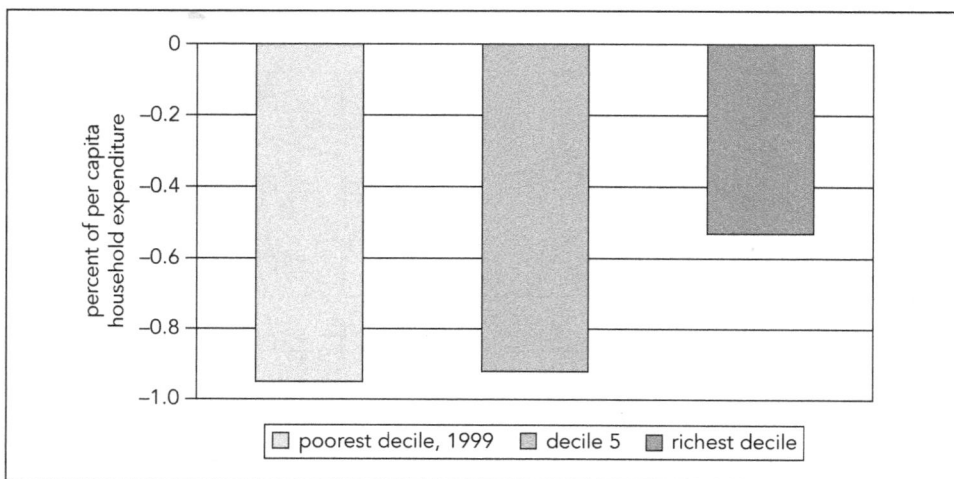

Source: Barja, McKenzie, and Urquiola 2005.

increase substantially. For households that gained access, there was a large positive impact on welfare. If it can be proved that this improved access was caused by privatization, privatization might have had a huge impact on consumer welfare.

In Cochabamba privatization was very short-lived. The privatization took place in October 1999. In March 2000 widespread protests occurred—the so-called Water War—and the government decided to give the water operation back to the original SOE. Barja, McKenzie, and Urquiola (2005) estimated the impact of the price increase on income groups in the population, looking simply at the share of water expenditure in household budgets and calculating how much households would have to pay in addition. Figure 10 shows that the impact of privatization in Cochabamba was highly regressive, with all deciles losing welfare because of this price effect but with the poorest decile losing much more than the richest decile.

The last example in this discussion is from a well-known study by Galiani, Gertler, and Schargrodsky (2005), who exploited variation in ownership across time and space to identify the causal effect of privatization of water distribution on child mortality in Argentina (figure 11). From 1993 onward, several municipalities privatized the distribution of water, whereas other municipalities kept their initial arrangement with public companies, either national or local, thus providing a control group, or counterfactual.

The evidence suggests that after 1993 child mortality rates in municipalities with privatized water distribution dropped faster than in those with nonprivatized water distribution. This is an interesting result. If we believe that changes in child mortality are mostly attributable to changes in the subgroups of the population in which child mortality is highest—often, the poorest people—this would mean that the privatization of water in Argentina had a progressive effect. But the difficulty with the

FIGURE 11.
Child Mortality Rates in Municipalities Served by Privatized and Nonprivatized Water Companies, Argentina, 1990–99

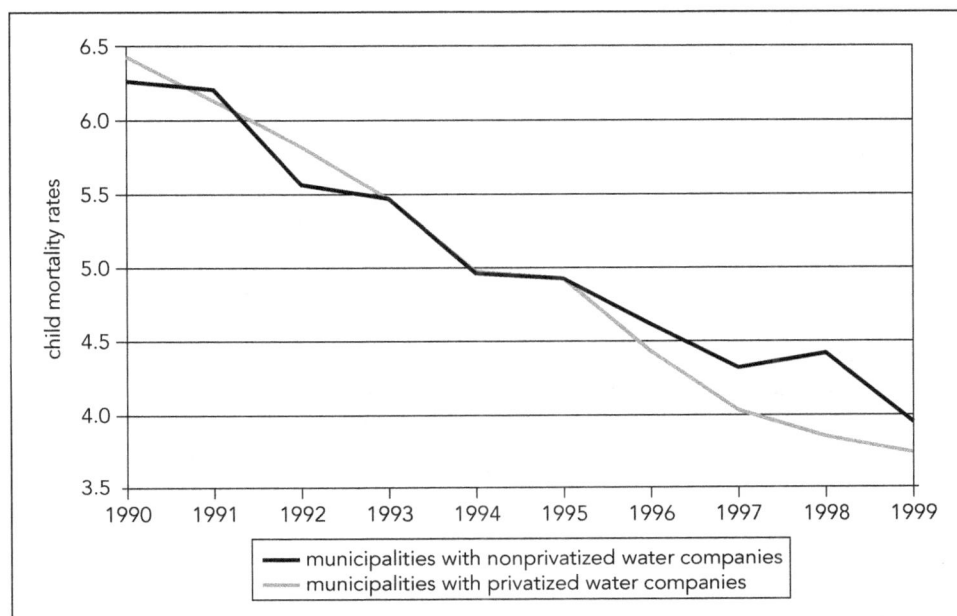

Source: Galiani, Gertler, and Schargrodsky 2005.

approach taken in the paper is that it is a highly reduced form. We do not know through what channels the reduction in the child mortality rate took place. Did it occur because there was better access under privatized water companies? Or was it because the quality of water was better? We do not know. But this certainly is the type of evidence that is needed in order to understand the distributional impact of privatization.

Concluding Remarks

The paucity of full evaluations of privatization operations in developing countries is surprising. There are some analyses of the efficiency gains of privatization, but there is very little assessment of the distributional impact of privatization, and most of the studies that do exist only consider the effect of price changes on consumers. Evaluations of the indirect effects of privatization—for example, the study of child mortality discussed earlier—are much rarer. The complete picture that was described in the analytical section of this paper is simply not available in the empirical analyses. Thus, one important conclusion of this brief review of privatization and development is the need to pursue this type of empirical analysis more exhaustively. If there is scope for privatization in some countries, we need to have more in-depth evaluations to guide our policies.

The efficiency gains of privatization seem warranted in many cases. Moreover, gains in productivity and output do not always imply a loss in employment. There is little doubt that when we consider privatization in a competitive environment, the change is almost certainly positive. The distributional effects, however, are uncertain and opaque. The negative attitude toward privatization in Latin America that was described at the beginning of this paper may well be the result of that opacity. People are preoccupied with the impact on consumers and do not look at taxpayers at all, or they ignore the issue of access, or they simply follow the general negative political discourse against privatization or are concerned with the macroeconomic impact of privatization. This lack of knowledge is not a desirable state of affairs.

Much more remains to be done at this stage toward evaluating the ex ante and ex post impacts of privatization, the most effective types of regulation and ownership regimes, and the way in which losers—when there are any—can be compensated. We have to rely on serious evaluations of different designs for those privatization operations. This is a need that must be met by the community of academics and development agencies, including the World Bank and regional development banks. We should try to exploit all the occasions when those institutions are involved in privatizations to extract the maximum information on the distributional impacts of these operations.

Notes

1. The state may be the central government or local governments.
2. These years were chosen simply because 1998 was the peak year of the second and last big wave of privatization in Latin America and 2005 is the most recent year for which information on attitudes toward privatization is available in Latinobarómetro.
3. Although we lack information on the share of SOEs in GDP in China, it does not seem unreasonable to assume that it should be about half their share in GDI. Then SOEs would still be responsible for 10 percent of GDP in 1997; privatization might have reduced that share by roughly 2 percent since then.
4. In private firms the discrepancy among objectives is reduced by the threat of takeover and bankruptcy, a managerial labor market, and the existence of ownership rights that allow the principals to sell the firm if they are not satisfied with managerial performance.
5. This corresponds to the area below the demand curve at the rationed quantity 85.
6. We assume that the wage rate is the same, but it might also be allowed to vary.
7. The assumption that all consumers are rationed in the same proportion would make the correction for rationing unnecessary.
8. Gupta, Ham, and Svejnar (2000) present evidence of nonrandomness in privatization in the Czech Republic.
9. Other useful surveys are Kikeri and Nellis (2004) and Shirley and Walsh (2000).
10. According to Megginson and Netter (2001), the most compelling studies, taking into account sample size, coverage, and methodological rigor, are for nontransition economies: Galal et al. (1994); La Porta and López-de-Silanes (1999); Dewenter and Malatesta (2001); and the three articles summarized in D'Souza and Megginson (1999). For transition economies the best studies (using the above criteria) are Dyck (1997); Weiss and Nikitin (1998); Claessens and Djankov (1999); Lizal, Singer, and Svejnar (2001); and Frydman et al. (1999).

11. The definitions of competitive or noncompetitive industries are based on the description of the industry provided in the privatization prospectus.

12. Djankov and Murrell (2002) use the term "restructuring measure" to capture both quantitative (performance) and qualitative indicators. Employment is not used as an indicator in their study because of the substantial disagreement in the literature on the impact of privatization on employment.

13. Djankov and Murrell (2002) use 11 categories of ownership, some of which overlap: (a) traditional state ownership (enterprises that are 100 percent state owned and have not been part of a privatization program); (b) state ownership in enterprises that are treated as private under the corporate governance laws and, usually, have been part of a privatization program; (c) insiders (a composite group that includes both workers and managers); (d) outsiders (a composite group consisting of all nonemployee, nonstate owners); (e) workers; (f) managers; (g) foreign owners of all types; (h) banks, except those included in (g); (i) investment funds, unless ownership of the fund is such that (b), (g), or (h) applies; (j) blockholders, that is, outsider ownership concentrated in the hands of large individual owners, unless the blockholder could be classified under (b) or (f)–(i); and (k) diffuse outsider—the residual outsider ownership category, when outsider owners are not identified as belonging to categories (g)–(j).

References

Alchian, Armen. 1965. "Some Economics of Property Rights." *Il Politico* 30: 816–29. Reprinted in *Economic Forces at Work,* ed. A. Alchian, 127–49. Indianapolis, IN: Liberty Fund, 1977.

Atkinson, A. B., and Joseph E. Stiglitz. 1980. *Lectures in Public Economics.* New York: McGraw-Hill.

Barja, Gover, David McKenzie, and Miguel Urquiola. 2005. "Capitalization and Privatization in Bolivia: An Approximation to an Evaluation." In *Reality Check: The Distributional Impact of Privatization in Developing Countries,* ed. John Nellis and Nancy Birdsall. Washington, DC: Center for Global Development.

Birdsall, Nancy, and John Nellis. 2003. "Winners and Losers: Assessing the Distributional Impact of Privatization." *World Development* 31 (10): 1617–33.

Claessens, Stijn, and Simeon Djankov. 1999. "Ownership Concentration and Corporate Performance in the Czech Republic." *Journal of Comparative Economics* 27 (3): 498–513.

Dewenter, Kathryn L., and Paul H. Malatesta. 2001. "State-Owned and Privately Owned Firms: An Empirical Analysis of Profitability, Leverage, and Labor Intensity." *American Economic Review* 91(1): 320–34.

Djankov, Simeon, and Peter Murrell. 2002. "Enterprise Restructuring in Transition: A Quantitative Survey." *Journal of Economic Literature* 40 (3, September): 739–92.

D'Souza, Juliet, and William L. Megginson. 1999. "The Financial and Operating Performance of Newly Privatized Firms during the 1990s." *Journal of Finance* 54 (4, August): 1397–1438.

Dyck, I. J. Alexander. 1997. "Privatization in Eastern Germany: Management Selection and Economic Transition." *American Economic Review* 87: 565–97.

Estrin. Saul, Jan Hanousek, Evzen Kočenda, and Jan Svejnar. 2007. "Effects of Privatization and Ownership in Transition Economies." CERGE-EI Discussion Paper 181, Center for Economic Research and Graduate Education, Economics Institute, Prague. Forthcoming in *Journal of Economic Literature.*

Frydman, Roman, Cheryl W. Gray, Marek P. Hessel, and Andrzej Rapaczynski. 1999. "When Does Privatization Work? The Impact of Private Ownership on Corporate Performance in the Transition Economies." *Quarterly Journal of Economics* 114 (4): 1153–91.

Galal, Ahmed, Leroy Jones, Pankaj Tandon, and Ingo Vogelsang. 1994. *Welfare Consequences of Selling Public Enterprises: An Empirical Analysis.* New York, NY: Oxford University Press.

Galiani, Sebastian, Paul Gertler, and Ernesto Schargrodsky, 2005. "Water for Life: The Impact of the Privatization of Water Services on Child Mortality." *Journal of Political Economy* 113 (1, February): 83–120.

Gupta, Nandini, John C. Ham, and Jan Svejnar. 2000. "Priorities and Sequencing in Privatization: Theory and Evidence from the Czech Republic." Williamson Davidson Institute Working Paper 323, University of Michigan, Ann Arbor.

Kikeri, Sunita, and John Nellis. 2004. "An Assessment of Privatization." *World Bank Research Observer* 19 (1): 87–118.

Kirkpatrick, Colin, David Parker, and Yin-Fang Zhang. 2006. "An Empirical Analysis of State and Private-Sector Provision of Water Services in Africa." *World Bank Economic Review* 20 (1): 143–63.

Laffont, Jean-Jacques, and Jean Tirole. 1993. *A Theory of Incentives in Procurement and Regulation.* Cambridge, MA: MIT Press.

La Porta, Rafael, and Florencio López-de-Silanes. 1999. "The Benefits of Privatization: Evidence from Mexico." *Quarterly Journal of Economics* 114 (4): 1193–1242.

Lizal, Lubomir, Miroslav Singer, and Jan Svejnar. 2001. "Enterprise Breakups and Performance during the Transition from Plan to Market." *Review of Economics and Statistics* 83 (1): 92–99.

Megginson, William L., and Jeffry M. Netter. 2001. "From State to Market: A Survey of Empirical Studies on Privatization." *Journal of Economic Literature* 39 (2): 321–89.

Shapiro, Carl, and Robert D. Willig. 1990. "Economic Rationales for the Scope of Privatization." In *Political Economy of Public Sector Reform and Privatization,* ed. Ezra Suleiman and John Waterbury, 55–87. Boulder, CO: Westview Press.

Shirley, Mary, and Patrick Walsh. 2000. "Public vs. Private Ownership: The Current State of the Debate." World Bank Policy Research Working Paper 2420, World Bank, Washington, DC.

Shleifer, Andrei. 1998. "State versus Private Ownership." *Journal of Economic Perspectives* 12 (4): 133–50.

Shleifer, Andrei, and Robert W. Vishny. 1994. "Politicians and Firms." *Quarterly Journal of Economics* 109 (4, November): 995–1025.

Ugaz, Cecilia, and Catherine Waddams Price, eds. 2003. *Utility Privatization and Regulation: A Fair Deal for Consumers?* Cheltenham, U.K.: Edward Elgar.

Vickers, John, and George Yarrow. 1988. *Privatization: An Economic Analysis.* Cambridge, MA: MIT Press.

———. 1991. "Economic Perspectives on Privatization." *Journal of Economic Perspectives* 5 (2): 111–32.

Weiss, Andrew, and Georgiy Nikitin. 1998. "Performance of Czech Companies by Ownership Structure." Williamson Davidson Institute Working Paper 186, University of Michigan, Ann Arbor.

World Bank. Various issues, *World Development Indicators.* Washington, DC: World Bank.

Keynote Address

JANEZ POTOČNIK

Ladies and gentlemen, good evening. First of all thank you for the opportunity to speak to you and second, welcome you to Slovenia, my country. I would like to congratulate the World Bank on choosing an excellent venue for this year's ABCDE conference. The British writer Somerset Maugham once said that at a dinner you should eat wisely, but not too well, and talk well, but not too wisely. You will be the judge of whether I follow this advice tonight, but I ask for your patience.

The theme of this year's conference is the private sector and development. It is a short title but a long story. You will probably not be surprised if I concentrate on research and innovation on the development side. Allow me first to say few words about the global picture and the things that are crucially influencing our lives.

People often divide the world into distinct camps: the developed world, the developing world, emerging economies, the First World, the Third World, and so on. As we all know, these are just short terms for very different and complex stages of the same more and more interconnected world. The reality is that our Earth is getting smaller; we are living faster, and we are, from day to day, becoming more interconnected. Globalization is a fact. You can hate it, you can love it, you can see opportunities if you want, and you can see the side effects that are also obvious; but one thing is quite clear: you cannot ignore it. The world is becoming more and more multipolar. China, India, Brazil, and others are developing rapidly and rightly so. I am pleased to see the developments in these countries. Challenges are also becoming more and more global, and so is the need to address them. Whether you look at health, climate change, drinking water, energy supply, security, or food, all these issues are effectively global ones. Addressing them together is logical and necessary.

The other issues in today's world worth mentioning are the effects of the aging of the population and the new emerging technologies and, even more than that, the

---

Janez Potočnik is European Commissioner for science and research. From 1998 until 2004 he headed the negotiating team for Slovenia's accession to the EU, and from 2002 to 2004 he was Slovenia's Minister for European Affairs.

Annual World Bank Conference on Development Economics 2008, Global

connection between the two. We have fewer children, and we are living longer. If you ask an insurance company in Germany what life expectancy they calculate for a girl born today, the answer is 104 years. That is the reality they use in their calculations. Technological development—unfortunately and fortunately for us who are getting older—is happening faster and faster. We need to work longer, but technology is becoming outdated faster.

There is obviously a need for a sustainable approach to life, and I do not mean sustainable only in the context of the environment. I think of it more in the context of being friendly toward people, toward all human beings on this planet, and of course, toward the planet itself. That kind of sustainability is extremely important for the future. Why do we need to pursue a sustainable future? If you ask a child of 5, the answer would be quite simple, and I would stick to that type of answer: because all other futures are unsustainable. Global partners are moving increasingly in the direction of knowledge societies. This is an inclusive concept, and it is the only concept that allows us to talk about social security, environmental sustainability, and business competitiveness at the same time. That is why so many people today understand that this is a move in the right direction.

It is interesting to look at the Eurobarometer results, which are regularly produced in the European Union (EU). A recent poll examined attitudes toward globalization. Something like 65 or 66 percent of the people surveyed believed that the most positive effect of globalization is cooperation in research and development. The negative effects cited had to do with the environment, economic growth, and so on.

In Europe we have seen the biggest enlargement yet, and we have experienced the failure of the constitutional treaty discussions. We are modernizing the necessary treaties. We are preparing the new financial perspective, and much will depend on it. In short, we are in the middle of a difficult but necessary transformation: from a resource-based economy to a knowledge-based economy and society. Some believe that we have gone too fast and too far, that enlargement was too rapid, and that the deepening of Europe is also proceeding too hastily. I think that enlargement had nothing to do with the progress of today's Europe, in an economic sense; or if so, it has been helpful. The old, traditional Europe would have had to face the problems of reconstruction and modernization, with or without enlargement.

In 2000 we decided to pursue the Lisbon strategy. In reality, the Lisbon story is quite simple. Are we able to sustain and even improve our quality of life and remain globally competitive? It is a question with a very difficult answer. We know that we should not lower wages because that would not be accepted. When we talk about social security standards, although knowing that we have to undertake reforms because of the aging of the population and the rigidities of the market, reducing the standards is not a path that Europe could competitively choose relative to other global competitors and partners. If we talk about the environment, it becomes ever clearer that reducing standards would be a disastrous decision. Europe does not have a lot of natural resources, so we have to perform better and know more than some. And this is why the orientation toward a knowledge society was the only wise and reasonable direction.

The EU strategy for growth and jobs launched by the European Commission was actually a confirmation that we have to do things in a different, more focused way, when we talk about the knowledge economy as well; and that we need a different model of management. Governance has not been well established. Today we have national reform programs and all the member states are heading in the same direction, each on the basis of its own environment and characteristics.

The role of knowledge in research and development in Europe is now well recognized. As an illustration, I would just use the debate on adoption of the energy package, which was a courageous move. Many people are saying that this is a new industrial revolution, and I personally believe that it is true, but let's wait and see. This was actually the first time that we discussed all the issues at the same time. Whether the concern is the environment, the energy shortage and the need for environmentally friendly solutions for the future, or the need to remain globally competitive, if you put these issues on the table at the same time, the answers are quite simple. The increased globalization of trade and knowledge means that business and research offer more than merely solutions. They offer innovation, economic development, and answers to our major challenges.

I will use climate change as an example of why getting the private sector on board is so crucial and important. At the recent meeting of the International Panel on Climate Change (IPCC), we heard three basic conclusions. First, there is a very high probability, a 90 percent probability that the climate process we are facing today is caused by human beings. To simplify, we created the mess, and nobody else can clean it up. Second, the 20 percent of the world's population that lives in rich countries generates almost half of the world's greenhouse gases. Per capita consumption of energy in the United States is much higher than in Europe, and it is much higher in Europe than in Asia. Finally, poor countries will be more adversely affected than rich ones by climate change effects such as increased desertification, floods, mass migrations, and loss of biodiversity. These are the facts and the major conclusions.

As you all know, growth rates are very much interconnected with energy consumption, and since countries like China and India are developing rapidly (and they have the right to do so), it is obvious that they will use more energy than they are using today. If we want seriously to deal with that process and problem, the only way is to show, by example, that we want to reverse the trend and that we are ready to work together to find mutual, technological solutions not yet available. We have to go in this direction together, and we have to go rapidly. But this can only be done if political signals are strong and clear and if they include major private capital investments. In other words, only if we change the difficult reality into a major business opportunity can we truly succeed. The key words are research, innovation, market rules, both cooperation and competition at the same time, and business investment. This is not an option; it is our duty.

The next point I want to mention is that development, like research, does not necessarily start and end at a country's borders. Look at places like Mumbai. That one Indian city has more millionaires than many individual EU countries. And a recent American Express study found that the Indian city now producing new millionaires faster than any other is Bangalore. India has the fastest-growing wealth base in the Asia and Pacific region, and Bangalore is growing faster than the Indian rate. And what is Bangalore famous for? For its research and development base. Just ask Google, or Nokia or Bell, or the many other companies that are already there. So, there are poles of development in the heart of the Third World, and there are pockets of poverty at the center of the First World. Both can be addressed through increased involvement in research, especially by the private sector.

In Europe, the European Council decided in 2002 that EU countries should invest an average of 3 percent of our gross domestic product in science and research. It was also decided that two-thirds of that should come from the private sector. Today we are at 1.84 percent, which is far from the target, and even if the national reform programs of the member states were fully fulfilled, we would reach only 2.6 percent in 2010. But even these programs are quite optimistic. The factors for attracting investment in research, innovation, and development are, first, the existence of the market; second, a strong knowledge pool; and, third, a high-quality public research base. Surprisingly, wage levels are not much of a factor. Of course, other conditions are important, such as tax incentives, state aid, and intellectual property rights. In Europe we are heading toward the much-needed European Community patent, public procurement, risk venture capital conditions, mobility of people, the higher education system, financial labor markets, coherence between macroeconomic and microeconomic policy, structural policies, and so on.

You may have noticed that I have not mentioned any of the topics for which I am responsible. Actually, I am measuring how others are doing, which is a nice position. Of course, it is also very important to understand how universities, institutes and business are connected, and how the education, research and innovation triangle is working. We have many activities in the EU, from the European technology platforms to joint technology initiatives and lead market initiatives. Then there is the idea of creating a European Institute of Technology. All of this goes exactly in the direction that I have tried to address.

Attracting research and development-intensive investment, especially foreign direct investment (FDI), is a challenge for everyone, but it is one worth addressing because the rewards of this kind of investment are undeniable. It brings not only capital and jobs but also knowledge, skills, technology, and, most important, new opportunities. This is a lesson for all of us. If developing countries are to attract quality FDI, they must first invest in their knowledge base—in education, research infrastructure, and training. By doing this, they will be better positioned to tap into the world economy. The EU research policy is helping to create this base in the developing world. We know that cooperation is one of our biggest weapons. That is why more than half of the EU Framework Program budget is dedicated to cooperative research projects, including international cooperation. And we also know that the private sector is fundamental if internal research is to become external innovation.

My final point concerning research is that research, like development, is never static. We need to keep our eyes and ears open to the latest needs and the latest directions. That is why the European Commission opened up a public consultation on how to develop the European Research Area. We want to introduce a fifth freedom in Europe: the freedom of movement of knowledge, which does not yet exist. We want to strengthen European research capacities.

When we had discussions recently with people who were conducting a serious analysis of how Europe was perceived from the outside—they came from the United States, China, India, South Africa, practically everybody was present around the table—their conclusion was straightforward. Europe is definitely an economic power; there is no doubt about that. Europe is the top exporter in the world and the second-largest importer. Europe is a potential emerging political power. We have the potential for policy leadership in areas such as climate change, energy, and the social model. In many areas of the world Europe is seen as a model for regional cooperation and integration. The question is, are we ready to exercise this soft power? Are we ready to turn the team of stars into a star team? Don't forget what happened to a team of stars from Brasilia in the last world football [soccer] championship! So, we need an ability to dream, but we need, at the same time, an ability to fulfil this dream. Or as our American friends from Nike would say, "Just do it."

And what about the role of a new EU member state such as my country, Slovenia? I will say just a few things, not connected to research or to the topics I mentioned earlier. There is no reason at all for Slovenia to feel small or inferior. On the contrary, what I have learned when I have travelled around is that nobody really expects us to feel like that. The problem is basically one of self-confidence—but it is our problem. Slovenia is an important member of the EU family. It has recently adopted the Euro, and it will hold the Presidency of the European Union, with its population of 2 million, in the first half of 2008. But it is small, relatively new member state, which has travelled through many troubled waters; and since it is a neighbor of the fragile Western Balkans, Slovenia can probably understand some of facts better than others. We can see, for example, that sometimes the most important national interest is actually a European interest, or even a global interest; that when it comes to Europe, in this global world, we all win or we all lose; that it is necessary to explain how important the European Union is for peace, stability, security, and prosperity; that we should continue with the EU enlargement process; that we should consolidate and improve our efficiency and functioning, and so on. Our role—your role, dear friends—is to explain and repeat this loud and clear because you know and understand it better than many others do. That is your duty, and my duty.

To conclude, the British film director Alfred Hitchcock once said that good wine and good food do not go with a lot of talking, so I will stop here. I wish you a pleasant meal and, of course, "Dober tek" ["Bon appétit"].

Keynote Address
Informality, Productivity, and Growth in Mexico

SANTIAGO LEVY

Good morning. I would like to begin by thanking the World Bank, and in particular François Bourguignon, for inviting me here. It is a pleasure to be with you this morning.

I want to share with you some work that I am doing on an issue that is, I think, particularly relevant for Mexico and many Latin American countries and perhaps for some countries in Africa and Asia. I am not sure to what extent it applies to European countries. It has to do with the existence of a very large informal sector. I will start by giving you a little background.

Over the past decade Mexico's growth has been disappointingly slow. There was a large set of reforms associated with the North American Free Trade Agreement, deregulation of some sectors, privatization of some firms, and, of course, macroeconomic stabilization. Yet growth, particularly productivity growth, has been very slow. This creates many problems for the government. In particular, slow growth of formal sector employment generates great political pressure to deliver some sort of social benefits to the informal segment of the labor force. There are many reasons why Mexico is not growing, but one of them is that the government continues adding to a system of perverse incentives that, in my view, is not conducive to the growth of productivity, rather than correcting some distortions that were already a hindrance to growth. There are, to be sure, commitments to macroeconomic stability and to free trade, and these are credible commitments; so in that sense macroeconomic and trade issues are no longer at front center. But a mix of higher oil rents and neglect of public investment has generated sufficient revenues for the government to provide social benefits to workers in the informal sector (which, in my view, are a source of inefficiencies) and reduce the rate of growth and which, as I said, add to rather than subtract from the existing distortions.

Santiago Levy is a vice president at the Inter-American Development Bank. He was general director of the Mexican Social Security Institute from December 2000 to October 2005 and served as Mexico's deputy finance minister from December 1994 to December 2000.

Annual World Bank Conference on Development Economics 2008, Global
© 2009 The International Bank for Reconstruction and Development/The World Bank

I would first like to talk about a framework for thinking about informality and, in particular, for showing why social programs can themselves be a source of informality. Second, I want to show why informality reduces the rate of growth of productivity and gross national product (GDP) in the country. In a nutshell, I interpret informality as a large tax on formal salaried employment and a subsidy to informal sector employment that, together, lower the average productivity of labor. In addition, the wedge between the costs of labor across firms translates into differences in the rates of return to capital across firms. Investments are allocated to firms that have high private rates of return but low social rates of return. This distorts the allocation of investment and results in a higher incremental capital-output ratio that, for a given volume of investment, lowers the rate of growth of GDP.

Why does Mexico have such a policy? As with many other Latin American countries, we have a system of parallel benefits for the workforce. Formal workers come under a European style of social security that includes many benefits such as health insurance, housing loans, and retirement, work-risk, and disability pensions. But workers in the informal sector also receive benefits from the government that, over the last few years, have become increasingly closer substitutes for social security benefits. Critically, these two types of benefits are financed from different sources, and the result is large distortions within the economy.

In this talk, I will focus mostly on the economic implications of informality. The social implications are equally important, but I do not have time to discuss that topic here. I begin with some numbers: excluding public sector workers, Mexico's labor force in 2006 had about 41 million people. The informal sector is very large, amounting to over 60 percent of the labor force (see table 1). Only 34 percent of the nonpublic labor force, about 14 million workers, is in the formal sector, with access to social security. More than 8 million workers are hired illegally—that is, they are workers who by law should receive social security benefits because they are salaried but do not because firms and workers jointly evade the law. As table 1 shows, evasion of the law is massive; more than 50 percent of the workers who should be covered by social security are not.

Of the 3 million firms in Mexico, only about 760,000 are registered with formal authorities—the tax authority, the social security authority—and are complying with the official governance mechanisms that apply to salaried labor such as social

TABLE 1. Distribution of Mexican Workers among Formal and Informal Sectors, 2006

Type of worker	Number of workers	Share of total
Formal	14,080,367	33.9
Informal	25,807,529	62.2
Illegal salaried	8,122,517	19.5
Self-employed and nonsalaried employees	17,685,012	42.6
Open unemployment	1,600,891	3.8
Total	41,488,787	100.00

Source: Levy (2008, table 5-1).

TABLE 2. Size Distribution of Mexican Firms, Total and Contributing to Social Security, 2003

Number of workers	All firms (1)		Firms contributing to social security (2)		Difference (1) − (2)	
	Number of firms	Number of workers	Number of firms	Number of workers	Number of firms	Number of workers
0–2	2,118,138	3,011,902	350,459	488,727	1,767,679	2,523,175
3–5	581,262	2,078,023	183,432	686,515	397,830	1,391,508
6–10	153,891	1,135,021	95,886	725,253	58,005	409,768
11–15	47,601	604,387	38,855	494,430	8,746	109,957
16–20	24,361	433,741	21,342	379,795	3,019	53,946
21–30	25,171	627,011	22,399	556,830	2,772	70,181
31–50	20,927	812,729	19,125	743,225	1,802	69,504
51–100	16,100	1,135,608	15,337	1,077,909	763	57,699
101–250	10,898	1,683,740	10,526	1,629,298	372	54,442
251–500	4,029	1,379,532	3,804	1,314,357	225	65,175
501–	2,636	3,199,628	2,626	3,082,169	10	117,459
Total	3,005,014	16,101,322	764,791	11,178,508	2,241,223	4,922,814

Source: Levy (2008, table 7-2).

security and other labor regulations (see table 2). Up to 75 percent of all firms in Mexico are illegal. This figure excludes firms that are on the street, engaging in ambulatory commerce and ambulatory trade. The definition of a firm here corresponds to the one used in the economic census: an establishment with fixed premises and two or more workers that produces output for sale. The size distribution of firms is strongly biased in the direction of very small firms, and this distribution is endogenous to the incentive structure generated by social programs—in particular, to the tax on formal labor and the subsidy to informal labor. Finally, note that over the past decade, the resources allocated to social programs for workers not covered by social security have grown at almost double the rate of resources for social security (see figure 1).

Let me now briefly describe how social programs affect the labor market. Social security for formal sector workers is a bundled set of benefits—an all-or-nothing package. That is what the law states. A formal sector worker in Mexico is entitled to health insurance, a retirement pension, a work-risk and disability pension, housing loans, daycare centers, severance payments, and so on. It is a vast protection system, modeled to some extent on the European style of the 1950s. The important point is that these benefits cost a certain amount per worker, which I denote as T_f, but the workers themselves might place less value on them; in particular, I assume that workers value them at $\beta_f T_f$, with $\beta_f < 1$. There are many reasons why workers undervalue T_f: a person wants to consume things separately rather than bundled, there are quality deficiencies, and, ultimately, the government is imposing its preferences on the individual, forcing the person to save when that person might not want to save, and so on. As a result, the utility of being a formal sector worker is the wage received

FIGURE 1.
Subsidies for Social Security and Social Protection Programs, 1998–2007

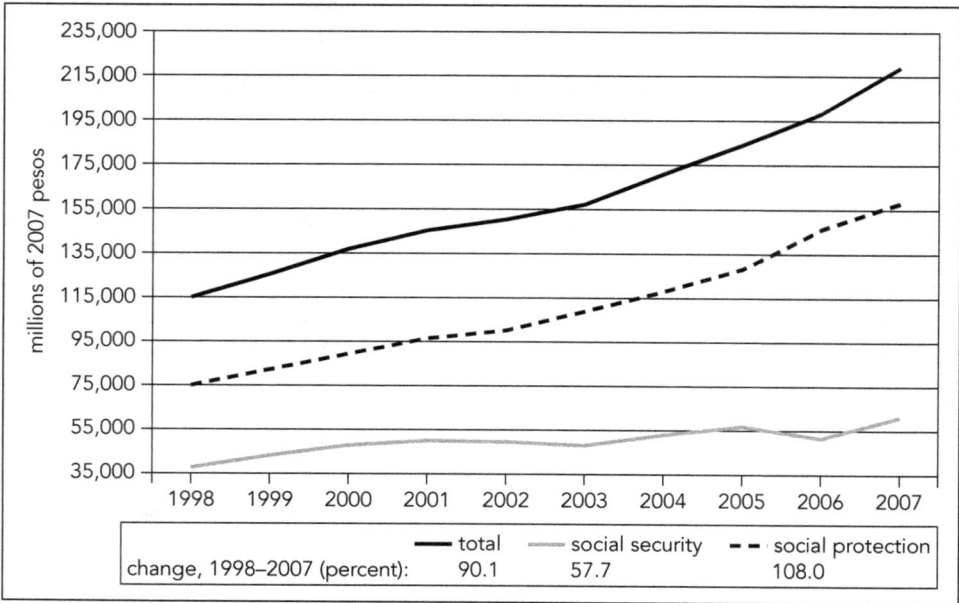

Source: Levy 2008, figure 1-3.

for working in the formal sector, denoted as w_f, plus the value to the worker of the benefits of social security.

Informal sector workers, who, as noted before, are the majority of workers in Mexico, are not forced to consume a bundled set of benefits. They have access to an unbundled set of benefits that could include health insurance programs, housing, and so on. The government, however, does not realize that its social protection policy will generate more rather than fewer informal workers (as shown in calculations). A worker in the informal sector may discount the benefits because of quality provision issues; the benefits may not be as good as they could be. But, critically, these social protection benefits are not paid by the worker (if self-employed), or by the firm that could potentially hire him or her. So the utility of working in the informal sector is $w_i + \beta_i T_i$, where w_i is the wage in the informal sector (or the implicit wage for the self-employed), T_i is the per-worker cost of social protection programs for informal workers, and β_i is the value that workers attach to those benefits.

The Mexican labor market is characterized by a high degree of mobility across sectors; it is not really the case that this market is segmented. The data show that workers go into and out of the formal labor force and that there is considerable fluidity. The best way to describe the labor market is that it satisfies an equation in which workers are not moving between the formal and the informal sectors to equate wages. In my view, the literature that looks at wage differentials as a measure of market segmentation is mistaken because it does not take into account that there is a large set of benefits aside from wages. The arbitrage equation for the labor market should tell us that workers move between the formal and informal sectors to equate utility.

From the point of view of firms, the differences in how social security and social protection benefits are financed imply that the cost difference between hiring a worker formally and hiring a worker informally is very high. Firms have to pay the full amount of social security when they hire workers formally, even if workers do not fully value that social security. The distortion in the labor market created in this way is large; the cost difference to a firm hiring workers formally rather than informally can be up to 50 percent. That difference consists of undervalued social security contributions, on the one hand, and free social protection benefits, on the other. The empirical evidence for Mexico shows that for low-wage workers, up to 75 percent of those nonwage costs are not valued by them, and this is equivalent to a 25 percent pure tax on labor. In addition, the government channels almost 2 percent of GDP to social protection programs, which is equivalent to an 8 percent subsidy to informal labor.

So this is the structure of the problem. Formal sector firms maximize profits. To do that, they equate the value of the marginal product of labor to the sum of wages and social security contributions, or the total cost of labor. Informal firms also maximize profits, but they do not have to pay for social benefits. Workers search for jobs to maximize utility. Everybody is employed and, of course, a budget constraint has to be satisfied; overall social spending has to be equal to revenues, which consist of taxes on profits, value-added taxes, and oil rents.

The standard solution to this problem tells you that if workers fully valued social security, so that $\beta_f = 1$, and there were no social programs for informal workers, so that $T_i = 0$, the equilibrium would be efficient. There would be an efficient distribution of the labor force between the formal sector and the informal sector. The informal sector would consist only of nonsalaried workers, and there would be an efficient level of informal employment because there are many good reasons why not all employment should be salaried—contracts to diversify risk and elicit effort, for instance, or efficient levels of self-employment. The result is an efficient distribution of labor force between formal (L_f) and informal (L_i) employment. This is represented as point A in figure 2, where L is the total labor force, L_f^* represents formal workers—informal workers would then be $L_i^* = (L - L_f^*)$—and the arbitrage condition in the labor market is satisfied, since $w_f^* + T_f = w_i^*$. But if workers do not fully value social security, so that $\beta_f < 1$, there is a wedge between what firms pay for social security and what workers get that is equivalent to a tax on salaried labor. In figure 2, formal firms move to point C, and formal employment falls to L_f'. Wages in the informal sector have to decrease to w_i' to absorb workers coming from the formal sector. There is a wage differential between the formal and informal sectors, but this differential is consistent with an arbitrage condition which tells you that workers are indifferent to moving between the formal and informal sectors, so that $w_f' + \beta_f T_f = w_i'$. So, workers are in equilibrium and firms are in equilibrium. However, this is an inefficient equilibrium to the extent that the average productivity of labor in the economy is now lower than before.

FIGURE 2.
Social Security with Labor Mobility

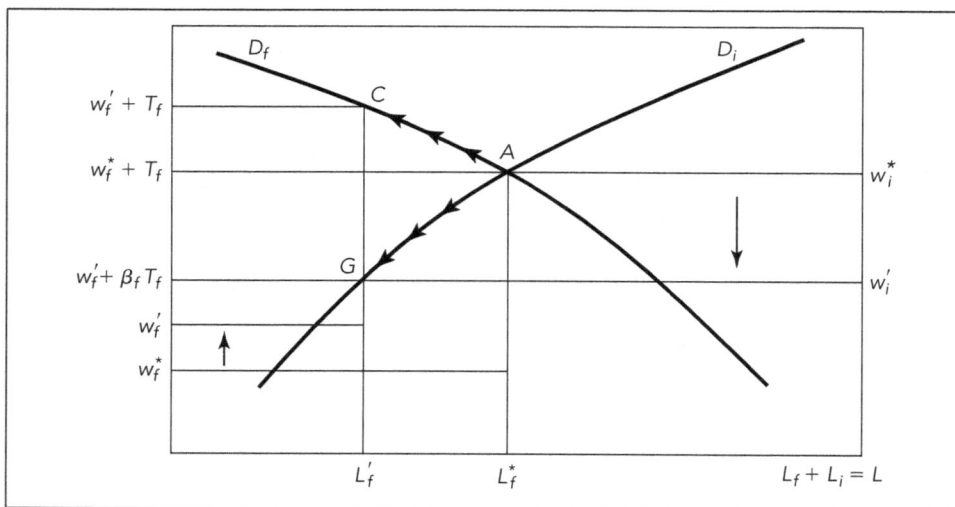

Source: Author's elaboration.

Let us take the argument one step further. The government realizes that informal workers have no social benefits and decides to remedy this situation. It will now provide benefits to informal sector workers who are not paid by firms (or are self-employed), as opposed to the case of firms hiring workers formally. This is the policy that I referred to at the beginning of this talk which has been growing in importance. Note now in figure 3 that setting $T_i > 0$ will actually increase the size of the distortion and make firms reduce formal sector employment even more, to L_f''. In parallel, informal sector employment increases further, and wages in the informal sector fall to w_i''. Note that aggregate labor productivity falls further because the allocation of labor is becoming even more inefficient. The informal sector is growing; the formal sector is getting smaller. And then you get a crazy result: although average labor productivity is falling, workers' utility is rising. The reason, of course, is that the government is providing "free social benefits" to part of the labor force, which is getting larger. Of course, someone has to pay for all of this. Oil rents are used, and all sorts of other fiscal adjustments take place in the background. But the point I want to emphasize is that the government's intervention generates an equilibrium in which utility goes up and labor productivity goes down.

So far, I have left evasion of social security out of the picture, but in Mexico it is very large. "Informal salaried employment" is a commonly used expression, but the proper expression really is illegal salaried employment. Evasion of social security makes sense because firms and workers realize that they are paying some amount for something that is not worth that amount to them. Evasion will create an equilibrium distribution of the rent between workers and firms, which is equivalent to $(1 - \beta)T_f$, and both workers and firms will benefit from it. Evasion now generates a labor

FIGURE 3.
Interaction of Social Security and Social Protection Programs

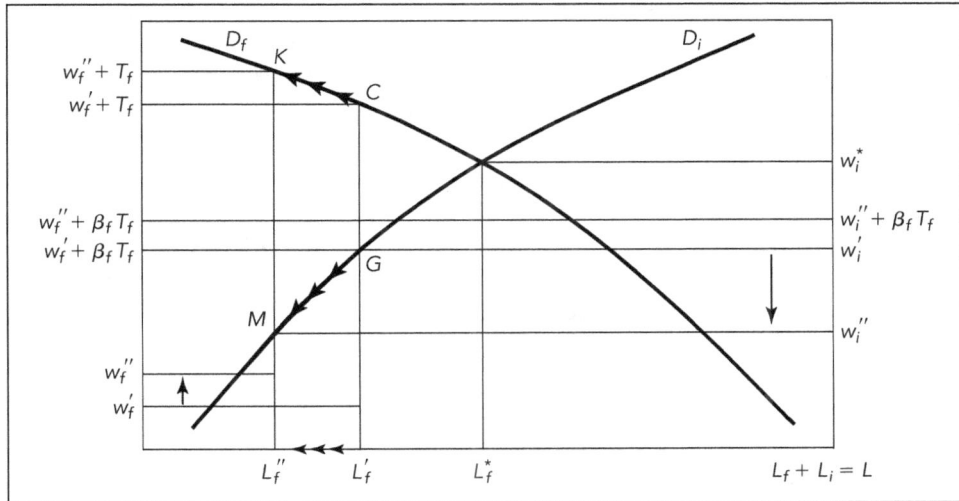

Source: Author's elaboration.

market in which there are formal salaried workers, informal salaried workers, and nonsalaried workers.

So, there are three types of workers in the economy: salaried workers hired formally (L_f), salaried workers hired informally (L_{if}), and nonsalaried workers, including the self-employed (L_i), with the last two constituting the informal sector. Note that this implies that informal employment has a legal segment (the self-employed and nonsalaried employees) and an illegal segment (salaried employees). Put differently, informality and illegality are not the same, although they overlap. As before, workers are all moving between one form of employment and another until they satisfy an arbitrage condition where utility is equalized across the different forms of employment. And there is a wage structure characterized by a wage for formal sector workers (w_f), an implicit wage for nonsalaried workers (w_i), and a wage for illegal salaried workers, which I will denote as w_{if}.

The point I want to make here is that the observed structure of wage rates in Mexico is strongly influenced by social programs. Even the formal wage reflects the effects of a large amount of evasion. And, of course, the allocation of labor in Mexico is also very strongly affected by social programs and by the responses of firms and workers to these social programs through evasion. It is useful to recall here that informal (or, better, illegal) salaried employment is about 20 percent of all non-public employment in Mexico and more than half of formal (or, better, legal) salaried employment. These are large numbers.

Let me turn now to firms and look at them more carefully. In particular, I want to tell a story about how firms behave in Mexico in the context of this incentive structure. Firms optimize. They mix legal and illegal workers depending on how strictly they think the government is going to enforce the law. There are 3 million firms in Mexico, so for a firm of four or five workers, the chances of being found and fined by the government are very small. If the firm is larger, with more than, say, 100 workers, the government will certainly find it, and the firm will not cheat. But a firm with 20 or 30 workers, or 35 or 40 workers, may cheat a little. Perhaps, out of 50 hired workers, it will register 40 with the social security authorities. Cheating behavior is elaborate because it depends not only on the firm's size and how visible it is but also on whether the firm has many illegal workers or just a few. It is not the same thing to be a firm of 50 workers with 45 illegal and 5 legal, or with 45 legal and 5 illegal. The proportion of legal and illegal workers matters to the firm.

On the basis of the Mexican census data, one can infer that in firms with zero to two workers, 84 percent of all workers are hired illegally. The proportion of legal to illegal workers hired decreases with increasing firm size. For firms with over 100 workers, the probability of engaging in illegal behavior is very small, and therefore most workers are legally hired.

In this incentive context, the problem for the firm can be stated as that of maximizing profits by mixing workers hired legally and illegally, subject to the costs of each type of worker and the expected costs of fines when workers are hired illegally (given by the size of the fines times the probabilities of being caught). This is a complex problem because labor costs depend on the firm's behavior. Wage rates are not determined by the firm. But the firm endogenously determines its labor costs because the more it cheats (or, the more workers it hires illegally), the higher is the expected marginal cost of labor (because the probability of being caught increases). If the firm gets caught, that could be catastrophic for it, as the fines are large. This implies that there will be three types of firms: those that hire all their workers illegally (fully illegal firms); those that mix legal and illegal workers; and those that only hire workers legally (fully legal firms). The distribution of firms across these legal statuses has implications for productivity, as the expected marginal cost of labor is different in each case, and to maximize profits firms equate the value of the marginal product of workers to their expected labor costs.

I try to depict this in figure 4, where, as noted before, w_{if} is the cost of labor for illegally hired workers and $(w_f + T_f)$ is the cost of labor for legally hired workers. Of course, w_{if} and w_f are determined simultaneously along with w_i so that the labor market clears, although they are exogenous to individual firms. Small firms, in the neighborhood of A, are only going to hire workers illegally. Firms in the neighborhood of B will hire a mix of legal and illegal workers. These firms will be registered with the social security authorities (the Mexican Social Security Institute, or IMSS, from the Spanish name), but some of their workers will not be. Finally, firms in the neighborhood of C will hire only legal workers, and so the firms and all of their workers will be fully registered with the IMSS. How many and what kind of firms will fall in each range depends on many factors, among them indivisibilities of capital and the nature of the production function. If there are large indivisibilities of capital, some firms might have to hire labor at a level that, relative to the probabilities of being found and fined, induces them to be in the third category. Think of steel or

FIGURE 4.
Distribution of Firms: Illegal, Mixed, and Fully Legal

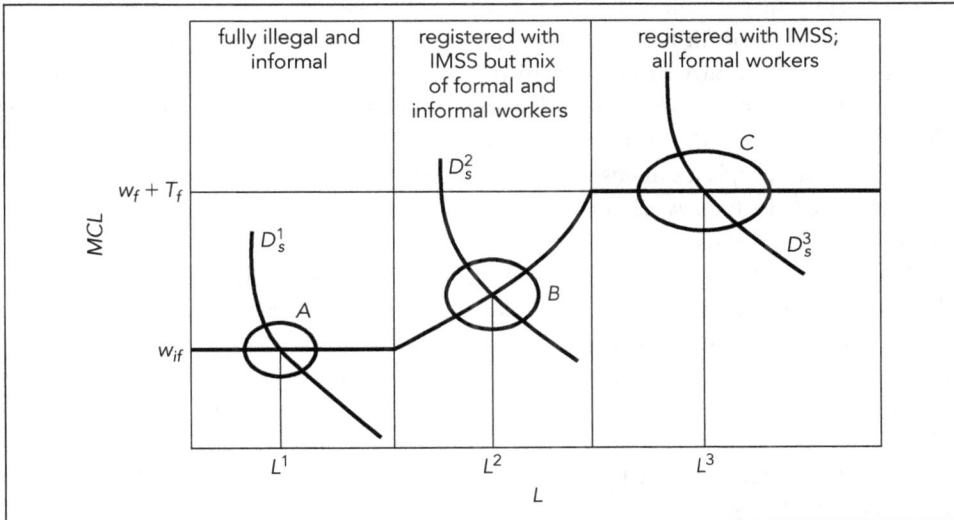

Source: Author's elaboration.

automobile production. Why are there no informal firms making automobiles? Why are there no informal firms hiring informal labor in steel production? The reason is that the minimum size for a firm that produces cars or steel is 200, 300, or 500 workers, so that the firm is not going to cheat because doing so would actually decrease its profits (as the probability of being fined is practically 1). But it will cheat if, with a relatively small size, it produces textiles, or toys, or other light manufactures, or if it is in retail distribution or retail transportation. The important implication is that similar workers with similar abilities have very different productivities depending on the type of firm where they are hired, because the cost of labor to firms will be different.

I want to highlight three interesting implications of this simple set-up. First, one can no longer speak about the productivity of labor in the formal and the informal sector; rather, there is a continuum of productivities, from w_{if} to $(w_f + T_f)$. Therefore, the average productivity of labor will depend on the distribution of workers among firms that are engaging in various levels of illegal behavior. Differently put, the size distribution of firms will have a strong impact on labor productivity, to the extent that the size of firms is strongly correlated with their cheating behavior. In particular, the more the size distribution of firms is tilted toward small informal firms, the lower is the average productivity of labor in the economy.

The second implication is that as firms grow, they not only expand employment but also change the proportion of legal to illegal labor; they hire proportionately more workers formally than informally. In other words, when there is a positive shock and the total demand for salaried labor shifts outward, formal employment will expand more proportionately than the increase in total salaried employment. This implies that in a boom period the growth in employment as measured by the registries of the IMSS overstates the growth in salaried employment, as some of that growth consists of conversion of illegal salaried labor to legal salaried labor; firms are not really hiring that many new workers. Conversely, when there is a negative shock, firms do not, in fact, fire as many workers as the IMSS measurement of job losses indicates; in part firms react to the negative shock by cheating more—hiring more illegal workers relative to legal workers. The fact that at times in the same firm there are formal and informal workers, and that these proportions change in response to shocks, is a dimension of informality that, in my opinion, has been largely overlooked. In fact, workers can change from formal to informal, or vice versa, without changing jobs.

The third implication is that when T_i increases, w_{if} will fall, and w_f will increase. All other things equal, this will induce more firms to be illegal or semilegal, and the result will be to lower average labor productivity. The reason is clear: more social programs for informal workers reduce the supply of labor to the formal sector, increasing w_f, and augment the supply of labor to the informal sector, lowering w_{if}. Of course, the government increases T_i to provide more social benefits to informal workers, but the point is that in doing so, it fosters the evasion of social security and lowers productivity.

I now want to call attention to another effect of informality: it distorts the composition of aggregate output. A simple description of this is provided in figure 5, in which there are five goods produced whose output prices are given, say, by world prices. (The assumption is that this economy is small, which is a sensible assumption for Mexico.) In the absence of informality, the fact that all producers face the same fixed world prices would imply that the economy produces the right bundle of

FIGURE 5.
Informality and the Composition of Output

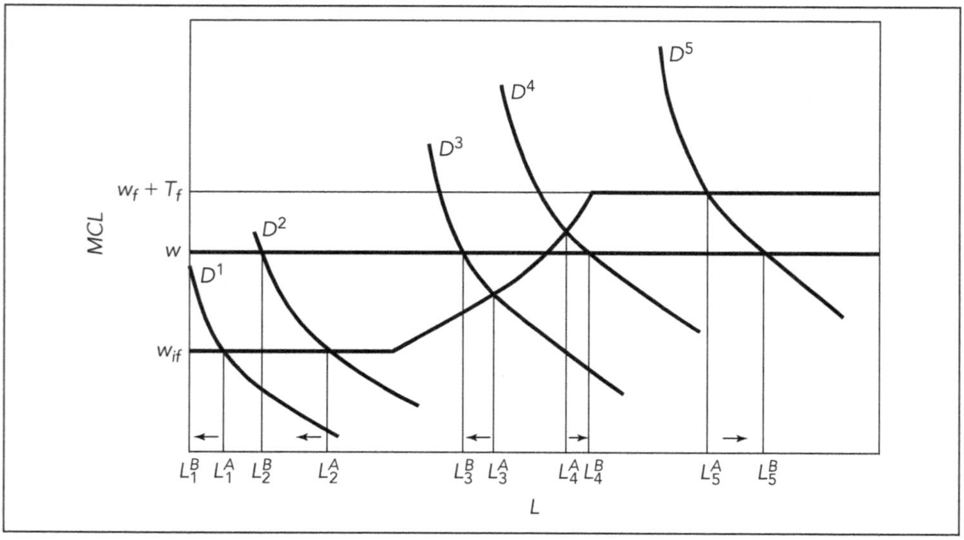

Source: Author's elaboration.

goods—the one that maximizes the value of GDP at world prices. But under informality, this is not so. In figure 5 the value of the marginal product of labor at world prices in the production of these five goods is D^1 to D^5. Contrast now the shape of the marginal cost of labor (MCL) curve with and without informality. As in figure 4, under informality the MCL curve has a lower bound at w_{if} and an upper bound at $(w_f + T_f)$ resulting from the interaction of social security and social protection programs; in the absence of the formal-informal dichotomy the marginal cost of labor is horizontal, at w. Employment levels under informality are designated by L^A (and L^B, without informality). Of course, $\sum L^A = \sum L^B = L$.

What would be the composition of output in this economy if there were no social programs creating a wedge between the costs of salaried and nonsalaried workers and between the costs of legally and illegally hired salaried workers? There would be more output in sectors producing goods 4 and 5, and less in sectors producing goods 1 to 3. Most likely, the former are larger firms with higher capital-labor ratios, while the latter are very small firms. Under informality, output composition is distorted in the direction of goods that can be produced by small and very small firms. These are activities that are subject to more cheating because firms can get by with more illegality. So, the combination of the existence of a large tax on salaried labor, the fact that this tax cannot be equally evaded by all firms, and the fact that there is a subsidy to nonsalaried labor implies that the economy produces more services provided by the self-employed (or one-man firms), more commerce and light manufactures produced by small firms, and so on, and less of the goods that require large-scale production. Differently put, the composition of output is strongly tilted toward what I call informality-prone sectors, and this tilt is not innocuous, because it is associated with lower average labor productivity.

Of Mexico's 3 million firms, half (1.5 million) are in commerce and an additional 1 million are in services, for a total of 2.5 million firms. Most of the country's 3 million firms have between 1 and 5 workers; in fact, less than 35,000 firms have more than 50 workers, while 2.1 million firms have only two workers. From the private point of view, the latter are very profitable firms. Informal firms have very high rates of return relative to formal firms, but only if they are small. As firms grow larger, rates of return decline quickly because, de facto, the tax on firms increases steeply with size (measured by the number of workers).

What happens to the rates of return on investments in different firms and the allocation of total investment resources in the economy when social programs change? It turns out that as social security contributions increase, or as the valuation of social security decreases, the rate of return on informal firms will increase relative to the rate of return on formal firms; the same happens as T_i increases. Better social protection programs, or deteriorating social security programs, make formal firms less profitable and informal firms more profitable. The allocation of investment in the economy changes. Basically, it tilts toward informal firms and toward firms that hire informal labor. And now I have a very important result. What this will do is to generate a growth path characterized by persistent informality. It is not the case that in these economies economic growth will reduce the size of the informal sector and that eventually all workers will be drawn into the formal labor market, with social security benefits. Rather, there will be a positive growth rate that is nevertheless below the potential growth rate as a result of large static inefficiencies that translate into dynamic inefficiencies because in every period the allocation of investment is going into sectors where, from the social point of view, one does not want it to go. And in this growth path informal employment will persist. One can see that this can create a vicious circle, as the presence of informal workers induces the government to increase social protection benefits (see figure 1), which then further lowers the rate of growth, and so on.

To sum up, from the economic point of view, the coexistence of social security programs for salaried labor and social protection programs for nonsalaried labor generates a tax on formal firms and a subsidy to informal firms, creating static and dynamic inefficiencies. I think this is one of the explanations—although not the only one—for the fact that Mexico has been caught for about 15 years now in a slow-growth, high-informality, low-productivity growth path. The real challenge, of course, is not to dismantle these social programs. The real challenge is to understand that social programs cannot be allowed to segment the labor market on the basis of the legal category of salaried or nonsalaried labor because the reaction of firms and workers to this legal structure will be counterproductive from the point of view of productivity and growth (and also from the point of view of the government's social objectives). Escaping from this predicament is politically very difficult because of another problem, which has to do with the fact that many of these social programs not only seek to provide benefits to workers but are also meant to enhance the political legitimacy of the government. A discussion of this problem, however, must wait for another occasion.

Reference

Levy, Santiago. 2008. *Good Intentions, Bad Outcomes: Social Policy, Informality and Economic Growth in Mexico*. Washington, DC: Brookings Institution Press.

Keynote Address

ABDOULAYE SARRE

Good afternoon, ladies and gentlemen. It is a pleasure and an honor for me to address this assembly. I will be discussing three points: the contribution of the private sector to economic development; problems and obstacles facing investors in Africa, and specifically in Senegal; and the expectations that some members of the private sector might have with respect to the World Bank. I will try to focus on specifics that I think are not often taken into consideration.

The Private Sector and Development

On the first issue, if we exclude certain industries such as the upstream oil sector, I think we could say that 99 percent of the world economy is driven by the private sector. In Africa, however, the public sector is still largely overweighted in gross domestic product (GDP) in comparison with other countries because most utilities—water, telecommunications, and energy—are still state-owned companies.

We all agree that in general the private sector is more competitive, more productive, and more efficient than the public sector, in Africa and in Senegal. Of course, the public sector has its own responsibilities, but the driving force should be and should remain the private sector, for various reasons. Today I will focus on one point: education.

A great deal of literature and many essays and conferences have emphasized the need for appropriate education for development. Yet in many African countries education, especially at the university level, is not really on a par with the needs and the expectations of investors. In Senegal, for example, a large portion of the state budget, almost 40 percent, is invested in education; so clearly the government understands that education is the foundation of development. Yet from my perspective, as an investor who uses a lot of human resources—I think my firm is the second-largest

Abdoulaye Sarre is founder and chief executive officer of PCCI, an offshore call center firm headquartered in Senegal.

Annual World Bank Conference on Development Economics 2008, Global
© 2009 The International Bank for Reconstruction and Development/The World Bank

private sector employer in Senegal—there are sometimes difficulties in finding appropriate staff. The private sector has no formal say in discussing the education programs that have to be put in place to meet needs today and in the future.

The university in Senegal, for instance, has roughly 5,000 students studying history and geography. Of course, it is absolutely necessary to have trained people in that discipline; but it is largely overweighted, and it is costing the government and, ultimately, the population considerable money. What can the country, what can the private sector, do with 5,000 persons studying history and geography when other sectors cannot find appropriate staff? Fewer than 200 students are pursuing information technology (IT) training—yet the market for IT is very important, as India understood 10 or 20 years ago, when it implemented a program putting the emphasis on IT engineers, to be able to snap up an industry.

In Senegal we are investing a lot of money, but it is still in traditional sectors. The private sector cannot employ these students who lack necessary knowledge of the potential jobs offered by various employers. I took the case of history and geography, but we also have a few thousand studying sociology, philosophy, and so on. Education is completely desynchronized with the needs of corporations, of small and medium-size businesses. Very often, firms have positions that they cannot fill because people do not have the necessary training or skills.

Very often, the training itself is obsolete and far from the latest developments in today's world. In the case of IT, an industry in which I am involved, we are obliged to take students who have completed a four- or five-year course and retrain them just to be able to bring them to the level of the latest technologies. They are still studying programs that are not in use anymore, that were designed perhaps five or seven or eight years ago. This is one example where the private sector should be relied on more in establishing the programs and academic orientations of the public universities. It would be a valuable contribution by the private sector because the firms in that sector will ultimately be employing these students.

Problems Facing Investors in Africa

I next address the problems with investment in Africa. I have the impression that the image of the private investor held by lower-ranking officials is not what it should be. Private investors are often seen not as partners but—I want to use this word with caution—almost as enemies. Lower-ranking administrative officials are not trained and aware of the important role of the private sector in the economy. Member of the private sector are often perceived as individuals only interested in making profits. This is unfortunate, and it is mainly because of the non-market-economy philosophy of public servants. At least, it was so in the countries where I have worked. This is something that has to be ameliorated, probably through training and through improving government officials' understanding of the role of the private sector. Just because businessmen always strive to make profits doesn't mean striving for profit isn't good for the country.

Another problem is the legal environment, which too often is not adapted to new sectors of the economy and is not agile. When we were setting up our company in 2001, we could not benefit from certain tax incentives because the law that was enacted back in the 1980s understandably did not provide for activities that involved exporting anything but goods. Exporting services was simply not covered by the law, so the law had to be changed. Even though all the political authorities were very keen about doing that, it took roughly five years to have some laws revised to allow us to export our services.

Labor laws in Senegal mostly date from the late 1950s and are completely inappropriate today for private sector development. Fiscal laws and customs laws do not take into consideration new sectors and new ways of doing business. For instance, for a firm to benefit from an *entreprise franche d'exportation*, a free enterprise zone, all the exported services were supposed to pass through customs. It took months for our company to discuss with the customs authorities how it was just bits and bytes going through the Internet and being exported, and it was not physically possible for a service to clear customs. Besides, these data are sometimes confidential; they can include credit card numbers and the like that cannot be shown at customs. But explaining this to administrative authorities who initially did not even understand what we were talking about took a lot of time. In brief, raising government officials' level of awareness of the new economy could have a very positive effect.

There are other small details. For example, today, if you use INCOTERM products, you don't just buy a computer, but you buy a solution with licenses to be used. However, you cannot expect such products to clear customs in the same way as hardware because the transfer of property and of risk is concluded only after the purchaser's provisional acceptance.

Another problem is human resources. It used to be that the most brilliant people taught at the universities. We appear to be seeing the contrary situation, and the consequence is that there is a vicious tendency toward lower quality. Many private schools without appropriate certification provide diplomas without real added value.

In the cultural and business environment, the values of entrepreneurship, innovation, and creativity are not omnipresent, whether we speak of the media or the environment in general. If these values are not inculcated in the population, especially the youth, a rich and strong private sector cannot emerge.

Today, most of the private sector creations in Senegal are basically for import and commerce, inside the country, and this type of economic activity does not raise GDP. To increase GDP, the economy has to export goods and services. I believe that there should be an emphasis on encouraging businesses to enter exporting activities, but no real concrete policies are in place today to promote export.

I come now to financial issues, beginning with interest rates. The average small or medium-size business in Senegal borrows at a rate of 12 or 13 percent, which is totally unsustainable. No economy can thrive with such high interest rates. If you add that to the poor environment, small market size, low purchasing power, lagging productivity, and so on, you have all the necessary conditions for impediment to invest in the private sector.

Another obstacle is the financial resources market. Small and medium-size businesses only have access to traditional retail bankers that require collateral amounting to 100 percent of the loan requested. No alternatives are available, such as the venture capitalist form of funding, which in certain economies today is the basis of development. If you have a good idea but you don't have any collateral or anyone that can put up 100 percent collateral, your business will never start up. So this is a major barrier.

Another problem in certain cases is utilities. Performing and affordable utilities—telecommunications, energy, water supply—are very important. Senegal has technically sound and state-of-the-art telecommunications operators, but costs are irrational. A two-megabit line costs roughly US$200 per month for high-speed Internet because the service is provided by the former national monopoly that is now a private monopoly. Even though the quality is very good, this kind of pricing model can be a drawback for development.

Considerable effort has been made by both sides—by the government and by the private sector—but I believe that a 360-degree view, and better synchronization and implementation of strategies to improve investment, are lacking. The National Agency for the Promotion of Investment and Large Infrastructure Works (APIX) was set up—funded, I think, by the World Bank—but it doesn't have executive decision-making power. A decision has to go through the ministry and through parliament. That makes for a great deal of red tape and inefficiency.

The Private Sector and the World Bank

I will conclude with the expectations that we have for the World Bank. Something that really has to be done, if possible, is to help small and medium-size businesses gain access to capital markets, through small venture capitalists or business angels. It is essential to lower interest rates for small and medium-size businesses because the rates that companies are paying today are unsustainable. Projects and companies have difficulty repaying loans because a project has to have a very high yield in order to sustain a 12 or 13 percent interest rate. Entrepreneurship, creativity, productivity, and innovation should also be promoted—through support to programs and seminars by appropriate experts, to raise the level of education. Today many private schools have curricula that are interesting, offering bachelor's or master's degrees, but the level of instruction is insufficient. It would be useful to be able to fund international groups of experts or professors to come in and to conduct seminars with young people in the various schools, thus raising the quality of education and training. And finally, one point that is often raised by the private sector is how to simplify and accelerate the procedures for World Bank–sponsored programs.

Finance and Economic Opportunity

ASLI DEMIRGÜÇ-KUNT AND ROSS LEVINE

An influential body of theoretical research and an emerging line of empirical work suggest that the operation of the formal financial system affects the degree to which economic opportunities are defined by talent and initiative rather than by parental wealth and social connections. Considerably more research is needed to identify which formal financial sector policies enhance the operation of the financial system in ways that expand the economic horizons of the economically disenfranchised.

In this paper we argue that there are good conceptual and empirical reasons for dramatically intensifying the study of how formal financial sector policies affect the economic opportunities of the poor. While not conclusive, an influential body of theoretical research and an emerging strand of empirical work imply that the operation of the formal financial system arbitrates who can start a business and who cannot; who can pay for education and who cannot; who can exploit economic opportunities and who cannot. Research suggests that finance, although not the only determinant, affects the degree to which economic opportunities are defined by talent and initiative or by parental wealth and social connections. In light of the enormous welfare consequences of expansion of economic opportunities and the existing evidence on the role of the financial sector in defining economic horizons, research on formal financial sector policies should play a much more prominent role in efforts to identify welfare-enhancing reforms.

A corollary of our argument is that economics has done an inadequate job of examining how formal financial systems affect poor people. We find this surprising because many of the profession's most influential theories on intergenerational income dynamics advertise the central role of financial market imperfections in shaping the economic

Asli Demirgüç-Kunt is senior research manager in the World Bank's Development Research Group. Ross Levine is the James and Merryl Tisch Professor of Economics and director of the Rhodes Center in International Economics, at Brown University, Providence, RI.

Annual World Bank Conference on Development Economics 2008, Global

opportunities of the poor. Researchers, however, generally take financial market frictions as unchanging features of economies and examine how changes in schooling, saving behavior, and fertility decisions influence poverty. In fact, financial market frictions are not immutable, and so such analyses, and the resultant policy recommendations, are based on an erroneous treatment of these frictions. The integration of endogenously changing financial market frictions into studies of intergenerational income dynamics may thus also modify existing studies of the effects of schooling, saving behavior, fertility, and redistributive policies on poverty, inequality, and economic opportunities.

Although the impact of financial development on inequality is theoretically ambiguous, the evidence suggests that financial development disproportionately helps the poor. Not only does financial development accelerate average economic growth rates (Levine 1997, 2005; Barth, Caprio, and Levine 2006); we find that improvements in the functioning of the formal financial system exert a particularly beneficial impact on the economic opportunities of the poor.

We stress the formal financial system, which includes banks, securities markets, and the full range of institutions covered in standard finance textbooks. We do not cover microcredit programs and informal systems, which have received considerable attention from development economists. On a conceptual level, there is no need to distinguish between formal and informal financial arrangements. Financial development includes contractual and institutional arrangements that lower transaction and information costs associated with the evaluation and monitoring of projects and the management of risk; it does not matter who provides these functions. Nevertheless, we focus on formal systems for three reasons. First, all countries have extensive laws and regulations governing formal financial systems. Second, when informal financial arrangements become economically substantive at a national level, these arrangements come under the umbrella of formal regulations. Third, there is an extensive literature on informal microcredit programs that is reviewed elsewhere (see, for example, Cull, Demirgüç-Kunt, and Morduch, 2009). We therefore choose to focus on how formal financial systems—and formal financial sector policies—affect poverty and the economic opportunities of the poor.

Conceptually, we define poverty in terms of economic opportunity. In theory and public policy debates, economists, politicians, and the general population frequently focus on the degree of equality of economic opportunity, not the equality of economic outcomes. People are often concerned with whether an individual's opportunities are severely limited by parental wealth, religion, or race. Comparatively talented and industrious individuals may face extraordinary obstacles and limitations because their parents lack resources, or the right religion, or the right pigment in their epidermis. Economic opportunity is exceptionally difficult to measure empirically. Thus, empirical work frequently focuses on changes in income inequality and the fraction of the population living below the poverty line. In this paper, we discuss this line of work, as well as recent efforts to examine opportunity more directly.

We first discuss the theory of how financial markets influence economic opportunity and review recent empirical work on the relation between formal financial systems and poverty, income inequality, and economic opportunity. We then describe recent efforts to measure the ability of households and small enterprises to access financial services, the impact of this access, and the mechanisms through which finance affects poverty and inequality. We end by drawing some conclusions.

Theory

Financial market imperfections are a keystone of many influential theories of persistent poverty. In these theories, perfect financial markets imply that individuals have access to capital to fund education, training, or business endeavors and that access is based only on individual talent and initiative, not on parental characteristics. Perfect financial markets provide equality of opportunity and do not produce a self-perpetuating class of poor dynasties. Financial development exerts a disproportionately positive influence on the poor by expanding their opportunities.

We are not arguing that this is the case for every model of poverty. We are not issuing a challenge for people to develop models in which financial market frictions are irrelevant for yielding perpetually poor dynasties. Rather, we simply observe that an influential line of research advertises that the operation of the financial system is critical for the poor. Examples include Becker (1957), Stiglitz (1969), Becker and Tomes (1979, 1986), Bourguignon (1981), Loury (1981), Banerjee and Newman (1993), Galor and Zeira (1993), Benabou (1996a, 1996b), Aghion and Bolton (1997), Galor and Tsiddon (1997), and many others, as discussed in review articles by Bardhan, Bowles, and Gintis (2000), Bertola (2000), and Piketty (2000).

Basic Framework

Consider the following equation:

$$y(i, t) = h(i, t)* w(i, t) + a(i, t)* r(i, t) \qquad (1)$$

where $y(i, t)$ is the income of dynasty i in generation t; $h(i, t)$ is the corresponding level of human capital in dynasty i; $w(i, t)$ is the wage rate per unit of human capital, which might be dynasty specific, as we discuss later; $a(i, t)$ is dynastic wealth in generation t; and $r(i, t)$ is the return on assets, which may also vary by dynasty, also discussed later. From this simple framework, it is easy to see that if the bequest rate— that is, bequests as a fraction of parental wealth—increases with parental wealth, initial wealth differences will persist in the long run. In other words, initially poor dynasties will remain perpetually poor. Since there is no strong evidence that bequests behave in this manner, we emphasize the role of finance in affecting the evolution of other factors in equation (1) that drive dynastic income.

Human Capital Accumulation

Next, consider the accumulation of human capital as being a positive function of both ability, which we designate by the letter b for brains, and schooling, designated by the letter s:

$$h(i, t) = H\{b(i, t), s(i, t)\} \quad \text{where} \quad \partial H/\partial b > 0 \quad \text{and} \quad \partial H/\partial s > 0 \qquad (2)$$

Further, assume that brains and schooling are complementary inputs into the production of human capital, so that schooling is more beneficial to those with more brains. Finally, assume that brains are not strongly persistent across generations within a dynasty, which is consistent with research suggesting that ability is mean-reverting across generations.

From equation (2), social efficiency requires that kids with lots of brains receive lots of schooling. Where perfect capital markets exist, the economy achieves this social efficiency. People with lots of brains get schooling irrespective of parental wealth, so that schooling is simply a function of brains: an individual's economic opportunities are determined by his or her abilities.

With imperfect capital markets, however, schooling is jointly determined by brains and parental wealth, as discussed by Becker and Tomes (1979, 1986), Loury (1981), Galor and Zeira (1993), and Galor and Tsiddon (1997). Dumb rich kids get too much education. Smart poor kids get too little: their parents do not have the resources to pay for schooling, and imperfect capital markets create a barrier to financing the education of the poor. This increases the cross-dynasty persistence of poverty and lowers the socially efficient allocation of resources.

Entrepreneurship

Some theories highlight the role of financial market frictions in determining who can become entrepreneurs and who cannot. In these models, individuals who become successful entrepreneurs have access to higher investment returns than individuals who do not become entrepreneurs. Individuals are endowed with different levels of entrepreneurial ability, $e(i, t)$, and the return to opening a business depends positively on entrepreneurial ability. Finally, there is a fixed cost associated with becoming an entrepreneur.

With perfect capital markets, those with the most entrepreneurial talent have access to the required funding at the economywide interest rate. Entrepreneurial activity is a function of entrepreneurial ability, not familial wealth. Thus, the rate of return on savings is a function of entrepreneurial ability, not dynastic assets. Furthermore, society's resources are funneled to those with the most talent, not to those with the most assets.

In a situation of imperfect capital markets, lenders demand large amounts of collateral before funding a business endeavor. The accumulated assets of a dynasty, therefore, influence the ability of that dynasty to attract outside funding and to open a business. The rate of return on savings is a positive function of both entrepreneurial ability and dynastic assets. Society's resources are not exclusively funneled to those with the most talent (see Banerjee and Newman 1993; Aghion and Bolton 1997). Rather, society's savings flow disproportionately to those with accumulated wealth. In particular, a poor person with a great idea might not be able to get funding for the project, while a rich person with a mediocre idea might have easier access to credit. Where financial market imperfections exist, the initial distribution of wealth influences which dynasties can obtain external finance and which dynasties are essentially cut off from entrepreneurial endeavors.

Discrimination

Finally, from equation (1), consider the wage rate. It is common to think of the wage rate per unit of human capital as not varying across individuals. Yet, as Gary Becker clearly articulated in 1957, employers might discriminate by particular characteristics, such as race. Blacks with exactly the same skills as whites might receive lower wage rates because employers are willing to lose some profits in order to satisfy their preferences for hiring only white workers. Discrimination might contribute to the intergenerational persistence of relative incomes across different groups.

As Becker (1957) stresses, discrimination is cheaper when there is little competition. When an owner is earning large rents, the marginal cost of hiring a more expensive white worker rather than an equally productive and less expensive black worker is not a very large share of the profits. With more intense competition and smaller profit margins, the cost of discrimination increases. Thus, competition reduces discrimination in wage rates and employment.

Now add financial policy to Becker's theory of competition and discrimination. Some financial sector reforms will spur financial intermediaries to expend more resources to seek out the best firms rather than simply grant credit to incumbents. For example, if a bank has a monopoly, it might lend comfortably to those with whom it has a long, multidimensional relationship. There might be other existing or potential firms with better ideas, but the bank can earn comfortable profits by lending to its friends. If the bank's monopoly position is threatened by regulatory reforms that expose the bank to more competition, however, the intensified competition might weaken long-standing bonds between the bank and firms. Competition might spur the bank to screen borrowers more carefully, and firms will compete more intensively to attract bank capital. Firms will have to demonstrate their superiority in product markets to attract bank capital. Thus, heightened competition in banking intensifies competition throughout the economy, which makes discrimination more expensive and hence expands the economic opportunities of the historically disadvantaged.

Alternative Views and Discussion

Theory does not unambiguously assert that the financial system exerts a first-order impact on the poor. Indeed, if the poor are simply excluded from access to financial services, improvements in the financial system will help only the rich, as noted in Greenwood and Jovanovic (1990). Financial development might not operate at the extensive margin by providing a broader array of new and improved financial services to the poor. Does, in fact, financial development operate at the extensive margin, or does it only improve financial services available to the rich? More concretely, which types of financial policy reform reduce poverty, and how do they affect other policies that societies use to combat poverty, such as welfare and other transfer payments? We need concerted and coordinated theoretical and empirical research to address these very basic questions.

Evidence

We now turn to the results from our research on this topic. We use our own papers for two reasons. First, these studies span different conceptions of poverty, including measures that use a poverty line, income distribution, and economic opportunity. Second, we draw on the discussion to emphasize shortcomings in the literature as an additional mechanism to spur research in this area, and there are smaller adverse repercussions from critiquing our own work.

Cross-Country Evidence

Beck, Demirgüç-Kunt, and Levine (2007) examine the relationship between financial development and the proportion of the population living on less than US$1 per day. The analysis draws on data on poverty for a cross-section of up to 68 developing economies, averaged over the period 1980–2005, with one observation per country. We average over this long time period to aggregate away any business cycle fluctuations or crises that might distort our assessment of theories that focus on the long-run relationship between the operation of the financial system and changes in the fraction of the population living below the poverty line. We look at both the relationship between finance and the poverty level and the relationship between finance and the growth rate of poverty. Use of the growth rate offers statistical advantages because we can reduce the importance of country-specific factors. It also has conceptual advantages because then the analyses of poverty link directly with larger cross-country growth investigations. In any event, the results are similar whether the level or the growth rate of poverty is used. Here, we present the regressions using the growth rate of poverty.

Figure 1 is a partial scatter plot showing the relationship between the growth rate of poverty and financial development, while controlling for a number of other factors. These factors include such country characteristics as the initial level of poverty, initial income per capita, economic growth, population growth, the age distribution of the population, and measures of trade openness and inflation.

In defining and measuring financial development, theory focuses on what the financial system does. The financial system ameliorates informational problems before investments are made; it affects corporate governance by reducing informational problems after investments are initiated; it facilitates risk diversification and reduces liquidity risk by lowering transaction costs; and it directly influences the ease of exchange through its effects on information and transaction costs. Obviously, some financial systems perform these functions better than others. Poorly functioning financial systems do a poor job of reducing information and transaction costs; they do not allocate resources efficiently; and they frequently keep credit flowing only to cronies. Other financial systems are better at providing these financial services to the economy. Differences in the ability of financial systems to identify good projects, monitor firms, diversify risk, and ease transactions are what we mean by the level of financial development.

FIGURE 1.
Financial Development and Growth of Poverty, 68 Economies, 1980–2005

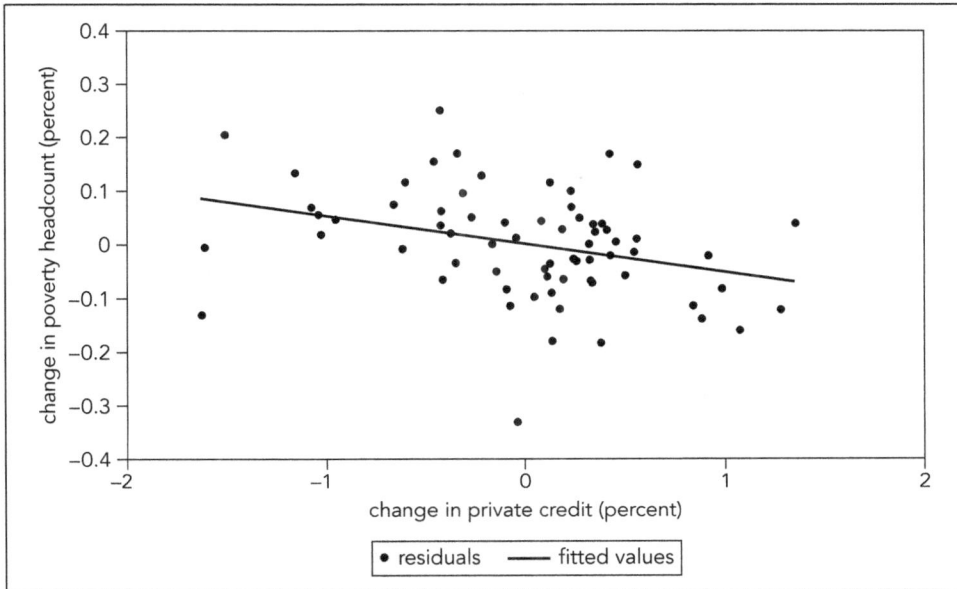

Source: Beck, Demirgüç-Kunt, and Levine 2007.

The empirical proxies for financial development, unfortunately, do not directly measure these concepts. A common measure of financial development is the variable "private credit," which is the value of credit going to privately owned firms as a fraction of a country's gross domestic product (GDP). The variable isolates the intermediation of credit that goes to private firms and excludes credit flowing to the state or to state-owned enterprises. Although private credit is not a direct measure of financial market frictions, it is a commonly used proxy.

In figure 1, the evidence is quite clear: there is a robust negative relationship between financial development and poverty alleviation that holds even when controlling for average growth, initial income, initial poverty, and the full range of country traits mentioned earlier. It is worth emphasizing that the negative relationship between financial development and poverty alleviation holds when controlling for average growth. We do not simply find that finance accelerates economic growth that helps the poor; we find that finance exerts a disproportionately positive influence on the poor. While illustrative, these results are suspect because of the small sample, which makes it difficult to use instrumental variables and panel procedures to control for endogeneity.

Figure 2 focuses on the Gini coefficient of income inequality, using data for 72 countries from 1960 to 2005. We use a dynamic panel instrumental estimator to control for potential endogeneity bias. We obtain the same results whether using the panel estimator or a simple cross-country regression with one observation per

FIGURE 2.

Financial Development and Income Inequality, 72 Economies, 1960–2005

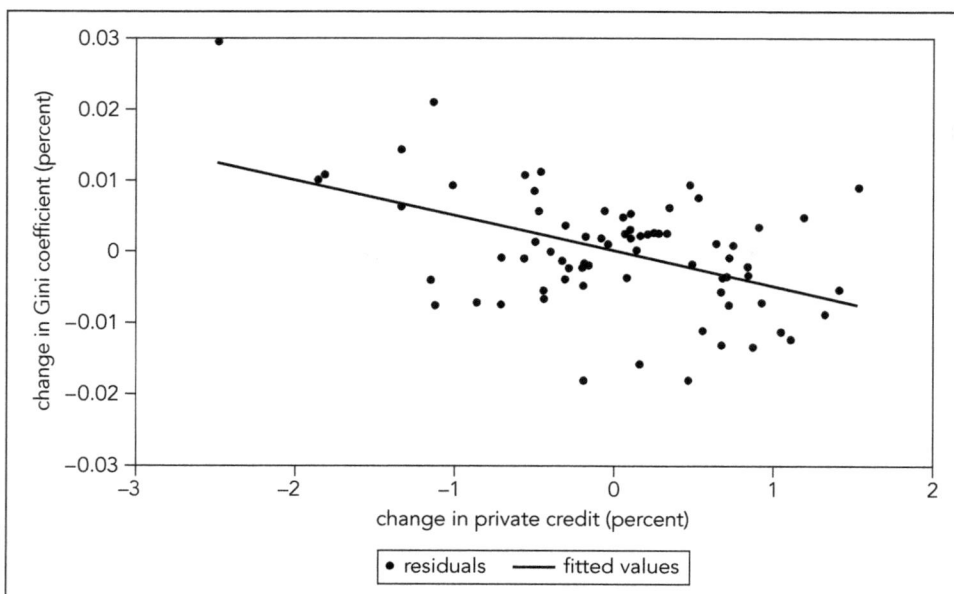

Source: Beck, Demirgüç-Kunt, and Levine 2007.

country. Therefore, we present only the partial scatter plot from the multivariate regression that controls for many country characteristics, including real per capita GDP growth and the initial value of income inequality for each country.

The figure shows a strong negative relationship between the level of financial development and income inequality. Financial development has an especially positive impact on those at the bottom of the distribution of income.

While illustrative, these results are not definitive. First, the measure of financial development is not closely tied to theory. Second, this research does not examine policy; rather, it examines a proxy for overall financial development that reflects many factors. Future work that develops better measures of financial development and uses exogenous innovations in particular policy changes will substantively improve our understanding of the impact of finance on inequality.

Deregulation across U.S. States

Next, we examine whether and how a policy reform that improved the quality of banking services affected the distribution of income. Beck, Levine, and Levkov (2007) examine the impact on income distribution from the deregulation of intrastate banking across the different U.S. states. The policy was implemented state by state over a 20-year period extending from the mid-1970s to the mid-1990s. By the end of this period, all states had removed regulatory prohibitions on banks' opening branches within state boundaries. Past work had shown that liberalization of restrictions on intrastate branching increased the average size of banks through consolidation, improved bank efficiency by reducing the difference between interest income received and interest income paid by banks, and accelerated the growth of average per capita income.

Methodologically, the deregulation of intrastate branching provides a natural setting for identifying and assessing the impact of regulatory reform on the distribution of income. Kroszner and Strahan (1999) show that national technological innovations triggered deregulation, which was exogenous to changes in income distribution within individual states. The invention of automatic teller machines (ATMs), in conjunction with court rulings that ATMs are not bank branches, weakened the geographic bond between customers and banks. Checkable money market mutual funds facilitated banking by mail and telephone, which undercut local bank monopolies; and improvements in communications technology lowered the costs of using distant banks. These innovations reduced the monopoly power of local banks and diminished their ability and desire to fight deregulation. Kroszner and Strahan (1999) further show that cross-state variation in the timing of deregulation reflects the interactions of these technological innovations with preexisting conditions. Thus, the driving forces behind deregulation and its timing were largely independent of state-level changes in income distribution. Consequently, Beck, Levine, and Levkov could exploit cross-state, cross-year variation in income distribution and deregulation to assess the impact of a single policy change on different state economies.

Beck, Levine, and Levkov use the difference-in-difference estimation technique to assess the relationship between branch deregulation and income distribution. Specifically,

$$Y_{s,t} = \alpha_s + \beta_t + \gamma D_{s,t} + \delta X_{s,t} + \varepsilon_{s,t} \; \mathrm{s} = 1, \ldots, 50; \; t = 1976, \ldots, 2005 \quad (3)$$

where $Y_{s,t}$ is a measure of income distribution in state s during year t; α and β are vectors of state and year fixed effects; $X_{s,t}$ is a set of time-varying state-level variables; and $\varepsilon_{s,t}$ is the error term. The variable of interest in equation (3) is D, a dummy variable that takes the value 1 after a state deregulates. The year-dummy variables control for economywide shocks that might drive income distribution over time, such as business cycles, long-term trends in income distribution, and changes in female labor force participation. The state-dummy variables control for unobserved, time-invariant state characteristics that shape income distribution across states. The coefficient γ therefore indicates the impact of branch deregulation on income distribution. A positive and significant γ suggests that deregulation increases income inequality, while a negative and significant γ indicates that deregulation pushes income inequality lower.

The major finding from the Beck, Levine, and Levkov study is that deregulation of branching restrictions reduced income inequality. After a state deregulates restrictions on bank branching, the Gini coefficient of income inequality drops relative to its long-run trend. The decrease becomes statistically significant three years after deregulation. The negative impact of bank branch deregulation on income inequality is a level effect that fully materializes over the six years following deregulation. The negative relationship between branch deregulation and inequality is robust to using different measures of income distribution, examining different components of income, controlling for many time-varying state characteristics, and conditioning on state and year fixed effects. The magnitude is consequential: deregulation explains 60 percent of the variation in income inequality during the sample period relative to state and year averages. Furthermore, deregulation reduces income inequality by exerting a disproportionately positive impact on the poor, not by hurting the rich.

Again, the analysis has its limitations. Do these results for the United States hold for other countries and for other policy reforms that boost competition among banks? While the shortcomings should be addressed, the empirical results thus far support a class of models predicting that better-functioning financial systems will help the poor.

Discrimination

Levine, Levkov, and Rubinstein (2008) examine whether the intensification of bank competition reduces discrimination. Again, they use branch deregulation across the states of the United States to identify an exogenous increase in competition. They then trace the employment and wage behavior of hundreds of thousands of individuals across the U.S. states over the period 1976 to 2005.

The authors examine the difference between the wage rates of white males and black males after controlling for a wide array of personal characteristics. The race gap is the difference between white and black wage rates that is unaccounted for by observable characteristics. As in other studies, they find a positive race gap: white wage rates are above black wage rates when other traits are held constant.

The study shows that this race gap decreases after bank branch deregulation. After conditioning on individual characteristics, as well as state and year fixed effects, the race gap drops by about 20 percent after a state removes restrictions on intrastate branching. More specifically, before a state deregulates, a white man earns 14 percent more than a black man with identical observable characteristics. After a state deregulates, the race gap falls to 11 percent. These findings suggest that formal financial sector reforms which improve the operation of the financial system reduce discrimination. Put differently, financial development expands the opportunities of people who have been disproportionately stuck at the bottom of the income distribution.

Access to Finance

Recent empirical evidence, reviewed in this paper, suggests that there is a strong negative relationship between financial development and poverty, inequality, and discrimination. These results survive rigorous robustness checks such as the use of instrumental variables and dynamic panel estimation to control for endogeneity bias. Analysis of specific policy reforms such as bank branch deregulation allows us to better deal with identification issues.

An area in which empirical work generally falls short is in the measurement of financial development. Development theory emphasizes that one of the crucial functions of a financial system is to allocate resources to the most productive uses, thus boosting economic growth, improving opportunities and income distribution, and reducing poverty. Access to finance for firms with growth opportunities, entrepreneurs with ideas, or individuals who wish to invest in their own education helps improve income distribution and promotes growth. But the measures of financial development commonly employed in the empirical literature do not reflect this access dimension that is emphasized in theory. For example, the private credit variable captures the depth of the financial system but not necessarily how widely access is available. One reason researchers have made extensive use of this variable to summarize financial development is that, unlike other measures, private credit is available for many countries over a long period of time. Indeed, although the financial sector is often thought of as being particularly well documented by statistical data, systematic indicators of access to different financial services are lacking. Accordingly, measurement of access to finance, its determinants, and its impact has been the focus of recent research that is described next (World Bank 2007).

Measuring Access

As figure 3 illustrates, access is different from use. Access is more difficult to measure because it is not directly observed. Indeed, some may have access but may not wish to use the services.

FIGURE 3.
Access to and Use of Financial Services

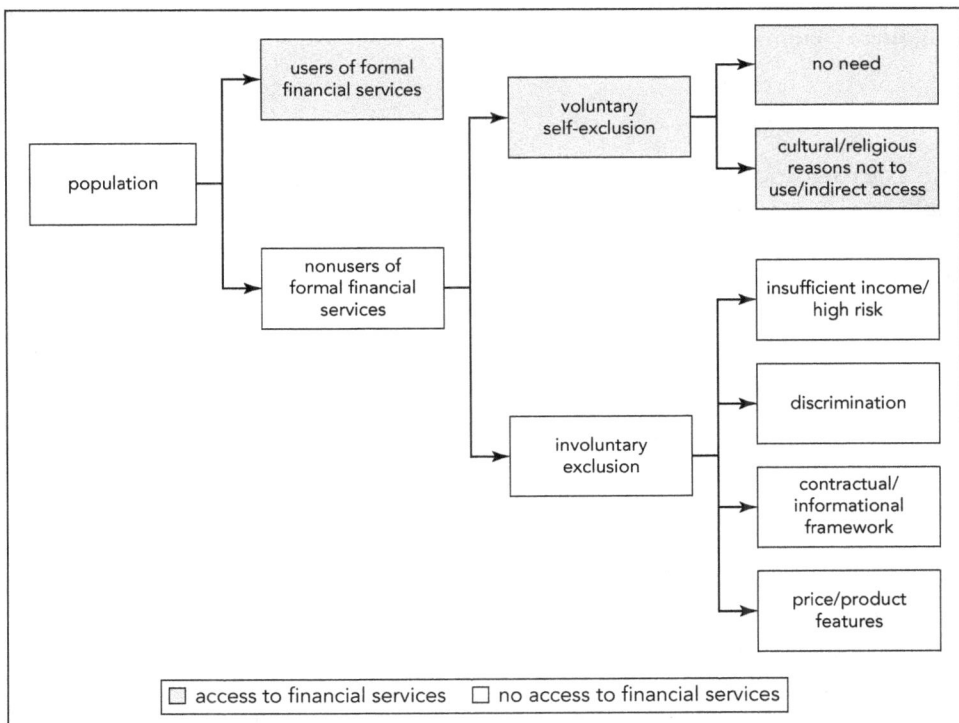

Source: World Bank 2007.

There are important distinctions among nonusers. Some people do not use financial services because they see no need for them or for cultural and religious reasons. This category includes households that prefer to deal in cash, as well as enterprises without any promising investment projects. Although this group has access, it does not use financial services. Then, there are the involuntarily excluded who demand financial services but do not have access to them. The involuntarily excluded can be divided into several groups. First, there are households and enterprises that do not have enough income or that constitute too high a lending risk to use financial services. This group can be considered unbankable by commercially oriented financial institutions and markets. Second, there may be discrimination against certain population groups on social, religious, or ethnic grounds. Third, the contractual and informational framework may prevent financial institutions from reaching out to certain population groups because the effort is too costly to be commercially viable. Finally, the price of financial services or the product features may not be appropriate for certain population groups. The first group of involuntarily excluded (the unbankable) cannot be a target of financial sector policy, but the other three groups demand different responses from policy makers.

To sum up, broad access to financial services is characterized by an absence of price and nonprice barriers to the use of financial services. The distinction between access and use suggests that it is important to collect information not only on the use of financial services but also on barriers to access in order to identify boundaries and causes of exclusion. These barriers, by excluding large parts of the population from access to finance, are likely to play an important part in perpetuating inequality and limiting economic opportunities for the poor.

Use versus Depth

An exact statistic on the number of households that use formal financial services can only be inferred from household surveys. Only around 34 countries, however, have household surveys that contain this information, and researchers have therefore turned to proxy indicators to estimate the share of the population using financial services.

Beck, Demirgüç-Kunt, and Martinez Peria (2007a) compile loan and deposit account data through surveys of bank regulators for a cross-section of countries and document the large variation in these indicators across countries. Whereas in Austria there are 3 deposit accounts for every inhabitant, in Madagascar there are only 14 per 1,000 inhabitants. In Greece there is almost one loan account for every inhabitant, but there are only four for every 1,000 inhabitants in Albania. The ratio of deposit and loan accounts per capita increases with income, although the average deposit or loan account balance relative to income per capita decreases with income, indicating that poor people and smaller enterprises are better able to make use of these services in more developed countries. Still there is great variation among developing countries. For example, in Bolivia the average loan amount is 28 times GDP per capita, while in Poland it is only a third of GDP per capita. In Madagascar the average deposit account balance is nine times GDP per capita, while it is only 4 percent of GDP per capita in Iran.

The authors show that these aggregate indicators are not only interesting measures in their own right but can also be used to predict the proportion of households using bank accounts when no household surveys are available. Regressing the share of households with deposit accounts obtained from household surveys on their aggregate indicators of deposit accounts and branch penetration, they show that the predicted share of households with deposit accounts from this regression provides a reasonably accurate estimate of the actual share of households with deposit accounts obtained from household surveys. Hence, using aggregate indicators, it is also possible to obtain out-of-sample estimates of the proportion of households using a bank account, although the fit is likely to be poorer.

Honohan (2006) combines these data from commercial banks with data from savings banks and other socially oriented institutions that target low-income clients (such as microfinance institutions, postal savings banks, and credit unions) to estimate a headline indicator, which provides the share of households with use of financial accounts in most of the world.[1] Figure 4 illustrates that use of finance is indeed very

FIGURE 4.
Use of Finance around the World

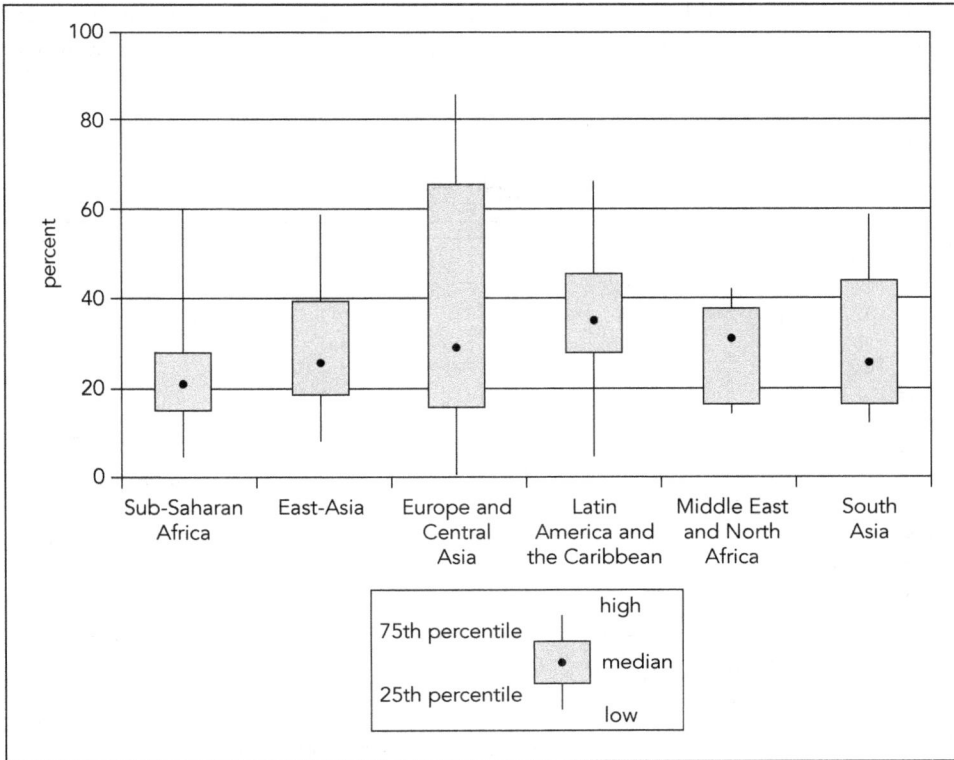

Source: World Bank 2007.

Note: Based on proportions of households with an account in a financial institution in each country averaged over world regions.

limited around the developing world: in most countries less than half the population has an account with a financial institution, and in many of the poorest countries the figure is less than one in five households. Those excluded often also include the non-poor, such as the middle class and small and medium-size enterprises.

Comparison of this indicator of use of finance with the commonly used financial depth indicator yields a positive but imperfect correlation (figure 5). This shows that access really is a distinct dimension: financial systems can become deep without delivering access to all. Take Colombia and Lithuania as examples. Both countries have similar ratios of private credit to GDP, at around 20 percent, but in Colombia 40 percent of households have accounts, whereas the ratio is 70 percent for Lithuania. Similarly, in both Estonia and Switzerland over 85 percent of households have accounts, but while Estonia's financial depth is around 20 percent, Switzerland's is over 160 percent. The positive but imperfect correlations of use of financial services with economic development and financial depth raise questions regarding what drives cross-country differences in financial use and access.

Barriers to Access

It is important to understand not only the actual use of financial services but also barriers to access to be able to design policies to broaden access. Beck, Demirgüç-Kunt, and Martinez Peria (2007b) conducted a survey of up to five large banks in over

FIGURE 5.
Financial Depth versus Use of Financial Services

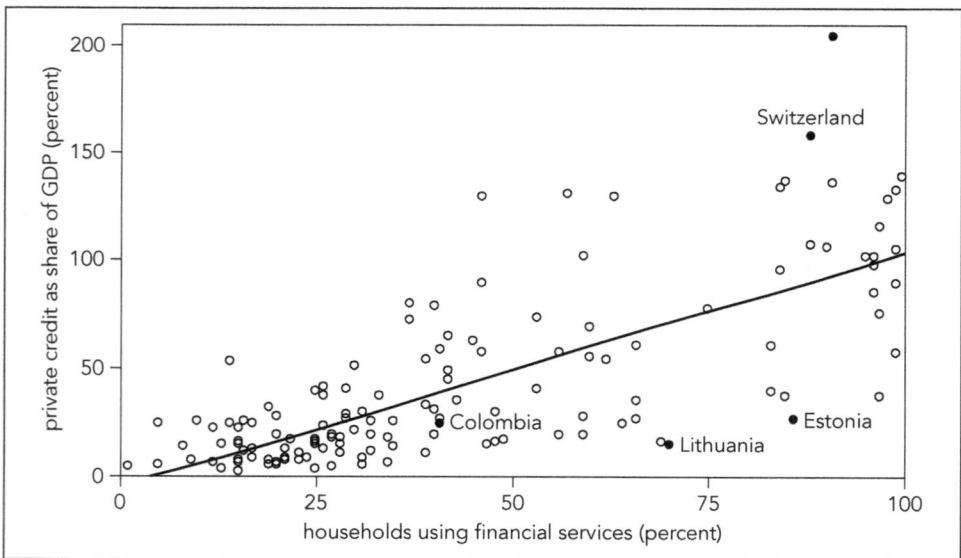

Source: World Bank 2007.
Note: GDP, gross domestic product.

80 countries and developed indicators of such barriers. They created barrier indicators for three types of banking services—deposits, loans, and payments—across three dimensions: physical access, affordability, and eligibility.

Barriers such as availability of locations for opening accounts and making loan applications, minimum account and loan balances, account fees, fees associated with payments, documentation requirements, processing times, and the like are found to vary significantly both across banks and across countries. Indicators of access barriers are found to be negatively correlated with actual use of financial services, confirming that these barriers can exclude individuals and small firms from using bank services.

Beck, Demirgüç-Kunt, and Martinez Peria (2007b) summarize the different access barriers measured by their survey by creating two aggregate principal component indicators, for access barriers for deposit services, and for access barriers for loan services. Table 1 reports partial correlations of these barriers with different country characteristics. These relationships are not necessarily causal; both the barriers and the country characteristics shown will have common underlying structural causes. Nevertheless, it is striking that indicators of competition, openness, and market orientation in overall financial sector and economic policy, such as the Heritage Foundation index of banking freedom and media freedom, are strongly correlated with access barriers.

As for the contractual and the informational infrastructures, better credit registries are associated with lower access barriers, but there is no evident correlation with creditor rights, suggesting that information infrastructures are more important than

TABLE 1. Correlation of Barriers to Access to Deposit and Loan Services with Country Characteristics

Characteristic	Access barriers: deposits	Access barriers: loans
Banking freedom	−0.563***	−0.474***
Media freedom	−0.327**	−0.425***
Credit information index	−0.302**	−0.275**
Official supervisory power	0.231**	0.071
Market-based supervision	−0.100	−0.374**
Physical infrastructure failures	0.264*	0.209
Government bank share	−0.002**	0.004***
Foreign bank share	−0.005**	−0.001
Creditor rights	−0.060	0.030

Source: Beck, Demirgüç-Kunt, and Martinez Peria 2007b.

Note: The entries in the table show the estimated impact of a one-standard-deviation change in each of the country characteristics on the two aggregate access barriers. The table is based on bank-level regressions using a dataset of 209 banks and 62 countries, regressing access to deposit or loan barriers on four bank-level controls (foreign ownership, government ownership, loan-to-asset ratio and log of asset size) and one country-level variable at a time. Significance tests are based on robust standard errors.

* Significant at 10 percent.

** Significant at 5 percent.

*** Significant at 1 percent.

stronger legal enforcement. Interestingly, government ownership of banks is associated with lower barriers on the deposit side (as is foreign ownership of banks) but with higher barriers on the loan side. Indicators of the approach to banking regulation are also correlated with access barriers. Countries that rely more on empowering markets (by enforcing accurate and timely information disclosure and providing the right incentives for market participants) tend to have lower barriers to accessing loan services. By contrast, the existence of all too powerful regulators (who may be subject to corruption and political and industry capture) is associated with higher access barriers, particularly for deposit services. Not too much should be read into these simple partial correlations, and much more research is needed to understand them. They do, however, have important policy implications for broadening access.

Impact of Access

How does improved access to finance affect the poor households, small businesses, and microenterprises that employ the majority of the workforce in developing countries? It is by now well established that in more developed financial systems, deserving firms have easier access to external finance, with positive implications for their growth and performance (Demirgüç-Kunt and Maksimovic 1998). More recent research has also identified a distributional impact. Using industry-level data for 44 countries and 36 industries and applying a difference-in-difference approach, Beck and others (2008) show that financial development disproportionately boosts the growth of small firms. Working with data from enterprise surveys for 54 countries and direct measures of credit constraints reported by firms, Beck, Demirgüç-Kunt, and Maksimovic (2005) demonstrate that the growth of smaller firms is significantly more constrained by financing obstacles, particularly in countries with less developed financial systems. Furthermore, they show that financial development is associated with a greater reduction in the financing obstacles faced by small firms and so disproportionately benefits this group. Research on microenterprises also yields consistent results. For example, De Mel, McKenzie, and Woodruff (2007) find that for a randomly chosen sample of entrepreneurs in Sri Lanka, credit constraints are the main reason for entrepreneurs' inability to expand their businesses.

What about the impact of access to finance by households? An extensive literature on microfinance addresses this issue (see Cull, Demirgüç-Kunt, and Morduch, 2009). Delivery of financial services to poor households can be quite challenging, since issues of risk management, monitoring, and transaction costs tend to make it very costly. Innovative techniques and products developed by microfinance institutions have helped overcome some of these difficulties and have attracted significant attention from the development community. Nevertheless, despite these innovations, microfinance services are costly to deliver and typically require extensive subsidies (Cull, Demirgüç-Kunt, and Morduch 2007). A review of the evidence suggests that the benefits of microcredit are not overwhelming and that there is considerable skepticism about the ability of microfinance programs to bring about large-scale reductions in poverty and inequality or to promote higher growth (World Bank 2007). Further research, ideally using more real experiments, is needed to convince the skeptics who continue to question whether subsidizing microfinance programs is the best use of scarce development assistance.

While still in its early stages, research on access using better indicators and micro-data on enterprises and households provide us with a glimpse into the mechanisms through which financial development is likely to affect poverty and income distribution. Comparison of the strong results on the impact of access for small and micro enterprises with the more mixed results for poor households suggests that the indirect effects of financial development on the poor, through labor and product markets, may be quite significant and that direct provision of credit to the poor may not be the most important channel.

Concluding Remarks

We end with an observation about financial sector policies. For purposes of comparison, consider redistributive policies. Many theories motivate redistributive policies as a mechanism for delinking an individual's opportunities from parental wealth, but one cannot simply change the distribution of income and hold everything else constant. Redistributive policies create disincentives to work and save. These tensions between efficiency and equity, however, vanish when the focus is on financial sector reforms. Financial developments that expand individual economic opportunity create positive, not negative, incentive effects, and avoid the adverse repercussions associated with attempts to equalize outcomes. Financial development boosts efficiency and the equity of opportunity. This observation further supports our core argument—that economists should devote considerably more resources to assessing how formal financial sector policies affect economic opportunity and poverty.

Note

1. Information on microfinance institutions, postal savings banks, credit unions, and state-owned agricultural and development banks comes from Christen, Rosenberg, and Jayadeva (2004); data on savings banks are drawn from Peachey and Roe (2006).

References

Aghion, Philippe, and Patrick Bolton. 1997. "A Theory of Trickle-Down Growth and Development." *Review of Economic Studies* 64 (2, April): 151–72.

Banerjee, Abhijit V., and Andrew F. Newman. 1993. "Occupational Choice and the Process of Development." *Journal of Political Economy* 101 (2, April): 274–98.

Bardhan, Pranab, Samuel Bowles, and Herbert Gintis. 2000. "Wealth Inequality, Wealth Constraints and Economic Performance." In *Handbook of Income Distribution,* vol. 1, ed. A. B. Atkinson and F. Bourguignon, ch. 10. 1st ed. Amsterdam: North-Holland Elsevier.

Barth, James, Gerard Caprio, and Ross Levine. 2006. *Rethinking Bank Regulation: Till Angels Govern.* Cambridge: Cambridge University Press.

Beck, Thorsten, Asli Demirgüç-Kunt, Luc Laeven, and Ross Levine. 2008. "Finance, Firm Size, and Growth." *Journal of Money, Credit, and Banking* 40: 1379–1405.

Beck, Thorsten, Asli Demirgüç-Kunt, and Ross Levine. 2007. "Finance, Inequality, and the Poor." *Journal of Economic Growth* 12 (1): 27–49.

Beck, Thorsten, Asli Demirgüç-Kunt, and Vojislav Maksimovic. 2005. "Financial and Legal Constraints to Firm Growth: Does Size Matter?" *Journal of Finance* 60 (1, February): 137–77.

Beck, Thorsten, Asli Demirgüç-Kunt, and Maria Soledad Martinez Peria. 2007a. "Banking Services for Everyone? Barriers to Bank Access and Use around the World." Policy Research Working Paper 4079, World Bank, Washington, DC.

———. 2007b. "Reaching Out: Access to and Use of Banking Services across Countries." *Journal of Financial Economics* 85 (1): 234–66.

Beck, Thorsten, Ross Levine, and Alex Levkov. 2007. "Big Bad Banks? The Impact of U.S. Branch Deregulation on Income Distribution." Policy Research Working Paper 4330, World Bank, Washington, DC. http://econ.worldbank.org/external/default/main?pagePK=64165259&theSitePK=469382&piPK=64165421&menuPK=64166093&entityID=000158349_20070827140607.

Becker, Gary S. 1957. *The Economics of Discrimination.* Chicago: Chicago University Press.

Becker, Gary S., and Nigel Tomes. 1979. "An Equilibrium Theory of the Distribution of Income and Intergenerational Mobility." *Journal of Political Economy* 87: 1153–89.

———. 1986. "Human Capital and the Rise and Fall of Families." *Journal of Labor Economics* 4: S1–S39.

Benabou, Roland. 1996a. "Equity and Efficiency in Human Capital Investment: The Local Connection." *Review of Economic Studies* 63 (2, April): 237–64.

———. 1996b. "Heterogeneity, Stratification and Growth: Macroeconomic Implications of Community Structure and School Finance." *American Economic Review* 86: 584–609.

Bertola, Guiseppe. 2000. "Theories of Persistent Inequality and Intergenerational Mobility." *Handbook of Income Distribution,* vol. 1, ed. A. B. Atkinson and F. Bourguignon, ch. 9. 1st ed. Amsterdam: North-Holland Elsevier.

Bourguignon, François. 1981. "Pareto Superiority of Unegalitarian Equilibria in Stiglitz' Model of Wealth Distribution with Convex Savings Function." *Econometrica* 49 (6, November): 1469–75.

Christen, Robert Peck, Richard Rosenberg, and Veena Jayadeva. 2004. "Financial Institutions with a Double Bottom Line: Implications for the Future of Microfinance." Occasional Paper 8, Consultative Group to Assist the Poorest (CGAP), Washington, DC. http://www.cgap.org/gm/document-1.9.2701/OccasionalPaper_8.pdf.

Cull, Robert, Asli Demirgüç-Kunt, and Jonathan Morduch. 2007. "Financial Performance and Outreach: A Global Analysis of Leading Microbanks." *Economic Journal* 117: F107–F133.

———. 2009. "Microfinance Meets the Market" *Journal of Economic Perspectives* 23(1): 167–92.

De Mel, Suresh, David McKenzie, and Christopher M. Woodruff. 2007. "Returns to Capital in Microenterprises: Evidence from a Field Experiment." Policy Research Working Paper 4230, World Bank, Washington, DC. http://www-wds.worldbank.org/external/default/WDSContentServer/IW3P/IB/2007/05/04/000016406_20070504134355/Rendered/PDF/wps4230.pdf.

Demirgüç-Kunt, Asli, and Vojislav Maksimovic. 1998. "Law, Finance, and Firm Growth." *Journal of Finance* 53 (6, December): 2107–37.

Galor, Oded, and Daniel Tsiddon. 1997. "Technological Progress, Mobility, and Economic Growth." *American Economic Review* 87: 363–82.

Galor, Oded, and Joseph Zeira. 1993. "Income Distribution and Macroeconomics." *Review of Economic Studies* 60 (1, January): 35–52.

Greenwood, Jeremy, and Boyan Jovanovic. 1990. "Financial Development, Growth, and the Distribution of Income." *Journal of Political Economy* 98 (5, part 1): 1076–1107.

Honohan, Patrick. 2006. "Household Financial Assets in the Process of Development." Policy Research Working Paper 3965, World Bank, Washington, DC. http://www-wds .worldbank.org/external/default/WDSContentServer/IW3P/IB/2006/07/11/000016406_ 20060711120153/Rendered/PDF/wps3965.pdf.

Kroszner, Randall, and Philip Strahan. 1999. "What Drives Deregulation? Economics and Politics of the Relaxation of Bank Branching Deregulation." *Quarterly Journal of Economics* 114: 1437–67.

Levine, Ross. 1997. "Financial Development and Economic Growth: Views and Agenda." *Journal of Economic Literature* 35 (2, June): 688–726.

———. 2005. "Finance and Growth: Theory and Evidence." In *Handbook of Economic Growth*, ed. Philippe Aghion and Steven Durlauf. Amsterdam: North-Holland Elsevier.

Levine, Ross, Alexey Levkov, and Yona Rubinstein. 2008. "Racial Discrimination and Competition." NBER Working Paper 14273, National Bureau of Economic Research, Cambridge, MA.

Loury, Glenn C. 1981. "Intergenerational Transfers and the Distribution of Earnings." *Econometrica* 49 (4, July): 92–6.

Peachey, Stephen, and Alan Roe. 2006. "Access to Finance: Measuring the Contribution of Savings Banks." World Savings Banks Institute, Brussels.

Piketty, Thomas. 2000. "Theories of Persistent Inequality and Intergenerational Mobility." *Handbook of Income Distribution*, vol. 1, ed. A. B. Atkinson and F. Bourguignon, ch. 8. 1st ed. Amsterdam: North-Holland Elsevier.

Stiglitz, Joseph E. 1969. "Distribution of Income and Wealth among Individuals." *Econometrica* 37 (3, July): 382–97.

World Bank. 2007. *Finance for All? Policies and Pitfalls in Expanding Access*. Policy Research Report. Washington, DC: World Bank.

Comment on "Finance and Economic Opportunity," by Asli Demirgüç-Kunt and Ross Levine

LILIANA ROJAS-SUAREZ

The paper by Demirgüç-Kunt and Levine presented in the plenary session, and the related paper by Beck, Demirgüç-Kunt, and Martinez Peria (2007), make important contributions to the growing literature on financial access and development.

The relationship between *financial depth*—defined as the ratio of key financial aggregates such as overall credit or deposits to gross domestic product (GDP)—has been shown both theoretically and empirically to be crucial for economic growth. Policy recommendations, including recommendations on the regulatory and supervisory side, have therefore been proposed to encourage financial deepening. The linkages between *financial access*—loosely defined as the percentage of the population that can freely use financial services—and development indicators such as reduction in poverty and inequality are less established. As indicated by Beck, Demirgüç-Kunt, and Martinez Peria (2007), a major reason is that data on access are scarce and inadequate. Another important reason is insufficient research on whether policy actions directly affecting the financial system can have an effect on poverty and inequality. (See, for example, Rajan and Zingales 1998.) This is where the paper by Demirgüç-Kunt and Levine advances the literature. A comprehensive review of existing theoretical research leads the authors to conclude that the relationship between income inequality and growth is affected by the degree of financial development, which in turn is identified with financial access.

On the basis of these findings, the authors argue in favor of more analysis (both theoretical and empirical) of policies that could remove financial market imperfections and thus improve access) as a mechanism for fighting poverty and persistent income inequality. Indeed, removal of barriers to financial access could well prove a more cost-effective means of poverty alleviation than programs aimed directly at reducing poverty.[1] However, until more research on this issue is undertaken, the jury is still out.

The 2007 study by Beck, Demirgüç-Kunt, and Martinez Peria examines the question, What are the barriers to financial access? Drawing on a global banking survey,

Liliana Rojas-Suarez is a senior fellow of the Center for Global Development, Washington, DC.

Annual World Bank Conference on Development Economics 2008, Global

the authors identify price and nonprice barriers that prevent large segments of the population from accessing financial services. Among the important barriers are fees charged by banks for loans and for maintenance of deposit accounts, and the number of documents and days required for processing loans and opening deposit accounts. The intensity of these barriers differs significantly among countries in their sample.

The authors argue that the factors explaining barriers to access are multiple and can be classified into two groups: (a) bank-level characteristics such as size, ownership, and degree of concentration and competitiveness, and (b) country-level characteristics such as physical infrastructure, contractual and information frameworks, regulatory policies, and degree of transparency. The authors then run regressions to assess the correlation between barriers to access and the suggested determinants of these barriers.

While fully acknowledging the high quality of this work, I would like to offer two main comments. First, in my view, the effects of macroeconomic stability on financial access are not sufficiently considered. Second, it is important to include among distortionary regulations inadequately designed capital requirements, which can adversely affect access to bank credit by small and medium-size enterprises (SMEs).

Let us start with the role of macroeconomic stability. In order to do business with banks, a country's population needs to trust the banking system. Yet the recurring economic and financial crises in many developing countries in the last three decades have resulted in significant losses for depositors in terms of the real value of their wealth. These losses have resulted from a variety of factors, including deposit freezes, forced conversion of deposits in foreign currency into deposits in local currency using undervalued exchange rates, and very high inflations or hyperinflations that practically destroyed the real value of bank deposits. Who lost the most in these periods of macroeconomic and financial instability? It was the poor and a large part of the middle class. Those segments of the population do not have the capacity to transfer money abroad in times of crisis. Furthermore, because of information asymmetries, these groups are the last to learn about banking problems and therefore are not in a position to exit the banking system in the early stages of the crisis.[2]

Macroeconomic instability has often translated into high volatility of real interest rates, which in some periods even took large negative values. Figure 1 shows the negative correlation between the volatility of real interest rates (approximated by the standard deviation during the period 1995–2006) and a composite measure of access to financial services constructed by Honohan (2008).

The figure shows a strong negative correlation between these variables. The message is clear: strengthening of demand for banking services requires that people have trust in the conservation of the real value of their deposits. Without that trust, not only will there be no incentives for bank usage, but the meager deposits in the banking system will tend to be short term in order to be available for quick withdrawal at the slightest sign of a problem. In turn, short-term liabilities limit banks' capacity to extend long-term financing, especially to relatively risky clients such as SMEs.

My second comment relates to the adverse effects of inadequate regulations on financial access. The authors rightly argue that straightforward government intervention in bank activities (such as limits on interest rates or government policies directing credit to particular sectors) induce banks to increase fees and commissions as

FIGURE 1.
Access to Finance and Real Interest Rate Volatility

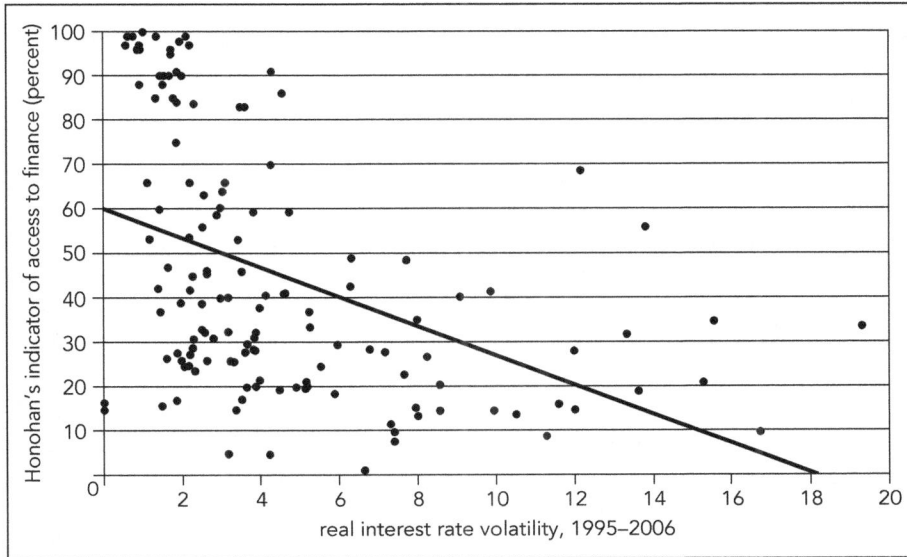

Source: Honohan (2008); International Financial Statistics Online, International Monetary Fund.

a way of compensating for the controls. There is, however, another form of regulation. Capital adequacy requirements can negatively affect financial access if inappropriately designed.

Most developing countries currently rely on the Basel I guidelines to estimate capital requirements. The Basel I Accord was proposed for the largest banks in industrial countries, with a significant level of international activity. In this context, the Basel recommendation established the calculation of capital requirements utilizing five weightings (0, 10, 20, 50 and 100 percent), which are assigned to bank assets according to risk category. One of these categories pertains to government bonds. Basel I recommends that banks assign a risk weighting equal to zero to the government debt of Organisation for Economic Co-operation and Development (OECD) countries and a weighting of 100 percent to non-OECD countries, unless the debt is issued and underwritten in local currency. The idea, of course, is that government assets in developed countries can be considered safe (nonrisky) assets.

Although the Basel recommendations were designed on the basis of the characteristics of industrial countries, most regulators in developing countries implemented the recommendations and assigned a risk weighting of zero to debt issues by their governments, whether issued in local or foreign currency. In other words, in the calculation of capital requirements, banks in most developing countries treat government debt as a safe asset—an assumption far removed from reality, given the frequency of crises in these countries. For comparison, Basel I recommended, and most developing countries implemented, assignment of a weight of 100 percent to all private-sector loans. The problem with the practice of weighting government debt at zero is that it creates an incentive for banks to keep a significant proportion of their assets in the form of government debt, to the detriment of credit to the private sector. This "crowding out" of credit to the private sector by government securities penalizes SMEs the most because this segment of firms is riskier and involves higher bank monitoring costs per loan than large corporations.

Can this problem be solved under the new Basel II accord? The greatest potential contribution of Basel II is the improvement of risk assessment, which would mean that many countries would have to increase the risk weighting assigned to government securities. But in reality, many developing countries are considering adopting the "standardized" Basel II approach, which contains a clause that allows banks, at supervisors' discretion, to continue applying a weighting of zero to government bonds if the bonds are denominated and underwritten in local currency. Proper risk assessment of government securities thus remains a challenge for supervisors and regulators in developing countries.[3]

All things considered, obstacles to financial access are multiple and involve the activities and decisions of banks, governments, businesses, and families. The papers reviewed here are important contributions to the advancement of our understanding of these complex issues.

Notes

1. Honohan (2004), for example, questions whether subsidized microfinance programs are the best policy instruments for poverty reduction.
2. See Rojas-Suarez (2007) for an application of this discussion to the Latin American experience.
3. See Rojas-Suarez (2002) for further discussion of these issues.

References

Beck, Thorsten, Asli Demirgüç-Kunt, and Maria Soledad Martinez Peria. 2007. "Banking Services for Everyone? Barriers to Bank Access and Use around the World." Policy Research Working Paper 4079, World Bank, Washington, DC.

Honohan, Patrick. 2004. *Financial Sector Policy and the Poor: Selected Findings and Issues.* World Bank Working Paper 43. Washington, DC: World Bank.

————. 2008. "Cross-Country Variation in Household Access to Financial Services." *Journal of Banking and Finance* 32 (11): 2493–2500.

Rajan, Rhaguram, and Luigi Zingales. 1998. "Financial Dependence and Growth." *American Economic Review* 88 (3): 559–86.

Rojas-Suarez, Liliana. 2002. "Can International Capital Standards Strengthen the Soundness of Banks in Emerging Markets?" *Capco Institute Journal of Financial Transformation* 5. Also published as WP-01-10, Institute for International Economics, 2001.

————. 2007. "The Provision of Banking Services in Latin America: Obstacles and Recommendations." Working Paper 124, Center for Global Development, Washington, DC.

Comment on "Finance and Economic Opportunity" by Asli Demirgüç-Kunt and Ross Levine

VICTOR MURINDE

The past two decades have witnessed an increased research focus on the role of finance in economic growth, as indicated in a recent survey of relevant theory, evidence, and policy by Green, Kirkpatrick, and Murinde (2005). A noteworthy insight, among the widely accepted findings from the recent work in this area, is that there are important relationships between finance and the development process. It is also acknowledged that there remain serious gaps in our knowledge regarding the mechanisms through which financial sector reforms can positively influence economic growth and poverty reduction. Specifically, there is a need to identify effective financial sector policies in relation to promoting poverty-reducing economic growth. The knowledge gaps are particularly important given the current commitment by the international community to the United Nations Millennium Development Goals (MDGs), which include a target of halving the number of people living on less than US$1 a day by 2015.

The paper by Asli Demirgüç-Kunt and Ross Levine presented in this session, and the related one by Beck, Demirgüç-Kunt, and Martinez Peria (2007), make important contributions to filling the gaps in the existing literature on finance and development and blaze the trail for future work in this area. Both papers are timely and policy-relevant, especially in emphasizing regulatory and other financial policy choices for governments and implications for private sector development.

My comments are organized around the two main contributions contained in these papers. I focus first on finance and opportunity across generations and then turn to barriers to bank access, before making some concluding remarks.

Finance and Opportunity across Generations

Demirgüç-Kunt and Levine seek to fill a critical gap in the literature with respect to how financial policy reforms and changes in financial system operations influence the evolution of poverty and the distribution of income. The paper emphasizes the dual

Victor Murinde is professor of finance and development at the Birmingham Business School, University of Birmingham, U.K.

Annual World Bank Conference on Development Economics 2008, Global

role of the financial system in shaping the economic opportunities faced by individuals and, consequently, in affecting the dynamics of the transmission of poverty and relative incomes across generations. An important message is that financial sector reforms create opportunities for households and firms, leading to an increase in the size of the economic pie and to reduction in poverty across generations.

The intergenerational dynamics of relative income is an important issue for researchers, as well as policy makers. There is already a large body of economics literature on overlapping-generations (OLG) models, which have been useful in informing key policy choices in public finance, especially taxation. It is encouraging that some of these ideas can be used innovatively to highlight the underresearched issue of the link between finance and poverty. Policy makers are also taking an interest in intergenerational issues, as indicated in recent work by Blanden and Gibbons (2006), which reports a government-supported pilot study on how best to overcome intergenerational poverty in the United Kingdom. The aim of the pilot study was to explore ways of offering opportunities to families that have been trapped in poverty for generations, in order to address the status quo of "born poor, die poor."

The paper by Demirgüç-Kunt and Levine offers abundant new ideas for further research, including new perspectives on existing knowledge. For example, the main idea of the study derives from the baseline theoretical model in equation (1) in the paper, in which the total income of dynasty i in generation t comprises wage income from human capital and the return on assets from physical capital. Not only does the paper recognize the role of human capital in the endogenous growth sense, but it is also consistent with recent evidence in Evans, Green, and Murinde (2002) that human capital is as important as finance in explaining economic growth across countries. Potentially, the insight offers a good platform for the promising extension of this work to consideration of new opportunities such as workers' remittances, which are now viewed as important in altering the future growth paths of household incomes.

In addition, the paper presents an important argument that a redistributive tax and benefits system may cause slower growth, mainly because of inherent perverse incentives. For example, if the unemployed are adequately protected by a comprehensive welfare system, they may not aggressively pursue every available job opportunity. In addition, the high taxes needed to pay for the benefits may discourage the wealthy from working as hard as they would under a low-tax regime. Pursuit of financial sector reforms rather than a redistributive tax and benefits system may expand individual economic opportunities and so create positive incentives for households to pursue welfare-enhancing economic opportunities, including employment. Researchers interested in randomized experiments on household incomes may find it useful to pursue these arguments further in order to generate new evidence.

In resonance with the 2007 paper by Beck, Demirgüç-Kunt, and Martinez Peria, Demirgüç-Kunt and Levine argue that the problem of financing constraints for small firms arises not only from lack of access but also from the cost of financing. In most developing economies this problem is exacerbated by a complete lack of innovative instruments for attracting and channeling savings at affordable rates to borrowers and potential investors. The high costs of working capital tend to squeeze potential profits that can be appropriated and thus to lower the private rates of return on investment.

The question of microfinance is relevant here. Various reasons are given for why the poor may not access financial services. These causes may in fact vary across developing economies. In some countries the poor may not access financial services because they are unable to fill in loan application forms or because they live in rural communities at a remote distance from financial institutions in urban areas. It may also be argued that although microcredit is successful in terms of reaching the poor, it is less successful in reaching the vulnerable, irrespective of village characteristics or other factors. There are compelling reasons why expanding the outreach of the banking sector may generate higher service delivery and even better welfare outcomes than existing microfinance approaches. Most important is the perverse role of subsidies when it is costly to reach the poorest of the poor in microfinance programs.

Specifically, there are at least two concerns. The first arises from empirical evidence showing that reaching the poorest of the poor is more costly than reaching other segments of the market, even in the absence of fixed lending costs (see, for example, Conning 1999). Are interest costs, salaries of service providers, the cost of staff training, and other administrative costs too high? The second question is, if the microcredit program is too costly to operate, is the optimal solution really extensive subsidy? The question of microcredit subsidies is a tricky one because subsidized credit tends to be politically manipulated and diverted from intended beneficiaries; without the subsidies, however, some microcredit programs are not sustainable.

As acknowledged by the authors, the main challenge in empirically pursuing the promising research ideas put forward in the Demirgüç-Kunt and Levine paper is methodological. For example, how do we measure intergenerational persistence of relative incomes? How do we model intergenerational portfolio choices by households? If, across generations, capital market opportunities and the stage of financial development change, what is the direction of causality between these changes and changes in poverty indicators? Recent empirical studies on the intergenerational persistence of incomes, earnings, and poverty may be helpful, especially on measurement techniques; see, for example, Restuccia and Urrutia (2004), Blanden and Gibbons (2006), and Blanden, Gregg, and Macmillan (2007).

Barriers to Bank Access

It is widely acknowledged that tackling financial exclusion is an important step in achieving poverty reduction. In this context, the 2007 paper by Beck, Demirgüç-Kunt, and Martinez Peria is valuable because it reports firsthand information gathered from a worldwide survey of banks. The paper endeavors to address an integral element of financial exclusion: banking exclusion. This is an assessment of how banking services such as deposits, loans, and payments are accessed (in terms of physical access, affordability, and eligibility) and the attributes of these services. The focus on banking exclusion is an important departure from existing literature, which tends to focus on exclusion from microfinance and aspects of financing micro and small enterprises. The paper also makes important contributions to knowledge by providing comprehensive cross-country coverage of the channels through which banking exclusion works. There is no doubt that the paper will stimulate further research on the mechanisms of banking exclusion.

Beck, Demirgüç-Kunt, and Martinez Peria (2007) take up one of the data challenges identified by Demirgüç-Kunt and Levine by developing indicators of barriers to banking services around the world. Their paper is rich in data. The dataset on bank access is valuable and facilitates cross-country comparisons, and even for the same country it allows some analysis of the impact of noninterest costs on access to local versus foreign banks. Among other applications, the dataset is particularly useful for researchers who want to delve into the gray area of what constitutes noninterest income.

It is important, however, not to sanctify the data. For example, it is reported that the survey was sent to the five most important banks in each of 115 countries. It is not clear how the authors selected the country sample, how they chose the sample period of 2004–5, whether regional differences and similarities were taken into account in the selection of the sample, and, if so, how the number of countries from each region was determined. Moreover, there is a limit to the usefulness of these comparisons simply because the banking services covered are not entirely homogenous of degree one. Also, in seeking to investigate the factors that explain banking barriers across banks and countries, Beck, Demirgüç-Kunt, and Martinez Peria draw data for country variables from a number of databases, and it is not clear how they resolve the problems of data inconsistency that typically arise from the various measurement methodologies used in different sources.

Arguably, the study suffers from sample selection bias in the sense that only the most important banks are selected for the sample. The conclusions drawn from a sample of large banks are unlikely to be representative of the banking sector. The main reason is that in developing countries the characteristics of large banks tend to be different from those of small banks, especially with respect to the financial products offered and the cost structure. For example, large banks tend to have a higher cost structure than small banks in terms of charges for cash withdrawals, overdraft fees, and money transfer costs. In addition, while large banks tend to offer a wide range of off-balance-sheet activities, small banks tend to concentrate on "bread and butter" on-balance-sheet products.

Concluding Remarks

Both papers highlight important issues for researchers and policy makers regarding the mechanism by which finance, growth, and poverty are linked through generations, as well as in the context of banking exclusion. There is no doubt that the two papers will stimulate new research within the spectrum of finance and development. Both papers point out promising directions for further research, including the starting point for constructing large datasets, in the case of Beck, Demirgüç-Kunt, and Martinez Peria.

In conclusion, at least two questions are imminent. First, what are the common barriers across countries at similar stages of development, and can financial policy or regulators break down these barriers? Second, what role can innovations in information technology and financial instruments play in shaping the economic opportunities faced by individuals and in affecting the dynamics of the transmission of poverty and relative incomes across generations?

References

Beck, Thorsten, Asli Demirgüç-Kunt, and Maria Soledad Martinez Peria. 2007. "Banking Services for Everyone? Barriers to Bank Access and Use around the World." Policy Research Working Paper 4079, World Bank, Washington, DC.

Blanden, Jo, and Steve Gibbons. 2006. *The Persistence of Poverty across Generations: A View from Two British Cohorts.* Bristol, U.K.: Joseph Rowntree Foundation Policy Press.

Blanden, Jo, Paul Gregg, and Lindsey Macmillan. 2007. "Accounting for Intergenerational Income Persistence: Noncognitive Skills, Ability and Education." *Economic Journal* 117 (519): C43–C60.

Conning, Jonathan. 1999. "Outreach, Sustainability, and Leverage in Monitored and Peer-Monitored Lending." *Journal of Development Economics* 60: 51–77.

Evans, Alun Dwyfor, Christopher J. Green, and Victor Murinde. 2002. "Human Capital and Financial Development in Economic Growth: New Evidence Using the Translog Production Function." *International Journal of Finance and Economics* 7 (2): 123–40.

Green, Christopher J., Colin H. Kirkpatrick, and Victor Murinde. 2005. *Finance and Development: Surveys of Theory, Evidence and Policy.* Cheltenham, U.K.: Edward Elgar.

Restuccia, Diego, and Carlos Urrutia. 2004. "Intergenerational Persistence of Earnings: The Role of Early and College Education." *American Economic Review* 94 (5): 1354–78.

Bring Me Sunshine: Which Parts of the Business Climate Should Public Policy Try to Fix?

WENDY CARLIN AND PAUL SEABRIGHT

This paper offers guidance to perplexed policy makers on how to draw practical lessons from the literature on the business climate and its role in economic development. We use the analogy of a doctor treating a patient, who must draw together information from the patient's subjective reports, clinical studies of average patient responses to treatment, and the patient's detailed case history. We argue that policy makers can use three complementary sets of findings: subjective reports by managers of firms, cross-country regression analysis, and case histories of countries or regions. These findings are less often contradictory than they sometimes appear, provided they are interpreted carefully. Although there is still much to learn, we give many examples of useful practical conclusions that can be drawn from this literature.

The purpose of this paper is to examine what policy makers can conclude from the large and often contradictory literature on the importance of the business climate for economic development. Over the past decade or so, a consensus has emerged in the research community that the quality of a society's institutions is of critical importance to successful development, but there is no agreement on how to identify the dimensions of institutional quality that matter most.[1] This divergence partly reflects the lack of a common definition of "institutions," without which it is easy for the term to serve purely as a cover for our ignorance as to what really determines differences in economic performance between societies. But even among researchers who use the term in the same way, there is little agreement about how to choose among rival institutional explanations. In these circumstances, what are policy makers to do? Should they ignore this literature until the researchers have got their act together?

Wendy Carlin is in the Department of Economics, University College London, and Paul Seabright is with the Toulouse School of Economics in France. Both are researchers with the Centre for Economic Policy Research (CEPR) in London.

This paper, especially the discussion of cross-country regression analysis, draws heavily on joint work with Mark Schaffer. The authors are also grateful for useful discussions with David Ulph and for the detailed comments by Jan Svejnar. Oleg Shchetinin provided excellent research assistance.

Annual World Bank Conference on Development Economics 2008, Global
© 2009 The International Bank for Reconstruction and Development/The World Bank

Should they dive in and hope to make sense of it themselves? Or are there some preliminary conclusions that can be drawn even if the remaining uncertainties are great?

This paper is intended as a guide to the research for the perplexed policy maker. We focus on those institutions that form part of what is commonly called the "business climate," namely, those aspects of the economic environment that are not under the control of individual firms but that affect the expense, ease, and reliability of doing business in a country. These factors have the advantage of being easier to define than institutions in general. Our intended typical reader is a senior civil servant advising the prime minister, the finance minister, or the minister of industry of a developing country. Policy makers will be very aware that it is not enough to understand what factors affect a country's economic performance unless those elements can be influenced by policy. We therefore focus on two questions on which existing research can shed some light:

- Which elements of the business climate make the most difference to the performance of firms?

- Which elements of the business climate have the highest priority for policy makers?

Some factors may be like the weather—impossible to control, but important to anticipate. Others may be like political crises—impossible to anticipate, but important to react to. Only a few can be both anticipated and controlled.

We start by asking what the business climate is and how we can find out about it.

What Is the Business Climate, and How Can It Be Measured?

Firms in any economy respond to their environments in ways that, in most cases, add value. That is, they transform goods and services (inputs) into other goods and services (outputs) which they can sell for more than it cost them to undertake the transformation. The terms under which they can do this are influenced mainly by technology and by the extent of competition in the market in which they sell. Two firms that use apparently similar technologies and face similar competition may have very different productivities, meaning that one of them can produce more valuable outputs for the same inputs. This difference in productivity may be the result of factors internal to the firm—the skill of its managers, for instance, or the motivation of its workforce. Alternatively, it may arise from factors outside the firm's control: one firm may be located in a violent neighborhood, for instance, that obliges it to spend more on security. The list of all the possible external factors that might influence a firm's productivity is what we call the business environment. We can therefore think of the state of the business environment as a series of constraints that prevents the productivity of firms in an economy from being as high as it could otherwise be.

In practice, and to enable comparison between different datasets, researchers use measures based on a number of commonly agreed dimensions, which typically include physical infrastructure, the legal system, the financial system, various aspects of the microeconomic and macroeconomic policy environment such as taxation, regulation, and macroeconomic stability, and social factors such as crime and corruption in a society. Physical infrastructure, for instance, counts as an aspect of the business environment because (unlike the case with such purely private goods as cars or refrigerators) firms cannot simply choose to buy as much of it in the market as they need. Firms can buy more private goods if they need them, provided they can pay for them by the productivity with which they transform them into outputs. But the state of the physical infrastructure is determined by factors in the economy (including government policy) that are not under the control of the firms that use it.

Although it is useful to think about the business environment as a kind of public good, it is important not to forget that even the terms on which private goods are available can be influenced by distortions, including those induced or sustained by poor policy. For example, trade barriers may raise the cost of inputs, and technological economies of scale may do the same for nontraded inputs if the size of the market is very small.

The question as to which elements of the business climate make the most difference to the performance of firms in a particular society therefore has, in principle, a simple interpretation: which of the constraints in that society costs firms the most in lost productivity? Alternatively expressed, if any one of the constraints on firm productivity could be relaxed, which one would have the biggest impact on productivity in the economy as a whole? Imagine that the legal system in Russia were as reliable as in, say, the Netherlands; would that make a bigger or smaller difference to the productivity of Russian firms than if the financial system were as developed as in the Netherlands? Or what if corruption were at Dutch rather than Russian levels? Or if Russian roads were as good as Dutch ones?

Once the question is posed in this way, we can see why it does not yet tell us what the priorities of Russian policy makers should be. Roads may be under policy makers' control, but corruption may be entirely outside their control (we are not claiming that this actually is so, but it may be). Alternatively, of any two constraints that are both under policy makers' direct control, some may cost much more to improve than others. Suppose, for instance, that we estimated that improving the Russian legal system to Dutch standards would make slightly less difference to productivity than improving the financial system but that it would cost only a fraction as much. Then, for the resources required to raise the Russian financial system to Dutch standards, it might be possible to improve the legal system *and* substantially improve the roads.

Still, finding out what factors make the most difference to firms' productivity is an essential first step toward determining what the priorities of policy makers should be. To move from the first step to the second, we need to add an assessment of the feasibility and costs of improving the relevant constraints. Unfortunately, as we shall see, research in this field has made less progress in identifying these costs than in identifying the impact of the constraints themselves. Nevertheless, a number of useful conclusions can be drawn.

To illustrate these conclusions we shall try in the course of this paper to answer a number of specific questions:

- Should governments in developing countries make large investments, financed out of public funds, in such items of physical infrastructure as electricity and telecommunications?

- In which countries should governments give high priority to improving law and order, and under what circumstances are there substitutes for improvements in law and order?

- Is labor regulation a major constraint on productivity?

- How much difference does the tax system make?

- What other regulatory reforms would have an important effect on the business environment?

We begin by looking at the different sources of evidence about the business climate, seeing what these different sources of evidence actually say, and asking whether they tell a consistent story.

What Are the Sources of Evidence about the Business Climate, and Do They Tell the Same Story?

We begin with a simple analogy. A doctor may be interested in knowing the major influences on the health of a particular patient being treated for some serious illness. She may have no doubt that her patient's health is determined by some complex causal process of which she could imagine having a reasonably full and reliable model. In practice, however, her model of that process is based on very limited information. For both practical and ethical reasons, she cannot subject her patient to all the experiments that would be necessary to determine how this patient's health responds to different influences. The doctor therefore has to rely on data generated by experiments (plus other, nonexperimental data) from other patients who are similar to her subject. She will be working with a model of the typical or average patient, albeit one who shares some of her subject's general characteristics, but she will not be able to control for unobserved ways in which her patient differs from those others and which may make treatments that are suitable for one patient quite unsuitable for another.

She can, of course, supplement her model with information designed to make it more sensitive to her subject's particularities. First, she can ask her patient for a full account of what he himself feels and any clues he may be able to give as to the origins of his condition ("I haven't felt quite right since I ate that hamburger . . ."). Such information may, of course, be misleading, as any medical professional knows ("I'm quite sure it's my heart, doctor"), but it can be useful if she has a way of integrating it with and testing it against information from other sources. Second, she can refer to her own or other doctors' detailed information about the patient's case history, including treatments to which the patient responds particularly well or particularly badly, plus any hunches she may have about his idiosyncrasies, his strengths, and his weaknesses. Such hunches, without necessarily constituting a basis for treatment in themselves, may suggest hypotheses that can help her in searching the medical literature. For instance, is the patient's adverse reaction to a certain treatment related to his weight problems, and have similar associations been documented elsewhere? She may also use case study material about subjects who are like her own patient in what seem to her particularly relevant respects.

In the spirit of this analogy, we distinguish three sources of information that a policy maker can use to understand the effects of the business climate on the productivity of the society for which she has political responsibility. There is cross-country evidence, generated by policy experiments and from other sources, about the average or typical response of the economy to various factors. There is what the managers of firms themselves say about the effect of various factors on their own productivity. Finally, there is case study evidence generated by the prior history of the country in question, or by that of relevantly similar countries. These three sources of evidence have many of the same strengths and weaknesses as their analogues in the medical example and need to be assessed together in something of the same spirit.

Countries are not the same as individual patients, and economic policy is not medicine. Among the most important differences is the presence of many interactions between firms; even if the managers of firms give accurate replies to questions about the constraints on their productivity, the effect of these constraints on the productivity of the economy as a whole may not be simply equal to the sum of their effects on individual firms.[2] Still, if we keep the limitations of the medical analogy in mind, we can explore it in a useful way.

The Causal Model: Cross-Country Regression Analysis

Just as the doctor will draw on studies based on samples of patients to derive evidence about the average causes of health, economists have now generated many studies based on samples of countries to derive evidence about the average determinants of economic performance.[3] No country is average, just as no patient is average, but a study based on averages can be a good place to start looking for explanations that fit the particular case.

One of the most difficult problems for studies of health is identifying the direction of causality. Depression and unemployment are correlated, but how much is this because unemployment causes depression and how much because depressed people are more likely to become unemployed? Studies purporting to find that breastfeeding raised babies' IQs turned out to have ignored the possibility that mothers with higher IQs, whose babies also have higher IQs on average, were more likely to breastfeed their babies (see Der, Batty, and Deary 2006 for a recent study controlling for maternal IQ). Much of the ancient medical lore that has now become discredited suffered from confusion about causality; an example is the common medieval belief that sickness could be caused by an excess of heat in the body, whereas we now know that high temperatures are typically a symptom of ill health rather than an underlying cause.

Exactly the same problem bedevils studies of institutions and economic performance: we all observe that richer countries have higher-quality institutions—a better business environment—but to what degree is this simply the consequence of economic development rather than the cause? (See Rodrik 2005 for a strong critique.) Would policy makers be better advised to focus on other fundamental causes rather than on the symptoms of development, leaving the business climate to improve as development proceeds? Real progress has been made in the past decade in identifying a causal role for institutional quality in development, and this has sharpened the incentive for researchers to pin down more concretely which aspects of the business environment matter for firm performance.

Recent cross-country econometric analysis is widely viewed as having established that institutional quality is causal in determining living standards (for a survey, see Pande and Udry 2006). The key to overcoming the reverse causality problem is to find a variable that predicts today's institutional quality but has no direct effect on today's living standards—an instrumental variable. In the best-known study (Acemoglu, Johnson, and Robinson 2001) the authors take a subsample of countries that had been colonized and use as the instrumental variable for today's institutional quality the disease environment faced by potential colonizers. They conjecture that the disease environment affected the nature of the colonies that were established but has no direct effect on living standards today. According to this hypothesis, where the disease environment was conducive to European settlement, so-called settler colonies were established. Settlers replicated their home institutions, which were associated with secure property rights and with successful capitalist development. The persistence of these high-quality institutions is reflected in current institutional quality, measured by the risk of expropriation of foreign investors. By contrast, in places where the disease environment for Europeans made settlement hazardous, extractive states were set up, with the main purpose of transferring resources to the colonial power. Australia is an example of a settler colony in which institutions to enforce the rule of law were paramount. The Belgian Congo was an extractive colony where the disease environment made it unattractive for the colonizers to settle and to invest in replicating home institutions. To complete the argument, Acemoglu, Johnson, and Robinson point out that the disease environment at the time of potential settlement is not related to current living standards because indigenous populations were already largely immune to the diseases that killed Europeans and because these diseases are no longer major killers.

Subsequent studies have tended to confirm the finding that historical and geographic factors are good instrumental variables for institutional quality. That is, their effect is indirect; they operate via institutional quality rather than having a direct effect on current performance outcomes. This literature does not help pin down which aspects of the business environment matter most, but it makes a highly relevant contribution by showing that countries are not doomed by their history or geography to be poor forever. A good example is the case of eastern and western Germany: longitude is a good instrumental variable for the role of institutional quality as a determinant of long-run per capita gross domestic product (GDP) by district (Rodrik 2004). A district lying further to the east was more likely to be organized as part of the planned economy during the 1949–89 period, but otherwise geography had no direct effect on 1989 living standards. The implication is optimistic rather than pessimistic, since if institutions can be changed, convergence of per capita GDP toward those in more westerly districts would be expected. This is what can now be observed in the eastern districts of unified Germany. The implications would be different if longitude had a direct effect on living standards, since policy aimed at changing institutions might be correspondingly less effective. (Latitude is more likely than longitude to have such an effect because it directly influences climatic, environmental, and epidemiological factors that have a known influence on economic outcomes.)

Unfortunately, many studies test for the importance of one aspect of the business environment against the null hypothesis that there is no systematic influence on productivity apart from some basic factor endowments. This is not an interesting null hypothesis. The source of the problem is the limited number of countries in the world and the shortage of convincing instrumental variables for different dimensions of the business environment; there are simply not enough degrees of freedom to choose between a significant number of alternative hypotheses.

One example where such a test has been implemented is the attempt of Acemoglu and Johnson (2005) to determine whether it is "property rights institutions" or "contracting institutions" that matter for long-run development. Property rights institutions regulate the relationship between the state and the private sector, and contracting institutions regulate the relationship between private sector lenders and borrowers. The authors use settler mortality as the instrument for property rights institutions and legal origin as the instrument for contracting institutions. Two important findings emerge. First, these are good instruments—and again, they have optimistic implications. For instance, a country's French legal origin helps predict the current nature of contracting institutions (as reflected, for example, in a greater degree of legal formalism and as measured by a greater number of steps required to resolve an unpaid check than in countries of English legal origin), but it has no direct effect on economic outcomes today. Second, they find that property rights institutions, and not contracting institutions, are causal for living standards today, as well as for investment share and overall financial development. By contrast, contracting institutions are causal for the structure of financial institutions and, in particular, for the significance of the stock market in the economy—more costly contracting institutions are associated with smaller stock markets. Other research suggests reasons why greater legal formalism may not be of first-order importance as a constraint on growth: there may be effective extralegal substitutes such as norms of tax enforcement and freely operating print and broadcasting media (Dyck and Zingales 2004).

The ability of cross-country regression analysis to reveal which institutions or elements of the business environment really matter for long-run development is severely limited by

- The correlation between the proxies that are used to characterize them
- Problems with measuring business environment variables
- The persistence of institutions over time
- The limited number of countries
- The paucity of credible instruments for dealing with the problem of reverse causality, as well as the problems of measurement error and omitted correlated variables.

In Appendix A.1 of this paper we provide an annotated guide to a selection from the vast number of cross-country studies that have sought to investigate the role of institutions or the business climate in long-run growth. Although most studies are conducted within a similar reduced-form framework, it is not easy to compare the findings. Different studies explore different ways of mitigating the problems listed above. Studies that appear to have identified one particular aspect of the business environment as explaining long-run performance should be treated with some skepticism. Just as epidemiologists are skeptical of the new study they receive each year claiming to have found that a particular foodstuff (broccoli one year, milk products another) raises or lowers the risk of breast cancer, economists should be wary of claims that the key dimension of the business environment has been revealed in a cross-country study. Corroboration from other sources of evidence is needed before any degree of confidence can be placed in the findings of a particular study. It is to these other sources that we now turn.

The Patient's Perspective: Surveys of Managers

Parallel with the emergence of more convincing evidence from aggregate data concerning the importance of institutional quality for long-run economic performance (using imaginative strategies for dealing with problems such as reverse causality) was a massive data collection effort that sought to document aspects of the business environment as experienced by managers. Two different kinds of data have been collected: quantitative indicators of the quality of physical and institutional infrastructure (for example, the length of time required to have a main-line telephone connection installed) and subjective assessments by managers of the impact of aspects of the business environment on the operation and growth of their firms. These data have been collected for fairly large cross-sections of firms in more than 70 economies, mainly developing and transition countries but also including members of the Organisation for Economic Co-operation and Development (OECD). The results of these surveys have been analyzed in a variety of ways, and a number of important lessons have emerged that are relevant to their usefulness for policy purposes. Appendix A.2 reviews a selection of business climate studies using firm-level data.

We concentrate on the use of the subjective evaluations collected from the surveys because this is a relatively new source of information that is different in character from the alternative measures of business climate. Commonly used measures of business climate include those collected from experts (for example, measures of the security of property rights) or from tabulation of objective indicators such as the numbers of procedures required to start a business or to cash a check in each country in the sample. Subjective evaluations of economic agents themselves are less commonly used in economics. We shall argue that they provide both opportunities and pitfalls in the context of business climate studies because of the public good character of at least some dimensions of the business environment (see Carlin, Schaffer, and Seabright 2007 for a more extensive discussion). The question asked of managers in the Productivity and Investment Climate Survey (PICS) and the Business Environment and Enterprise Performance Survey (BEEPS) conducted by the World Bank and the European Bank for Reconstruction and Development (EBRD) goes as follows:

> I would now like to ask you questions about the overall business environment in your country and how it affects your firm. Can you tell me how problematic are these different factors for the operation and growth of your business?

Aspects of the business environment managers are asked to evaluate are telecommunications, electricity, transport, land access, tax rates, tax administration, customs regulation, licensing regulation, employment regulation, access to finance, cost of finance, policy uncertainty, macroeconomic stability, corruption, crime, skills availability, and anticompetitive practices.

Thinking about the business climate as a public good highlights the potential role of the policy maker. In the theory of pure public goods, we face the questions of what is the optimal amount of the public good and whether the private market will provide it. The problem arises for policy because once a pure public good is provided, it is available to all. Those who do not wish to pay cannot be excluded from consuming the good, so either citizens must be coerced into paying for the good, or the good must be supplied at a zero price and funded out of coerced taxation or some uncoerced source such as foreign aid. Voluntary participation therefore cannot be used as a signal of citizens' willingness to pay for the good. Policy makers somehow have to determine the sum of their marginal valuations of the public good and compare it with the marginal cost of provision to determine the optimal quantity. Furthermore, different agents value the public good differently even when it is optimally supplied, unlike the case of (divisible) private goods, where the marginal valuations (determined by prices) of different citizens are the same, even if their average valuations are not.[4]

We can apply this insight to the interpretation of subjective ratings of the business climate by managers. A manager will value a public good according to how much an extra unit of that public good would improve the performance of the firm. In the language of microeconomics, this value is a shadow price—it represents the cost to a decision maker of the fact that some resource is in constrained supply. But even if the constrained supply of the public good is constant for all firms in a particular economy, different firms will be affected by it to different degrees. (Poor law and order will obviously hurt a firm that delivers payrolls much more than it will hurt a firm that delivers pizzas.) So, the shadow prices of the public good will vary across firms in the economy. Furthermore, it will often be the most productive firms that have the highest shadow prices, for reasons familiar from the case of ordinary public goods. Think of a park; assuming that we can elicit their true preferences, citizens who are fitter and anticipate using the park more intensively are likely to set a higher marginal valuation on it. Similarly, firms that make more efficient use of their resources will utilize the business environment more intensively and will place a higher value on the relaxation of its constrained supply than will less productive firms.

From the point of view of our original question, data about valuations have one great advantage over the results of cross-country regression studies: they already tell us how important different aspects of the business environment are relative to each other. Of course, this is of relative importance in the opinion of managers, who may be mistaken, just as patients may be mistaken about the relative importance of factors such as diet, genotype, lifestyle, and disease pathogens in affecting their health. Still, managers typically spend much more time systematically studying their business than most individuals spend analyzing their own health, so the value of their opinions about relative importance should not be underestimated.

We can now show how this simple framework can be applied to the data collected in the surveys of managers. For each dimension of the business environment, a higher score is recorded when the manager views that factor as imposing a stronger constraint on the firm. We interpret this as a higher shadow cost of the constraint to the firm. If we compare the scores across firms within a country, we would expect to find that better-performing firms would report higher costs of the constraint (higher scores), since these are the kinds of firm for which the constrained supply of good business environment services is most costly. By contrast, if we average across firms within a country and compare averages across countries, the variation is likely to be strongly influenced by variations in the supply of the public good (although not only by that, as we shall see). We would expect this average complaint score to be lower in countries with better economic performance, and vice versa. (The sum of the marginal valuations declines as the supply rises.)

Figure 1 illustrates these relationships in a simple way by showing, for three firms with different levels of productivity, their valuation of a public good as a function of the level of the public good supplied (a diminishing function, for familiar reasons—the more you have of something, the less you need still more of it). At any level of supply, the more productive firms will report higher valuations. The heavy line represents the sum of their valuations for any level of supply, and the optimal level of supply is where the heavy line intersects the marginal cost (shown here as constant, for simplicity). If the supply is less than the optimal level, the sum of the valuations will be higher.

Thus, we have two sharp empirical predictions: in any country, the more productive firms will complain more about the business environment, but when we take average complaints in a country, firms in more productive countries will complain less. What do the data actually show?

Figure 2 illustrates how these cross-country and within-country patterns are reflected in data from the PICS and BEEPS surveys of managers. Panel 2a reports a between-country relationship of the level of income per capita of the country and the reported importance of three kinds of constraints: physical infrastructure (specifically, electricity), customs regulations, and access to finance.

FIGURE 1.
Business Environment Constraints and Productivity: Between- and Within-Country Relationships

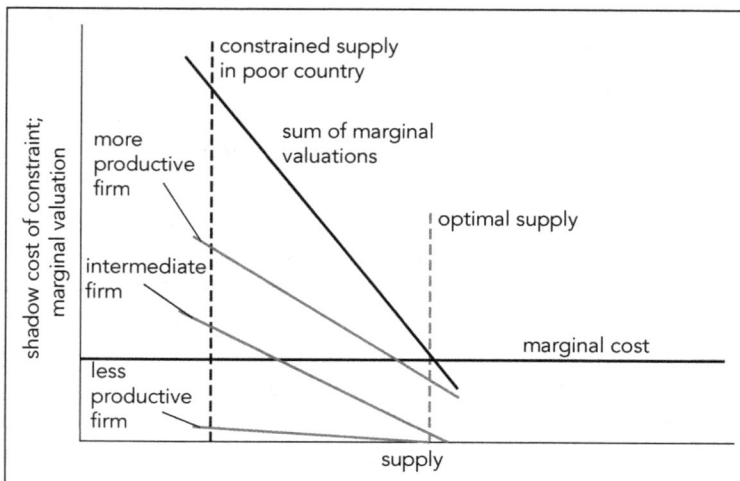

Source: Authors' construction.

FIGURE 2.
Between- and Within-Country Variation in Three Dimensions of the Business Environment

2a. Between-country variation in constraint, by country income

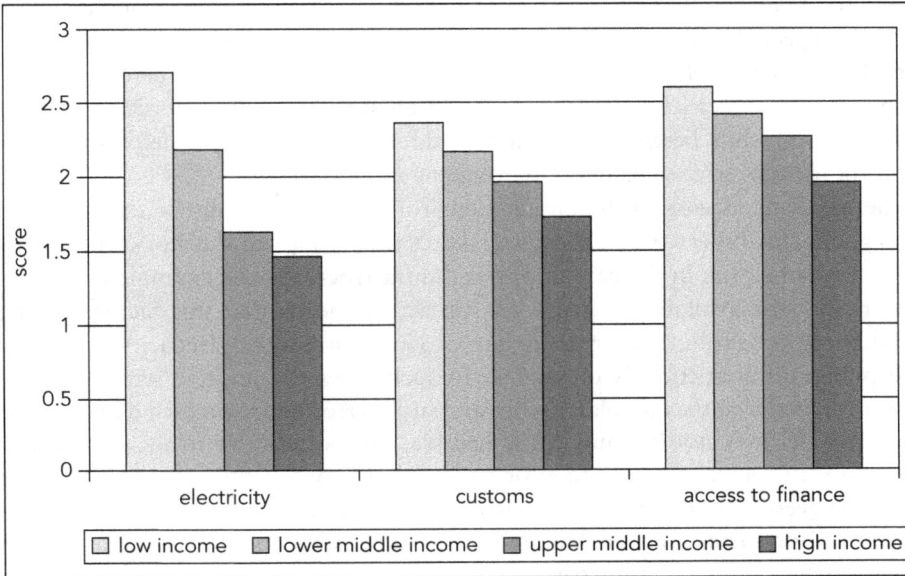

2b. Within-country variation in constraint, by firm-level TFP

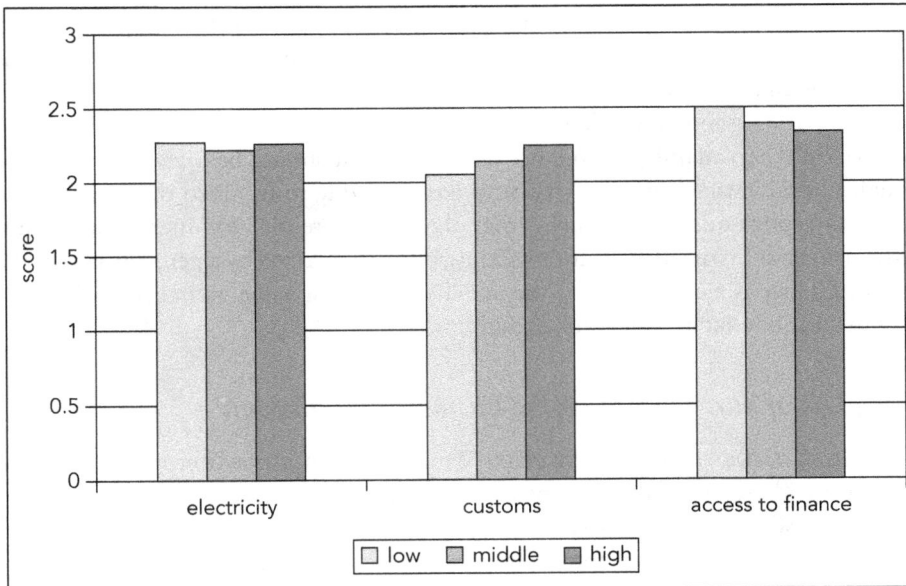

Source: Carlin, Schaffer, and Seabright 2007.

Note: TFP, total factor productivity. Country income categories are those defined by the World Bank. Data on importance of constraints are for 18,444 manufacturing firms. The severity of the constraint is measured on a scale from 0 (no obstacle) to 3 (major obstacle). For further details, see Carlin, Schaffer, and Seabright (2007).

As predicted, the first panel shows a declining relationship, with the reported importance of constraints falling as country income level rises. The second panel (2b) reports the equivalent within-country relationships. It shows that for customs regulations there is an increasing relationship between productivity and the score measuring the cost of the constraint to the firm. This is in accord with the earlier discussion, as would be expected, given that customs regulation has the character of a pure public good. The opposite relationship applies for access to finance, and there is no relationship at all for electricity. Exploring why different patterns characterize the within-country relationship between constraints and firm performance helps bring out important features of the business environment and its effects.

Whereas some aspects of the business environment can usefully be thought of as public goods, for others the public good aspect is only part of the story, and for yet others, it is unhelpful. In the case of physical infrastructure—the example in figure 2 is electricity—the availability of private substitutes means that this factor is not a pure public good. Productive firms are likely to invest in private electricity generation if the public infrastructure is unreliable. In such cases the positive within-country relationship between the complaint score and firm performance predicted by the public good model may not be found. It is necessary to be sensitive to the existence of private substitutes when assessing information about constraints drawn from survey data. As is even clearer in the case of telecommunications, where mobile telephony has replaced or substituted for landlines, technological progress can radically alter the public good nature of infrastructure.

Taking the third aspect of the business environment in figure 2, we note first that when managers are asked to evaluate the constraint imposed on their firm's performance by their access to finance or by the cost of finance, it is high-productivity firms that report lower constraints. This brings our attention to the fact that these aspects of the financial system—access to and cost of finance—do not have the character of a public good. Indeed, if the financial institutions are working well, the perception of the availability of finance as a constraint should be *inversely* related to the quality of investment projects the firm has available to fund, so that high scores may indicate poor-quality projects rather than the potential for increased output. An effective set of financial institutions should be characterized by a perception that the supply of finance is a constraint on the activity of at least some managers, unlike the case of institutions such as customs regulations.

Making Use of Survey Data on the Business Environment

Within- and across-country patterns. We are now in a position to examine the scores for a wide range of dimensions of the business environment across more than 60 countries. We concentrate here on the ranking of constraints relative to the average complaint level for the country. One way of looking at the data is to take each constraint in turn and count the countries for which that particular constraint is ranked as relatively important. This information is shown in figure 3, where the constraints are ordered by the total number of countries in which each constraint was rated as of above-average importance.

FIGURE 3.
Relative Importance of Business Constraints, by Country Group

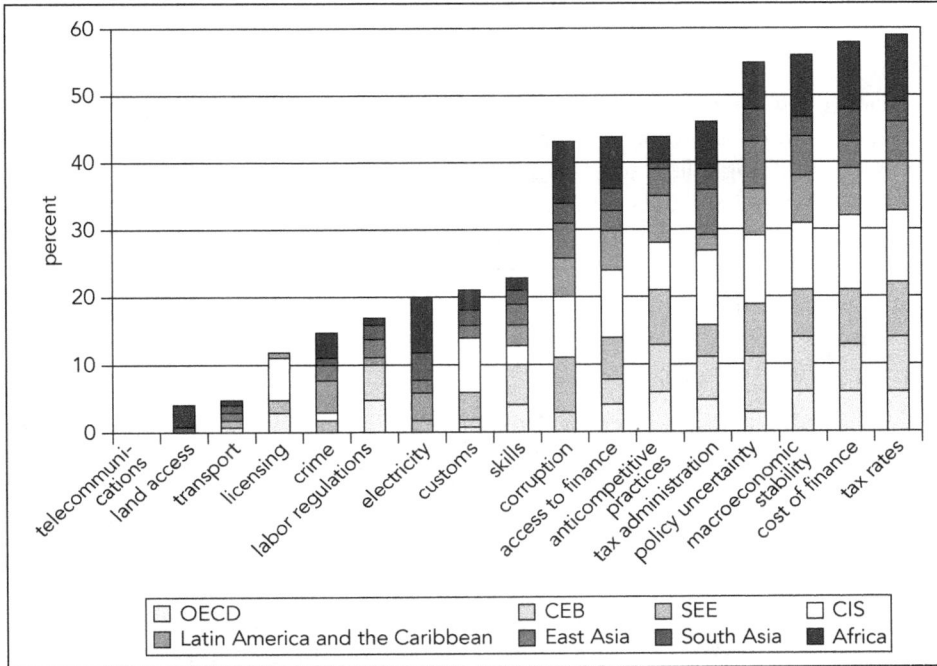

Source: Carlin, Schaffer, and Seabright 2007.

Note: CEB, Central and Eastern Europe and the Baltic states; CIS, Commonwealth of Independent States; OECD, Organisation for Economic Co-operation and Development; SEE, Southeastern Europe. Each bar shows the number of countries in each country group for which the constraint is ranked as more important than the average constraint for that country. Since the data for about half the more than 60 countries surveyed include only manufacturing firms, the data used in the figure are for responses from manufacturing firms only.

Another way of summarizing the data is to use the absolute rather than the relative value of the constraint score. In principle, the absolute score of a constraint is the correct measure of the shadow value of the constraint for that economy, and a country whose scores are higher, on average, than those of another is a country facing more constraints overall on the supply of public goods. Here, however, we use relative scores because from the perspective of the policy maker, the country is the right focus: in measuring the relative importance of a constraint, we are capturing where the priorities of policy makers in that country should be directed. Interestingly, there are few differences between the rankings of constraints by relative importance and by absolute importance (for details, see Carlin, Schaffer, and Seabright 2007). The differences that do exist concern constraints that affect countries which are either very poor or very rich. For instance, telecommunications constraints rank as absolutely important in four countries; but because these countries have many other problematic constraints, telecommunications never ranks as relatively important even there. Labor regulation, by contrast, ranks as relatively important for more countries than report it as absolutely important, since it is reported as important only in comparatively rich countries where other constraints score low.

The constraints fall into three groups: those that infrequently appear as of above-average importance (telecommunications, land access, and transport); those that are important in one-fifth to one-third of countries surveyed (from licensing through skills in figure 3, reading from left to right); and a final group comprising the constraints that appear to be of above-average importance in more than 70 percent of countries (from corruption through tax rates in the figure).

Countries are classified into eight groups: Africa (10 sample countries); South Asia (5); East Asia, including China and Vietnam (7); Latin America and the Caribbean (6); a group of European OECD members (6); and transition economies from the former Soviet bloc—Central and Eastern Europe, including the Baltic states, or CEB (8); Southeastern Europe, or SEE (8); and the Commonwealth of Independent States, or CIS, including Georgia (11).

When looking at the constraints reported as of above-average importance, some interesting patterns emerge:

1. Physical infrastructure rarely ranks high as an important constraint. Land access appears only in three African countries: Eritrea, Ethiopia, and Mali. Transport ranks high in a handful of poor or war-torn economies, including Sri Lanka and Kosovo, and in Ireland. Telecommunications does not appear at all, suggesting that the penetration of privately provided mobile telephony has much diminished the public good aspect of this traditional component of infrastructure. Electricity stands out as the key physical infrastructure problem that constrains firms; it is rated as of above-average importance in one-third of the countries, including all 10 of these African countries except South Africa, as well as South Asia. The only transition economies where electricity is cited as problematic are Kosovo and Albania, where it is the top-ranked constraint.

2. Problems with licensing and customs affect relatively few countries in aggregate (less than one-third) but are especially prevalent in the CIS countries, where tax administration is also of particular concern.

3. Crime or corruption, or both, show up as important constraints in all groups of countries surveyed except OECD members. Crime is top ranked in only one-quarter of countries and corruption in 70 percent. In five of the six sample countries in Central and South America, crime is ranked above average (Chile is the exception), and corruption is ranked above average in all six. For four of those countries, crime or corruption is the top-ranked constraint. The only other countries where corruption is top ranked are Cambodia, India, and Kenya.

4. There are seven dimensions of the business environment that are viewed as of greater than average importance in all country groups: anticompetitive practices, tax rates, tax administration, access to finance, cost of finance, policy uncertainty, and macro-economic stability.[5] Perhaps not surprisingly, complaints about the burden of the tax rate are virtually universal. Tax administration, however, is scored as more problematic than the tax rate in almost half of the CIS countries, including the Russian Federation, and is rated as more problematic than corruption in all CIS countries except Georgia. It is in the CEB and OECD countries that the tax rate most often shows up as the highest-ranked constraint. An exception is Estonia, where the tax rate attracts

a relatively low score and where skill shortages, followed by labor regulation, are ranked as the most important constraints. In Southeastern Europe policy uncertainty is the most common top-ranked constraint, in East Asia it is macroeconomic policy, and in Africa it is the cost of finance. Unsurprisingly, South Africa's profile is quite different from that of the rest of Africa; the constraints ranked most highly there are labor regulation, skill shortages, macroeconomic stability, and crime.

5. The broad similarity in the pattern of complaints between CEB and OECD countries is reassuring; complaints about labor regulation and skill shortages are much less in evidence in country groups at lower levels of per capita GDP.

Interpreting studies using firm-level business environment data. Since many studies have been carried out using business climate data, it is useful to draw attention to issues that arise in the interpretation of results. For illustrative purposes, we focus on four studies. The first, Dollar, Hallward-Driemeier, and Mengistae (2005), uses the investment climate surveys for four low-income countries: Bangladesh, China, Ethiopia, and Pakistan. The authors employ "objective" measures of the business environment collected in surveys similar to the ones we use in this paper. They restrict their attention to firms in the garment industry and use city averages as their measure of the quality of the business environment. They estimate a production function, which is augmented by the inclusion of five business environment measures. The authors conclude that the most significant bottleneck is the delay in getting a phone line, followed by customs delays and power outages. The number of inspections by government officials and the availability of an overdraft do not appear to be as important. The significance they report for delays in getting phone connections is quite at odds with the average subjective assessments by managers of the problems posed by telecommunications infrastructure recorded in the PICS–BEEPS data reported earlier. All four country surveys are in the PICS–BEEPS dataset, and telecommunications is not recorded there as of above-average importance (nor is it in any other country in the dataset, as we mentioned). What are we to make of this discrepancy?

Regression analysis of the PICS–BEEPS data casts an interesting light on this question. As reported in Carlin, Schaffer, and Seabright (2007), the severity of telecommunications constraints enters with a large and significant negative coefficient in the between-country production function regression (using country average scores), and this result is exactly consistent with the results of Dollar, Hallward-Driemeier, and Mengistae (2005). There seem to be two possible explanations for the discrepancy between the regression results and the low reported costs of the constraints in the raw data. One is reverse causality; that is, countries (or cities, in the Dollar, Hallward-Driemeier, and Mengistae analysis) that are prosperous—for a variety of other reasons for which it is not realistically possible to control econometrically—also happen to have higher levels of telecommunications services. In Carlin, Schaffer, and Seabright (2007), the equations were reestimated using a variety of instrumental variables to try to address this endogeneity problem, but without success. Any plausible instrument has to affect telecommunications infrastructure without being otherwise correlated with economic performance, and Carlin, Schaffer, and Seabright report that instruments which meet this challenging description could not be found.

An alternative explanation for the discrepancy could be the presence of network externalities. The subjective data measure the reported importance of telecommunications constraints to telecommunications users, not the network benefits that their use of telecommunications might have for others. But the direct importance of these externalities is small. The absolute level of the reported constraint is 1.74 in Pakistan, 1.91 in China, 2.43 in Bangladesh and 2.36 in Ethiopia. These absolute levels are unimportant in Pakistan and China and somewhat important in the other two countries. The relative levels show, however, that telecommunications is never a priority for any of these countries, compared with their other public good constraints. Whether network externalities matter remains a subject for further research, but the data suggest that they would have to be large in order to overturn the conclusion that telecommunications constraints matter little for firm performance.[6]

A second study that raises important issues of interpretation is that of Ayyagari, Demirgüç-Kunt, and Maksimovic (2006), who report, on the basis of regression analysis, that only constraints related to finance, crime, and political instability are important for firm performance.[7] Other constraints such as taxes and regulations are found to be unimportant. Yet other data show that tax rates and tax administration are reported as important by firms across the entire sample of countries. As argued in Carlin, Schaffer, and Seabright (2007), that makes it very probable that tax policy is indeed important, in the sense that policies to reduce tax rates while holding other aspects of public good provision constant (for instance, by improving administrative efficiency) would improve firm performance. However, constraints that score high in both rich and poor countries are likely to show up with low values of regression coefficients (as confirmed in the regression analysis by Carlin, Schaffer, and Seabright), no matter how important they are in fact, because regression analysis picks up *differences* in scores reported by high- and low-performance firms. This does not mean, as one might initially suppose, that tax constraints are unimportant, on the grounds that "if rich countries can maintain tax rates, that means they can hardly matter much for economic performance." Such an inference would be warranted only if tax rates were exogenous. But if, as seems overwhelmingly likely, countries that perform well demand higher levels of public good provision and have to maintain high tax rates to finance them, tax rates will not show up in the regressions, however important they really are. This suggests that we should be cautious about drawing policy implications from studies of this kind.

A third study is instructive for different reasons. Commander and Svejnar (2007) conduct an exhaustive regression analysis of the BEEPS business environment dataset for transition economies. Their analysis confirms that variations in firm-level performance within countries are positively influenced by foreign ownership and competition. Variations in the firm-level business environment within a country (where this is measured by the indicator averaged across other firms in the same sector, size class, year, and country) do not seem to be important. This reinforces the idea that the business environment is a country-level characteristic (although there may be important regional variations, especially in large countries for which the authors were not able to test). Their analysis also confirms that with a set of only 26 countries, regression analysis is unable to distinguish which elements of the business environment matter most—or indeed, to distinguish between business environment and other country characteristics.

Finally, we draw attention to how pitfalls can be avoided and policy-relevant use made of regression analysis on business environment data (see Carlin, Schaffer, and Seabright 2007 for more details). The standard regression approach discussed in this paper has a performance indicator as the dependent variable and business environment (and other) variables as explanatory variables on the right-hand side. Our earlier discussion about interpreting many dimensions of the business environment as public goods indicates that regressing firm-level performance on the firm's own evaluation of the business environment will not provide a good measure of how the business environment affects the firm. The reason is that the firm's assessment of the cost of a business environment constraint will reflect its own performance. As illustrated in figure 1, good firms will be more constrained by a shortage of public goods and will complain more. It would be a mistake to interpret a positive sign on the complaints score for, say, customs regulation as indicating that a policy to worsen customs regulation and thereby raise complaints would boost firm performance. This example suggests what not to do—but it also hints at another exercise that the policy maker might find useful. When considering whether to implement a policy to improve some aspect of the business environment, the policy maker may be interested to know the characteristics of firms most likely to benefit from the measure. Information on this comes from a regression of the business environment scores at firm level (as the dependent variable) on firm characteristics.

Carlin, Schaffer, and Seabright (2007) report that, controlling for other firm characteristics, firms with higher efficiency are more constrained by customs regulations and the legal system, and less efficient ones are more constrained by access to finance. More highly educated managers appear more sensitive to a broad range of constraints. Compared with domestically owned private firms, those with a foreign owner appear more sensitive to certain constraints, including aspects of physical infrastructure and a series of administrative and regulatory institutions. As we would expect, these firms complain less about access to or the cost of finance. State-owned firms rate many constraints as less of an impediment than other firm types, which suggests that improvements in the business environment may benefit private firms more.

Country-level diagnosis. The analysis of the data from manager surveys suggests that variations in the business environment across countries matter for firm performance. Countries, however, differ in many other ways. This highlights two problems noted earlier in the discussion of cross-country regression analysis: given the limited number of countries and the large number of potential country differences, it is next to impossible for a cross-country regression analysis to single out the most important factors. Moreover, cross-country analysis can only provide information about the relationship between performance and business environment variables for the average country or for particular sample splits—for example, by geographic location. The limited ability of cross-country regression analysis to provide direct policy guidance is reflected in the summary of studies in the appendixes to this paper. Dixit (2006) discusses this problem further. This problem points to the use of a different strategy when we seek to narrow down the aspect(s) of the business environment on which a policy maker in a particular country should concentrate. One approach is to

FIGURE 4.
Diagnosing the Binding Constraint in Country X:
Combining Growth Diagnostics with Data from Manager Surveys

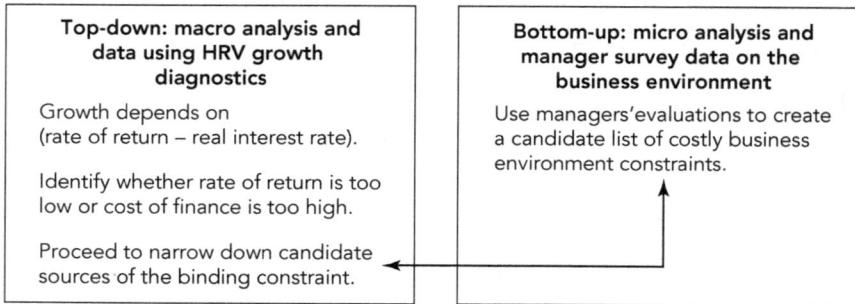

Top-down: macro analysis and data using HRV growth diagnostics	Bottom-up: micro analysis and manager survey data on the business environment
Growth depends on (rate of return − real interest rate). Identify whether rate of return is too low or cost of finance is too high. Proceed to narrow down candidate sources of the binding constraint.	Use managers' evaluations to create a candidate list of costly business environment constraints.

Source: Authors' construction; HRV, Hausmann, Rodrik, and Velasco 2006.

combine top-down "growth diagnostics" (Hausmann, Rodrik, and Velasco 2006) with the bottom-up survey data from managers. Figure 4 shows in a schematic way how these two perspectives may be combined.

We begin with the Hausmann, Rodrik, and Velasco macroeconomic (endogenous) growth framework in which output per capita grows at a rate that depends on three key variables: preferences about current consumption relative to future consumption; the rate of return to economic activity; and the real rate of interest that is relevant to domestic investment decisions. We ignore the first variable and concentrate on the rate of return and the rate of interest (figure 4, left-hand panel). The rate of return on investment depends on a technology indicator; on the availability of complementary factors of production, which include skills and infrastructure; and on the presence of externalities, which reflects both positive spillovers between firms and negative coordination failures. This rate of return is reduced by taxes, poor tax administration, and risks of expropriation. The rate of interest that is relevant to domestic investment decisions will be increased by high country risk and by poorly functioning domestic financial markets and institutions.

Hausmann, Rodrik, and Velasco (2006) suggest beginning the diagnostic exercise by reviewing the macroeconomic indicators of the economy as a way of making an initial determination as to whether the growth weakness reflects too low a rate of return or too high a cost of capital. The initial top-down diagnosis of the binding constraint on a country's growth evaluates whether the problem is that plenty of high-return investment projects are available but access to finance, including international finance, is lacking; or whether the problem is the reverse—adequate availability of finance but limited demand because of a predominance of low-return projects. The authors provide guidance about how to determine this. For example, if the problem is a shortage of finance (high real interest rates relative to the rate of return), the country will tend to be characterized by external deficits because of restricted access to international finance (the result, for example, of poor fiscal control), or low domestic savings, or both. Such an economy should display high returns to investment in physical capital but also in human capital (manifested, for instance, in high premiums for skilled labor). In the opposite case, where it is not the availability of finance that is the problem but the lack of high-return investment projects, the economy will be characterized by low rates of return and low skill premiums; and there will be few signs of its having exhausted its access to international capital markets.

This initial diagnosis is of crucial importance, since directing resources and attention to improving infrastructure or reducing regulation in an economy in which returns to investment are already high is likely to produce few gains for growth. It is much more important to try to understand why an economy's access to international finance is poor, domestic savings are too low, or the inefficiency of domestic financial institutions imposes such a large wedge between borrowing and lending rates in order to prevent advantage from being taken of the existing profitable opportunities in the economy. Conversely, in a country where access to finance at the macroeconomic level appears adequate, closer attention needs to be directed toward trying to understand why weak private returns from investment are the fundamental problem. The explanation here could be the poor quality of complementary inputs such as skilled labor or infrastructure (for example, poor transport or poor communications skills and infrastructure that prevent isolated entrepreneurs from effectively demanding capital that is potentially available); or it could be the inability of entrepreneurs to secure an adequate expected private return from investment because of high taxes, predatory or inefficient performance by the state (taxes, regulation, corruption, and crime), or prevalent macroeconomic instability. Figure 5 illustrates how a diagnostic tree diagram can be used to review possible constraints.

FIGURE 5.
Diagnosing the Binding Constraint in Country X: Top-Down and Bottom-Up Analysis of Business Environment

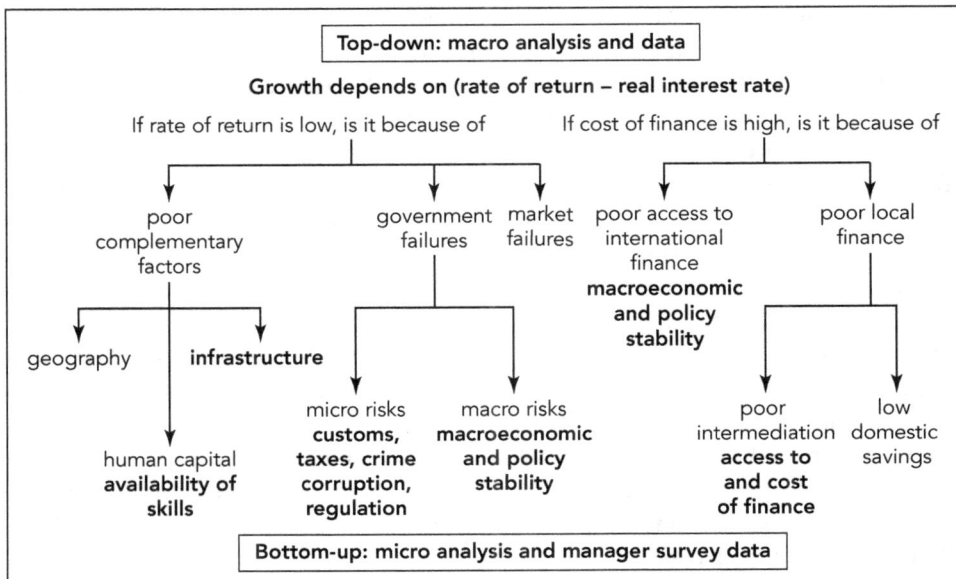

Source: Authors' construction.

Note: Bold face type on lower branches of tree diagram represent business environment.

As the tree diagram in figure 5 suggests, when assessing the relevance of the lower branches, the ranking of business environment constraints by managers in the economy in question provides a crucial input. To see how the top-down and bottom-up approaches can be combined, we look at two Latin American countries considered by Hausmann, Rodrik, and Velasco (2006): Brazil and El Salvador. In Brazil, situated on the right-hand side of the tree, the binding constraint is excessive macroeconomic risk and inadequate domestic savings. Brazil has had persistent problems with its external deficit. When external conditions have improved because of higher world commodity prices or a more favorable view of emerging markets by international capital markets, growth has revived. This points toward a constraint imposed by the availability of savings.

By contrast, in this analysis El Salvador is on the left-hand side of the tree diagram: its problem is not the availability of finance but the weakness of its investment projects. Unlike Brazil, the authors point out, El Salvador appears to have plenty of savings; when remittances went up dramatically, they were not converted into higher investment. Banks "have more liquidity than domestic credit demand can soak up" (Hausmann, Rodrik, and Velasco 2006, 13), and they lend to firms elsewhere in the region. From the perspective of the standard bundle of "good micro and macro policies," El Salvador looks puzzling. How can weak growth performance be reconciled with good institutions and infrastructure (as captured by standard country indicators) and the absence of macro imbalances? The authors conclude that El Salvador's problem must be lack of appropriate innovation. This would be captured in figure 5 under the heading "market failures," with the implication that poor information, abuse of market power, or externalities between firms (or potential firms) prevent entrepreneurs from discovering and exploiting the economy's comparative advantage.

What light is cast on the top-down diagnosis by the business environment rankings? According to the ranking of complaints by managers of manufacturing firms in the PICS–BEEPS dataset, the biggest problems in Brazil are policy uncertainty and macroeconomic instability, tax rates, and the cost of finance. All of these are consistent with high macroeconomic risk and the high cost of finance alluded to by Hausmann, Rodrik, and Velasco. It is clear from the lower panel of figure 6, which shows absolute rankings, that macroeconomic conditions, tax rates, and the cost of finance are viewed as less problematic in El Salvador than in the other Latin American and Caribbean countries represented, including Brazil. The survey data confirm that El Salvador's problems, unlike Brazil's, do not seem to stem from the right-hand side of the tree in figure 5. Rather, managers in El Salvador complain most about crime, anticompetitive practices, and corruption. But consistent with the Hausmann, Rodrik, and Velasco diagnosis using expert country ratings of the business environment, we can see from the upper panel of figure 6 that in terms of absolute complaint scores, El Salvador does not seem in particularly poor shape across these dimensions in the Latin American context. For example, complaints about corruption are lower than elsewhere in the region.

Figure 7 highlights the differences between the two countries in the relative importance of the two sets of constraints: institutions, and macroeconomics and

FIGURE 6.
Average Country Scores by Constraint (Absolute Measure)

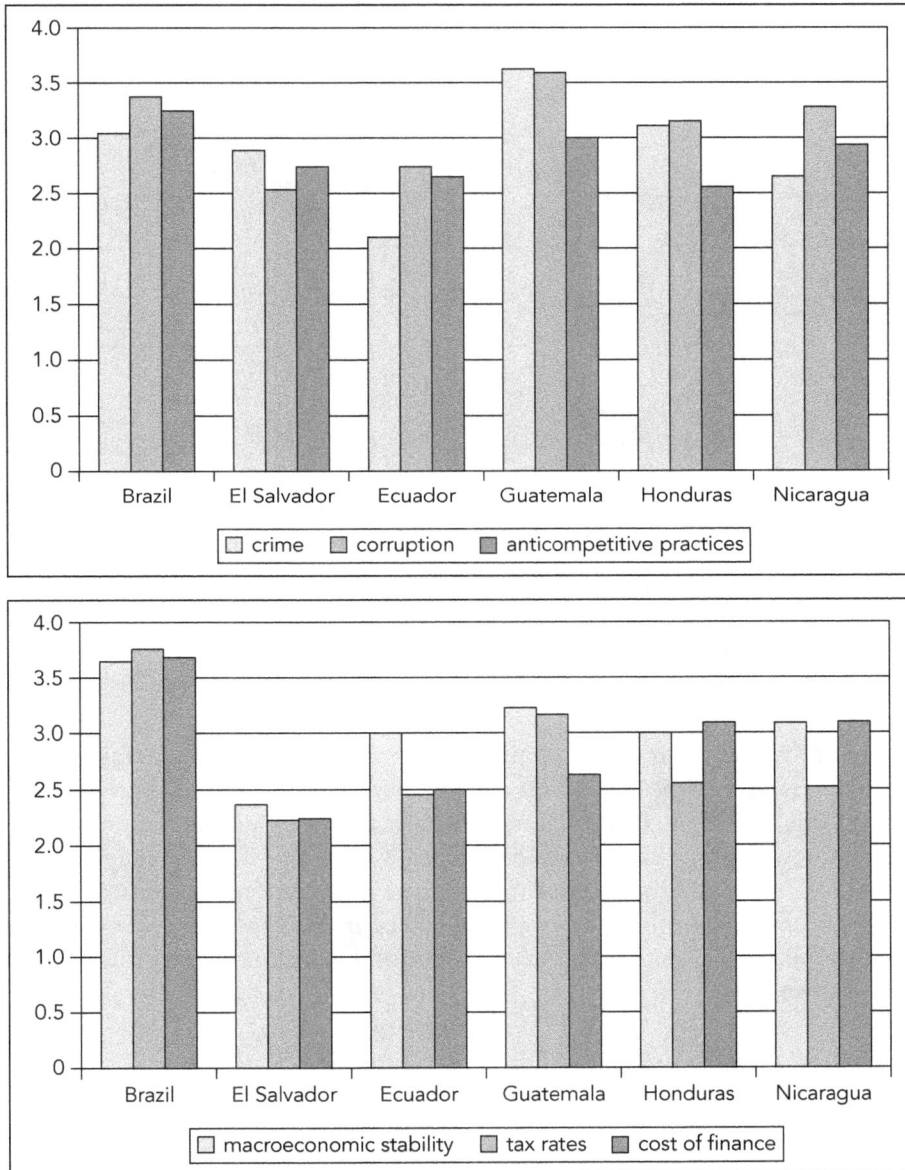

Source: Carlin, Schaffer, and Seabright 2007.

finance.[8] This suggests that there may be additional information in the subjective rankings by managers, who in El Salvador identify crime, corruption, and anticompetitive practices as the biggest barriers to the operation and growth of their business and in Brazil see macroeconomic and financing problems as the biggest constraints. Such information is not available in the cross-country benchmarking

FIGURE 7.
Country Scores by Constraint Relative to the Average Country Score across Constraints (Relative Measure)

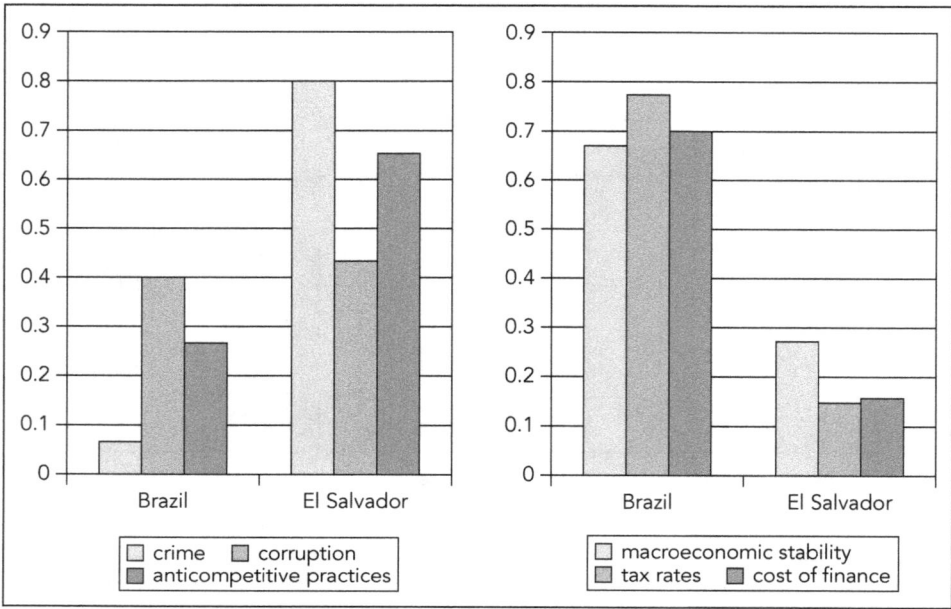

Source: Carlin, Schaffer, and Seabright 2007.

Note: The statistical significance of the differences shown here is confirmed in Carlin, Schaffer, and Seabright (2007).

indexes used by Hausmann, Rodrik, and Velasco to determine the quality of institutions in El Salvador, since these indexes have difficulty in identifying priorities for countries with low average constraints. The manager survey information suggests that in addition to investigating possible problems with innovation and appropriate specialization in El Salvador and the implied need for some kind of industrial policy intervention, there is a prima facie case for policy makers to look more closely at how anticompetitive practices, crime, and corruption may be depressing private returns to investment.

Case Histories: Individual Regional or Country Studies

The case-history literature on the effects of the business climate is vast; and we cannot even begin to survey it here because of its sheer size and because, without the pressure for methodological homogeneity imposed by a cross-country framework, many studies effectively study the business climate even when they do not call it that. We include in the category of case histories regional studies such as the famous East Asia study undertaken by the World Bank (1993). We doubt whether a simple set of rules of thumb could ever realistically be devised to enable policy makers to integrate the insights of case studies of their own countries with the comparative literature discussed in the previous section. We can, however, make a few remarks about some of the strengths and weaknesses of case studies and illustrate them with examples.

The methodology of cross-country regressions rests on the assumption that there is a common technology that transforms inputs, including business environment inputs, into output. This assumption has tended to go along with the idea that countries performing poorly relative to the average should be prescribed a set of reforms to improve their business environment. As we have seen, however, the regression methodology is not well suited to identifying the aspects of the business environment that matter most for the average country and cannot speak to the question of the likely effect of a given reform in a specific country. The use of manager survey data within a diagnostic framework, as illustrated in the previous section, can help fill this gap. So, too, can the case-history literature. However just as there are pitfalls in interpreting cross-country regression studies and managers' firm-level assessments of constraints, there are dangers in drawing implications for policy from case studies.

The first point to note is that case histories can be very good at suggesting causal hypotheses but very bad at testing them, since usually there is little basis for evaluating the hypotheses other than a general inclination or disinclination to take the author's word for it. Different authors may look at apparently similar facts and reach incompatible conclusions, sometimes giving the reader no means of choosing among them other than a preference for one author's prose style, political convictions, or general scientific distinction. The Asian "tigers," for instance, have inspired a range of country studies with wildly different implications both for the tigers themselves and for any other country that might be tempted to imitate them; compare Amsden (1989), Wade (1990), World Bank (1993), Young (1995), Fishlow and others (1996), Khan and Jomo (2000), Stiglitz and Yusuf (2001), Chang (2002), and Noland and Pack (2003).[9] This diversity reinforces the importance of using country studies together with other evidence; each time a country study suggests an apparently plausible hypothesis, we should ask what other evidence might help to decide whether it is in fact correct.

A second point is that case histories are often the only source of evidence about the relative feasibility and costs of improving various components of the business climate—an aspect of the problem on which, as we noted at the outset, much less work has been done than on the relative benefits. Case histories can reveal that policy makers tried something and then abandoned it, or tried several different initiatives and concluded that one was much harder to implement than the other, or found policies easier to implement in some circumstances than in others. For instance, Schrank and Kurtz (2005) argue on the basis of studies of Latin America and the Caribbean that trade openness changes the trade-offs in domestic industrial policy: they observe that "open economy industrial policies are costly to retain and easy to abandon, and therefore *tend* to be temporary" (Schrank and Kurtz 2005, 673). Case studies can also cast light on such issues as whether elements of a given culture undermine or reinforce components of the business climate. For instance, is corruption deeply ingrained and widely accepted in a given culture, as argued, for instance, by Ledeneva (2006) for Russia; or is it a more accidental and temporary result of the under-rewarding of bureaucrats? (See Rose-Ackerman 1999, especially parts I and II, for an illuminating general discussion of the difference between these perspectives.)

A third point is that case histories can sometimes suggest interactions between effects that cross-country studies can miss or that might apply only in rather limited circumstances. Some studies of interventionist industrial policy appear to have suggested that policies which have had credibility in the East Asian context (for instance, making state subsidies conditional on performance; see Wade 1990) have lacked credibility in Europe, where—far from picking winners—governments have often found themselves in a continual effort to prop up losers. It is one thing to argue (as we ourselves have argued) that in a modern industrial economy much productivity growth comes from the entry of new firms and the exit of old ones, a process that policy makers may wish to manage but should not seek to curtail (Carlin, Haskel, and Seabright 2001; Seabright 2005). It is quite another to identify the political and other circumstances under which public policy is able to commit credibly to allowing the sorting process in modern industrial capitalism to work, still less to document the subtle interactions that may indicate, in a society where firms are allowed to fail, fewer firms actually do so.[10] Nevertheless, case histories are far more likely than cross-country studies to support a plausible and sophisticated rationale of this kind.

A good example of these potential interactions was recently suggested by Paul Collier (2007), who proposed that an important difference between highly corrupt but relatively successful poor countries (such as Bangladesh) and equally corrupt but slower-growing countries (such as many natural resource exporters) may lie in the nature of comparative advantage and the differential vulnerability of different activities to the damage that corruption can cause. It seems likely that Bangladesh's reliance on low-cost manufactured textile exports created less of a tempting target for rent seekers than the great mineral resources of, say, Venezuela (or Russia, or Saudi Arabia). There is presumably even less incentive to avoid killing the goose that lays the golden eggs if the eggs, rather than having to be carefully and painfully laid, have already been laid and have only to be lifted out of the ground. Other writers, such as Mushtaq Khan (1998), have highlighted the way in which apparently similar degrees of corruption have had very different consequences for economic development in various countries of South and East Asia because of the different nature of patron-client networks in these economies.

Surely, an important source of future insights along these lines will be the comparison between growth in China and Russia during the last two decades of the twentieth century, and particularly the role of property rights and interregional competition in that process. Both of these vast countries experienced considerable regional competition, but with very different consequences. Neither country saw the development of what could be called clear systems of property rights along the Western European or North American model, but while it has often been argued that this was a serious handicap to Russian economic performance, it has yet to be convincingly explained why a similar absence should apparently have been no handicap at all in China. Once again, it is in the nature of the question that cross-country regression studies can hardly be expected to provide an answer.

These examples suggest that *comparative* case studies are of particular value. There is a sound economic reason why this is the case. Much of the methodology of growth analysis emerged from an essentially closed-economy framework—yet economic success hinges on a country's integration into the world economy. The comparative case studies highlight how a country's comparative advantage can interact with the business environment: that is, aspects of the business environment that are crucial for a country specializing in standard manufactures are likely to differ from those in countries specializing in traded services or in exports of minerals. As development proceeds, specialization evolves, and with it, the demands on the business environment. Surveying the advanced countries of the world, we see a considerable variety of business environments: countries differ greatly in legal formalism (the cost of doing business), the extent of employment protection, and tax and welfare regimes. In successful countries those arrangements complement the countries' comparative advantage. The principal message of this section is therefore that case studies can be of immense value provided they are treated as a complement to rather than a substitute for the other sources of evidence we have discussed.

Some Simple Messages

It may be helpful for the reader to see what all this analysis can lead to in a concrete setting. Here, in no particular order, are some conclusions that, in our view, emerge from a reading of the business climate literature that follows the kind of procedure we have outlined.

1. The supply of telecommunication infrastructure is not worth significant investment from the government budget; it is much better to let private entry take care of it.

2. Poor electricity supply can be a big problem, but primarily in Africa and some parts of Asia.

3. Tax rates and inefficient tax administration constitute a large problem almost everywhere. This does not mean that the public sector should be small but, rather, that it should be financed at lowest cost, including the cost implicit in slow and cumbersome procedures.

4. Labor regulation is not really a problem—except in some relatively rich countries. In poor and middle-income countries it is not worth incurring significant political costs to reform it.

5. Crime and corruption are serious problems in some parts of the world, though not in all. The problems may not be easy to fix, but further investigation is needed to determine whether affordable solutions exist.

6. Slow, inefficient, or corrupt customs procedures impose a high cost on firms and should be capable of being fixed at low cost.

7. Development of financial systems is important, but ambitious. Although it does not necessarily make it easier for all firms to have access to finance, it leads financial intermediaries to discriminate more effectively between good and bad investment projects.

We now draw the threads together and consider how perplexed policy makers should proceed.

Conclusions: What Should Policy Makers Do?

There are two main questions that policy makers might reasonably ask in the face of the large literature and many business climate studies that we have reviewed. The first is about the solidity of the scientific findings; the second is about how these findings can be used to decide on policy priorities.

What should policy makers conclude when there is disagreement in the literature or uncertainty about the findings?

One thing that becomes apparent from the foregoing review is that although there are many different findings in the literature, there are very few *incompatible* findings—because many of the studies ask different questions. This is not just true in the sense that the three categories of contribution (cross-country regressions, surveys of managers, and country studies) do different things; even within categories, it is rare for studies to come up with genuinely incompatible findings. For instance, regression studies often test the hypothesis that a particular set of institutions is important against the null hypothesis that no institutions are important, rather than against a rival hypothesis asserting the importance of different institutions. By contrast, surveys of managers are more informative about these hypotheses concerning relative importance. So, the findings of the regressions should be understood as preliminary and complementary rather than as definitive and contradictory. They establish that institutions matter, that we are not yet sure how they matter, and that we need to refine our conjectures about the causal channels involved. On its own, this might seem an inadequate consolation (like saying, "medical studies have established that diet is important for health, but we have no idea which is the best diet"). However, this is where the complementarity with other sources of information becomes important; managerial surveys and case studies can be used in the ways earlier. And as further research subjects more sophisticated data to the discipline of regression analysis, it will be possible to test the hypotheses suggested by these other sources in their turn.[11]

How can policy makers use these findings to help order their budgetary allocations and their political and legislative priorities?

Policy makers do not decide policy priorities in a vacuum: they face repeated lobbying for their budgetary resources and for their scarce legislative and regulatory attention. The lobbyists in question have their own agenda, and politicians should be wary of thinking that the strength of lobbying about some aspect of the business climate necessarily reflects the weight that this specific factor should have in public policy. We propose a checklist of questions that policy makers can ask themselves. Suppose that a lobby such as the chamber of commerce requests that the government spend money, or pass a law, to bring about an improvement in some aspect of the business climate—the tax administration, customs regulations, the functioning of the courts, the state of the electricity infrastructure, or the time it takes the banking system to clear a check. Policy makers can ask the following questions to establish the value of responding to such a request:

1. Where does a particular aspect of the business climate fit in the diagnostic tree diagram, and is its importance corroborated by the top-down analysis?

2. How high does that aspect of the business environment rank as a complaint in the surveys of managers in the policy maker's country? If it does not rank very high, it will take more argument and more evidence to establish that it should be a priority for public policy.

3. Does cross-country regression analysis suggest modifying the answer to question 2 because there are grounds for thinking that this aspect of the business climate is generally more important for economic performance than it appears to be in the surveys of managers? Network effects, or the impact on new entry (which creates benefits for the economy but costs to existing firms), might explain such discrepancies.

4. Do case studies suggest that this aspect of the business climate is more or less important for this country's performance than in other countries?

5. Are there alternative policies that would achieve similarly valuable results but at lower cost, or with a greater probability of success for the same cost?

6. Do the interest groups lobbying for this policy change represent firms that, on average, are performing relatively well, or relatively poorly? What are the other distinguishing characteristics of the firms concerned, and is it likely that a policy reform that aids these types of firms will benefit the economy as a whole?

Note that these questions closely parallel the questions a doctor would ask about the condition of a patient: what does the patient himself say about his condition; what do scientific studies suggest about the factors that influence the health of typical patients like this one; does the patient's personal history lead one to suspect particular susceptibilities that make him different from others; are there alternative treatments that would achieve the same outcome but with fewer side effects or with more certainty of success; and is the patient asking for treatment out of other concerns than his health (a desire to qualify for sick pay, recurrent depression, or whatever)?

Just as the answer will not be the same for each patient, so the answer will not be the same for each country. Earlier, we discussed at some length how the importance of constraints varied across countries. For example, physical infrastructure (with the exception of electricity) was rarely a constraint in the countries studied, except in some countries in Africa; crime and corruption varied in importance around the world; and labor regulation, a problem for rich countries, was of negligible importance in poor ones. But we can make sense of the differences between countries, as well as the points they have in common.

APPENDIX A.1. Summary of Results, Cross-Country Empirical Studies on Institutions (Long-term growth)

Study	Basic method and aim	Dataset	Dependent variable(s)	1. How is business environment measured? 2. Other key right-hand-side variables	Comments on methodology	1. Main findings 2. Explicit policy conclusions	Comments (quantitative importance)
Acemoglu and Johnson (2005)	Multiple IV *Aim: evaluate importance of property rights institutions versus contracting institutions*	Former European colonies (77 countries) GDP per capita, 1990s Property rights measures from Political Risk Services; Polity 4 dataset Contracting institutions measures from Djankov et al. (2003) WDI, PWT	GDP per capita Investment rate Level of financial development measured as: (a) (total amount of) credit to the private sector)/GDP, 1998; (b) stock market capitalization	1. Property rights institutions (protection against expropriation by the state; constraint on the executive) Legal formalism (steps to resolve bounced check) 2. No controls—only institutions on the second-stage regression	IV for institutions: mortality rate of European settlers or indigenous population density in 1500; legal origin	1. Can separate the IVs: settler mortality is good instrument for property rights institutions; legal origin, for contracting institutions. In second stage, property rights institutions have effect on long-run economic growth, investment, and financial development; contracting institutions appear to matter only for the form of financial intermediation (size of stock market).	1 SD (property rights) → 1.4 SD GDP per capita; coefficient on legal formalism not significant (IV). 1 SD (legal formalism) → 0.2 SD lower stock market capitalization (IV).
Acemoglu, Johnson, and Robinson (2001)	Single cross-section. Focus on endogeneity. *Aim: test whether "institutions matter"*	Years, 1985–95. 75 countries, world WDI, ICRG	Final year GDP per capita	1. Institutions: index of protection against expropriation; constraints on executive in 1990 2. Latitude; regional dummies; British or French colony; legal origin; health variables; historical variables (settler mortality, democracy in 1900); ethnolinguistic fragmentation	IV for institutions: settler mortality	1. Pioneering paper proposes settler mortality as an instrument for today's institutions in former European colonies. 2. "It is useful to point out that our findings do not imply that institutions today are predetermined by colonial policies and cannot be changed."	1 SD (protection against expropriation risk) → change in GDP per worker by 118 percent (OLS) and 309 percent (IV).

Study	Method / Aim	Sample	Dependent variable	Independent variables	Approach	Results
Aghion, Howitt, and Mayer-Foulkes (2005)	Cross-country OLS; IV *Aim: analyze role of financial intermediation for growth*	1960–95, use averaged 71 countries	GDP growth relative to that of United States	1. Financial intermediation measured as (bank lending)/GDP Alternative measures: (liquid liabilities)/GDP; bank assets; ratio of commercial bank assets to sum of commercial and central bank assets 2. Initial GDP relative to United States; schooling; other controls	Develop a theoretical model and estimate growth regression with financial intermediation IV for financial intermediation: legal origin; legal origin interacted with initial GDP relative to United States	1. Significant and sizeable effect of an interaction term (initial GDP per capita relative to United States) (financial intermediation), in otherwise standard growth regression, implies that likelihood of converging to U.S. level increases with financial development. Direct effect of financial intermediation on growth is not significant. Country converges to frontier only if its financial development exceeds a critical value: this is the case for 37 of 71 countries in sample.
Bardhan (2004)	Cross-section IV estimation Focus on endogeneity of institutions *Aim: alternative instruments (other than settler mortality), which allows larger sample size*	Year: 2000 Three samples, according to availability of data (n = 98, 69, 57)	2000 GDP per capita; literacy; life expectancy; human development	1. Measures of institutions: protection of property rights, as in Acemoglu, Johnson, and Robinson (2001); "voice" measure relating to democratic political rights 2. Ethnolinguistic fragmentation; population density in 1500; European settler mortality	Alternative IV for institutions, in particular state antiquity index	1. State antiquity predicts (in first stage) security of property rights, including in countries that were not European colonies. In second stage, for some aspects of development (e.g., literacy), an index of participatory rights and democratic accountability is a better explanatory variable than property rights institutions.

(Continued)

See note at page 135 for key to abbreviations in Appendix A.1.

APPENDIX A.1. Summary of Results, Cross-Country Empirical Studies on Institutions (Continued)

Study	Basic method and aim	Dataset	Dependent variable(s)	1. How is business environment measured? 2. Other key right-hand-side variables	Comments on methodology	1. Main findings 2. Explicit policy conclusions	Comments (quantitative importance)
Barro (1997)	OLS Standard growth regression	98 countries, 1960–85 PWT	GDP per capita average annual growth rate	1. Measures of infra-structure: government spending/GDP; public investment/total investment 2. Initial GDP per capita; education; regional dummies; number of revolutions; number of assassinations	OLS only	1. An increase in resources devoted to nonproductive (but possibly utility-enhancing) government services is associated with lower per capita growth. There is no separate effect on growth from the breakdown of total investment between private and public components.	
Bockstette, Chanda, and Putterman (2002)	OLS and IV cross-section Aim: investigate the impact on long-run growth of an early territorywide policy	ICRG	Average GDP growth, 1960–95 Output per worker, 1988	1. Index of social infra-structure; ICRG 2. Initial GDP per capita; schooling; population growth; investment rate; population density; ethnic heterogeneity; regional dummies	IV for institutions: distance from equator; English speakers; European-language speakers; predicted trade share; state antiquity	1, 2. Early territorywide polity and experience with large-scale administration may make for more effective government and for more rapid economic growth. Emphasis on capacity building and institutional quality is important to foster economic growth.	1 SD (= 0.25) index of social infrastructure increases output per worker by 126 percent (OLS) and 229 percent (GMM-IV).

Calderón and Servén (2004)	Panel data GMM estimators based on both internal and external instruments (Arellano-Bond)	121 countries, 1960–2000. Data averaged over five-year periods	Growth of GDP per capita	1. Aggregate index: telecommunications sector—number of main telephone lines per 1,000 workers; power sector—electricity-generating capacity of the economy (megawatts per 1,000 workers); transportation sector—length of road network (kilometers per square kilometer of land area) 2. Standard growth and inequality determinants IV: external—terms of trade; internal—lags of covariates (estimated equation is in first differences)	1. Growth is positively affected by the stock of infrastructure assets. Income inequality declines with higher infrastructure quantity and quality. 2. Infrastructure development can be highly effective in combating poverty.
Carlin and Mayer (2003)	Cross-section OLS and IV	Industry-level (manufacturing) data for 27 industries in 18 OECD countries + country-level data, 1970–95	Abnormal growth (also investment and research and development as percent of GDP) relative to country and industry average	1. Financial development: accounting standards; concentration of banking sector; ownership concentration 2. Interaction between equity-dependence of industry (also skill dependence and bank-finance dependence) and measure of financial development of country (e.g., accounting standards), structure of banking sector, ownership concentration IV for country variables: legal origin; rule of law; population United States used as benchmark for equity dependence of industries; Japan, for bank-finance dependence; and Germany, for skill dependence	1. Accounting disclosure is associated with faster growth of industries that are equity- and skill-dependent. Skill-dependent industries benefit from concentrated ownership. Equity-dependent industries grow more slowly where the banking system is concentrated. Bank-dependent industries appear to benefit from accounting disclosure and more concentrated banking, in poorer countries only.

(Continued)

See note at page 135 for key to abbreviations in Appendix A.1.

APPENDIX A.1. Summary of Results, Cross-Country Empirical Studies on Institutions (Continued)

Study	Basic method and aim	Dataset	Dependent variable(s)	1. How is business environment measured? 2. Other key right-hand-side variables	Comments on methodology	1. Main findings 2. Explicit policy conclusions	Comments (quantitative importance)
Clague, Keefer, Knack, and Olson (1999)	IV cross-section Aim: introduce a new proxy for contract enforcement institutions (contract-intensive money, CIM) and test in a growth regression	ICRG, PWT, IFS, BERI	GDP per capita annual growth, 1970–92; output per worker, 1988; capital per worker, 1988; years of schooling per worker, 1985; TFP, 1988	1. Contract-intensive money (CIM)—the ratio of noncurrency money to total money supply; ICRG index; BERI index	IV for institutions: colonial origin; ethnolinguistic homogeneity Use new measure of the security of contract enforcement and property rights (CIM)	1. CIM is positively related to investment and growth rates and to the relative size of contract-dependent sectors of the economy.	1 SD (= 0.14) (CIM) increases growth by 0.945 (OLS) and 1.739 (IV).
Djankov, McLiesh, and Ramalho (2006)	Develop an aggregate index of business regulations and use it in Barro-type growth regression Cross-section OLS + 2SLS (IV)	Doing Business database, 135 countries + country indicators: economic (1993–2002) WDI, ICRG, Transparency International	GDP per capita growth, 1983–92	1. Business regulation index; corruption; law and order; democratic accountability 2. Initial GDP per capita; education; civil conflicts; regional dummies; government consumption (as percent of GDP)	IV for business regulation: legal origin; commercial code or company law; absolute latitude; initial GDP per capita; religion; language	1. Business regulation remains a significant determinant of growth after controlling for other standard determinants. 2. Policy implications could be drawn, since index consists of reform-related components, but this is not done in the paper.	Shift from first to fourth quartile of business regulation index raises growth by 2.3 percentage points. Results are weaker in IV regressions.
Easterly and Rebelo (1993)	Standard Barro-type growth regression; pooled regressions with decade averages	100 countries, 1970–88 PWT; World Bank	GDP per capita growth	1. Transport and communication infrastructure 2. Initial GDP per capita; education, number of revolutions, assassinations		1. Investment in transport and communications is correlated with growth.	

130

| Esfahani and Ramirez (2003) | Aim: estimate a structural growth model (three-equation system), which includes infrastructure, based on both steady-state conditions and deviations from steady state. Estimated for 10-year periods by IV cross-country regression | 75 countries; 1965–75, 1975–85, 1985–95 | GDP per capita growth | 1. Infrastructure: telephone lines; power generation capacity Institutions: contract enforcement; centralization 2. Private ownership of infrastructure; population; urbanization; investment; democracy; ethnolinguistic heterogeneity (ELH); Gini coefficient; regional dummies; education; health variables; interactions between democracy, ELH, and Gini coefficient | Estimation results not robust to changing the specification Analyzes only two infrastructure sectors (lack of data) | 1. Private ownership of infrastructure speeds adjustment but does not affect long-run levels. Stronger institutions and private ownership matter more for infrastructure adjustment in richer countries; centralization and population density matter more in poorer countries. | 1 Examples: 5-percent annual increase in growth rate of telephones per capita raises annual growth of GDP per capita 0.4 percent; 4-percent annual increase in growth rate of electricity output per capita raises annual growth of GDP per capita 0.5 percent. Complexity of model makes interpretation of results difficult. |
| Giavazzi and Tabellini (2004) | Panel difference-in-difference estimation | 140 advanced and developing countries, 1960–2000 Indicator of economic liberalization; Polity 4 dataset; ICRG | Performance indicators: (a) growth in GDP per capita; investment; (b) macroeconomic: inflation, central government surplus; (c) governance indicators: perceptions of structural policies and institutional environments (Knack and Keefer 1997); corruption | 1. Openness to international trade—Sachs and Werner index of economic liberalization; democracy 2. Dummies for liberalization or democratization Dummies for pre- and postreform years | Identify reforms and consider them as "treatment" for the countries | 1, 2. Sequence of the reforms is important for economic performance. Economic liberalization should come first and receive the strongest priority; only afterward should the country worry about political reform. | When the second reform is democracy, growth is not affected; but investment accelerates by 2–3 percent of GDP. When the second reform is economic liberalization, growth falls or remains unaffected, and investment rises, but by less (about 1.5 percent of GDP). |

(Continued)

See note at page 135 for key to abbreviations in Appendix A.1.

Study	Basic method and aim	Dataset	Dependent variable(s)	1. How is business environment measured? 2. Other key right-hand-side variables	Comments on methodology	1. Main findings 2. Explicit policy conclusions	Comments (quantitative importance)
Glaeser, La Porta, López-de-Silanes, and Shleifer (2004)	Critical review of existing literature on the role of political institutions in economic development	ICRG Polity 4 dataset	GDP per capita, 2000; GDP per capita growth, 1960–2000, overall and by decade; five-year change in years of schooling; five-year changes in political institutions	1. Executive constraints (i.e., political institutions) 2. Initial GDP per capita, schooling (as human capital); share of population living in temperate zone	IV for institutions: settler mortality; legal origin; indigenous population density in 1500	1. Question the validity of settler mortality as an instrument for institutions, arguing that human capital performs better. Growth and human capital cause improvement of political institutions, not vice versa. Focus on role of dictators in raising human capital.	
Hall and Jones (1999)	Estimated equation based on production function IV cross-country	ICRG; PWT, 127 countries	Output per worker, 1988	1. Index of social infrastructure, which combines index of government antidiversion policies and index of country's openness	IV for institutions: distance from equator; English speakers; European-language speakers; predicted trade share	1. The large variation in output per worker across countries is only partially explained by differences in physical and human capital. Differences in social infrastructure → differences in capital accumulation, educational attainment, and productivity → differences in income. Type of social infrastructure is partially related to the influence of Western Europe.	1 SD (= 0.25) (index of social infrastructure) raises output per worker by 128 percent (OLS) and 261 percent (IV).

Kaufmann and Kraay (2002)	Cross-section OLS Aim: separate strong positive causal effect, from better governance to higher per capita incomes, and a weak or even negative causal effect running in the opposite direction	175 countries, 2000–2001 World Bank approach: indexing (aggregation) methodology to measure institutions WBES, ICRG, Country Risk Service, PWT, and others	GDP → institutions and vice versa to determine causality	1. Governance measures: voice and accountability; political stability; government effectiveness; regulatory quality; rule of law; control of corruption; overall governance	Strategy to infer direction of causality: use nonsample information to determine the variance of measurement errors in GDP and institutions (governance)	1. Reforms matter. Causality is from governance to GDP per capita. Evidence for virtuous circles, in which higher incomes lead to further improvements in governance, was not found.	1 SD (governance measure) raises per capita income in the very long run by 4 SD
Knack and Keefer (1997)	Cross-country OLS 2SLS	World Values Surveys, 29 market economies	Growth, 1980–92 Investment/GDP, 1980–92	1. Human capital—trust in society; civic cooperation; groups—density of associational activity; trust GDP_80 2. Education; initial GDP per capita	IV for institutions: ethnolinguistic homogeneity; law students as percent of postsecondary students in 1963	1. Where interpersonal trust is low and unlikely to improve rapidly, institutional reforms to provide better formal mechanisms for reliable enforcement of contracts and access to credit are even more important than where trust is higher.	1 SD (= 0.14) (trust) → raises average annual growth in per capita income by 0.011 (OLS) and 0.012 (IV).
Masters and McMillan (2001)	Cross-section of average data OLS and IV Aim: replicate standard growth regressions by augmenting them by a new climate variable (days of frost)	PWT panel for 1960–90. 90–125 countries, depending on specification (data availability) OLS	Output per worker, 1988	1. Index of social infrastructure as in Hall and Jones (1999) 2. Standard growth regression variables plus frost days and scale measures	IV for institutions: distance from equator; predicted trade share; English speakers; European-language speakers	1. Temperate countries have been on growth paths that converge toward a common high level of income, while tropical countries' growth paths converge toward income levels that depend on scale measures. Institutions matter more for tropical countries' growth.	1 SD (= 0.257) (index of social infrastructure) raises output per worker by 680 percent (IV) for "tropical" subsample of countries (average of fewer than five days per month of frost in winter).

(Continued)

See note at page 135 for key to abbreviations in Appendix A.1.

APPENDIX A.1. Summary of Results, Cross-Country Empirical Studies on Institutions (*Continued*)

Study	Basic method and aim	Dataset	Dependent variable(s)	1. How is business environment measured? 2. Other key right-hand-side variables	Comments on methodology	1. Main findings 2. Explicit policy conclusions	Comments (quantitative importance)
Mauro (1995)	IV and OLS cross-section for averaged data. *Aim: study the role of corruption with respect to growth*	Business International, 68 countries, 1980–83 PWT	Average growth of GDP per capita, 1960–85 Average investment/GDP, 1960–85 Average investment/GDP, 1980–85	1. Index of institutional efficiency Index of bureaucratic efficiency	IV for institutions: ethnolinguistic fragmentation, 1960	1. Corruption lowers investment, thereby reducing economic growth.	1 SD (= 2.16) (index of bureaucratic efficiency) raises average growth of GDP per capita by 0.006 (OLS) and 0.023 (IV).
Rajan and Zingales (1998)	Panel and cross-section	Industry-level (manufacturing) data for 41 countries + country-level data (average data for 1980–90)	Abnormal growth relative to country and industry average	1. Financial development: total capitalization (percent of GDP); bank debt (percent of GDP); accounting standards 2. Interaction between dependence of industry on external finance and measure of financial development of country (e.g., accounting standards)	United States used as the benchmark for dependence of industries on external finance	1. Financial market imperfections have an impact on investment and growth: inferred from the second-order effect of financial development on equity-dependent industries.	Possible reverse causality (but tested and not a problem).

Study	Method	Data source	Outcome variables	Institutions measures	Instruments	Findings	Magnitude
Rodrik (1999)	OLS and panel	World Bank Labor Market database compiled from UNIDO. U.S. Bureau of Labor Statistics (BLS); International Comparisons data series	Average dollar wages in manufacturing, 1985–89	1. Political institutions: two rule of law indicators, ICRG and bureaucratic efficiency; two democracy indicators, Freedom House and Polity 3 dataset. Labor market institutions: unionization rate; number of the ILO's six basic workers' rights conventions ratified by a country	IV for institutions: dummy for oil exporter; colonial origins. Each measure of democracy used as an instrument for the other one in different specifications	1. Institutions matter to distributive outcomes. Democratic institutions tend to be friendly to labor: they are associated with higher wages and a larger factor share for labor in manufacturing.	1 SD (= 0.33) (Freedom House index) raises average dollar wages in manufacturing by 0.198 (OLS) and 0.3762 (IV).
Rodrik, Subramanian, and Trebbi (2004)	*Aim: study the three clusters of factors of economic growth—institutions, integration, and geographic.* Repeat traditional regression by using larger set of instruments. IV cross-section	80 countries. ICRG; PWT; Polity 4 dataset	GDP per capita, 1995; output per worker, 1988; capital per worker, 1988; human capital per worker, 1988; TFP, 1988	1. Rule of law index; contract-intensive money (CIM) defined in Clague et al. (1999); Freedom House rating; rule of law (ICRG); war deaths. 2. Regional dummies; climate (frost); malaria; temperature	IV for institutions: settler mortality; European-language speakers; predicted trade shares	1. Once institutions are controlled for, measures of geography have at best weak direct effects on incomes, but strong indirect effect by influencing the quality of institutions. Similarly, once institutions are controlled for, trade is almost always insignificant and often enters the income equation with the "wrong" (negative) sign.	1 SD (= 0.94) (rule of law index) raises GDP per capita by 112 percent (OLS) and 205 percent (IV).

Source: Authors' compilation.

Note: Contract-intensive money (CIM) is the ratio of noncurrency money to the total money supply, or (M2 − C)/M2, where M2 is a broad definition of the money supply and C is currency held outside banks. 2SLS, two-stage least squares; BERI, Business Environment Risk Intelligence; GDP, gross domestic product; GMM, generalized method of moments; ICRG, International Country Risk Guide; IFS, International Financial Statistics (International Monetary Fund); ILO, International Labour Organization; IV, instrumental variable; OECD, Organisation for Economic Co-operation and Development; OLS, ordinary least squares; PWT, Penn World Tables; SD, standard deviation; TFP, total factor productivity; UNIDO, United Nations Industrial Development Organization; WBES, World Business Environment Survey; WDI, World Development Indicators.

APPENDIX A.2. Summary of Results, Firm-Level Empirical Studies

Study	Basic method and aim	Dataset	Dependent variable(s)	1. How is business environment measured? 2. Other key right-hand-side variables	Comments on methodology	1. Main findings 2. Explicit policy conclusions	Comments (quantitative importance)
Ayyagari, Demirgüç-Kunt, and Maksimovic (2006)	Panel and directed cyclic graph (DAG) methodology	WBES, 1999–2000, 80 countries	Firm growth	1. Financing; political instability; street crime; inflation; exchange rates; judicial efficiency; corruption; taxes and regulation; anticompetitive behavior; infrastructure Interactions: (financing, political instability, street crime) (size of firms, country income group dummies)	Panel contains only two years; regressions have weak explanatory power; weak instruments + still possible endogeneity.	1, 2. Only finance, crime, and political instability are binding constraints; therefore, maintaining political stability, controlling crime, and undertaking financial sector reforms to relax financing constraints are most likely to promote firm growth.	
Bastos and Nasir (2004)	Focus on investment climate OLS (production function estimation → TFP → regress TFP on investment climate factors)	World Bank investment climate survey, 2003 Kyrgyz Republic, Moldova, Poland, Tajikistan, Uzbekistan 362 firms total	Firm output and TFP	1. Foreign ownership; exports (percentage of sales); rent predation; infrastructure; competition 2. Age of firm	After regression, rank relative importance of each of the investment climate dimensions in explaining the variation in productivity across firms.	1. Results indicate that competitive pressure is the most important factor driving productivity levels. Good infrastructure and a nonpredatory regulatory environment are invaluable but are not sufficient.	

Study	Method	Data	Dependent variable	Variables	Notes	Findings	Conclusion
Beck, Demirgüç-Kunt, and Maksimovic (2005)	Panel + robustness check with IV	WBES, 1999–2000, 54 countries	Firm growth	1. Obstacles with financing, legal obstacles, corruption, as reported by firms. 2. Country characteristics: size; GDP per capita; GDP growth; inflation. Firm characteristics: size; ownership structure; sector of economy	Panel contains only two years; explanatory power of regressions is not always strong, especially within countries.	1. Provides evidence that small and medium-size firms face greater financial, legal, and corruption obstacles than large firms and that the constraining impact of obstacles on firm growth is inversely related to firm size. Small firms benefit most from improvements in financial development and a reduction in corruption.	The predicted effect of the legal obstacle on annual firm growth is highest for small firms and lowest for large firms. The difference between the predicted effects on large and small firms is statistically significant. The influence of corruption is qualitatively the same.
Carlin, Schaffer, and Seabright (2007)	Panel. *Aim: estimate the role of obstacles to firm growth by using public good framework*	PICS, BEEPS 53 countries, 1999–2005	TFP: firm-level (i.e., within regression) Country level (i.e., between regressions)	1. Business environment = obstacles for the business derived from subjective evaluations in firm surveys. 2. Capital and labor inputs; firm characteristics (foreign owned, state, SME, big city)	Production function assumed to be the same for all firms. Estimate between-country and within-country regressions.	1. Demonstrates that empirical results should be interpreted with care because of the public good nature of at least some features of business environment.	
Commander and Svejnar (2007)	1. Pooled 2002 and 2005 data estimated as 2SLS (IV). 2. Changes between 2002 and 2005; only 600 firms	BEEPS; 26 transition countries; up to 5,897 observations (depending on specification); 2002–5	Firm revenue or value added	1. Business constraints from firm surveys (objective and subjective evaluations); use value averaged across all other firms in same sector, country, and firm size class. 2. Export orientation of the firm; extent of product market competition; firm ownership, as reported by managers; capital and labor inputs	IV: Age; location; skill ratio interacted with region, firm age. Lagged values of employees; investment, export share. Possible multicollinearity of constraints complicate interpretation.	1. Firm performance is positively affected by foreign ownership and competition. Perceived constraints for business development do not explain much when country and sector fixed effects are included and when constraints are entered together.	Business climate factors vary at the country level but do not account for variation in firm performance within countries.

See note at page 138 for key to abbreviations in Appendix A.2.

(Continued)

APPENDIX A.2. Summary of Results, Firm-Level Empirical Studies *(Continued)*

Study	Basic method and aim	Dataset	Dependent variable(s)	1. How is business environment measured? 2. Other key right-hand-side variables	Comments on methodology	1. Main findings 2. Explicit policy conclusions	Comments (quantitative importance)
Dollar, Hallward-Driemeier, and Mengistae (2005)	Production function estimation (OLS, GLS) Compute TFP and regress it on business climate characteristics	Bangladesh, China, India, Pakistan; firm-level data; 4,000+ firms	TFP and annual growth Growth of fixed assets Growth of unemployment	1. Customs days for export and import; power loss (percent of sales); days to obtain phone line; overdraft facility; distance from market; distance from port 2. Industry dummies	Endogeneity: replace reported indicator of business climate by average value over (sector * location) of firms.	1. There is significant variation in the investment climate across locations within countries. Local governance is therefore important.	Problem of potential endogeneity of business climate at regional level remains.

Source: Authors' compilation.

Note: 2SLS, two-stage least squares; BEEPS, Business Environment and Enterprise Performance Survey (World Bank and European Bank for Reconstruction and Development); GDP, gross domestic product; GLS, generalized least squares; IV, instrumental variable; OLS, ordinary least squares; PICS, Productivity and Investment Climate Survey (World Bank); SME, small and medium-size enterprise; TFP, total factor productivity; WBES, World Business Environment Survey.

APPENDIX A.3. Examples of Studies Where the Dependent Variable Is Not a Performance Measure (e.g., GDP per capita or TFP)

Study	Basic method and aim	Dataset	Dependent variable(s)	1. How is business environment measured? 2. Other key right-hand-side variables	Comments on methodology	1. Main findings 2. Explicit policy conclusions	Comments (quantitative importance)
Djankov, McLiesh, and Shleifer (2005)	*Aim: examine the effect of private credit institutions on financial development.* OLS on averaged data + panel	129 countries; 25 years of data. Other sources: IMF, legal sources survey of 440 lawyers from 133 countries	Private credit (percent of GDP)	1. Creditor rights; public registry; private bureau 2. GDP; legal origins	No endogeneity issues discussed	1. Suggests that governments, especially in poorer countries, should facilitate information sharing.	
Djankov, Hart, McLiesh, and Shleifer (2006)	Focus on debt enforcement Index of efficiency of firm liquidation	88 countries	Index of efficiency of firm liquidation Measure of going concern	1. Index of efficiency of firm liquidation (standardized case study of an insolvent firm); measure of going concern 2. GDP; legal origins		Debt enforcement around the world is highly inefficient; is related to underdevelopment; and associated with insufficient public sector capacity of the country and with French legal system.	A 10-point increase in efficiency → a 5–6 point higher ratio of debt to GDP.
Djankov, La Porta, López-de-Silanes, and Shleifer (2003)	Focus on procedural formalism Construct index and subindexes of formalism OLS cross-section	Lex Mundi and Lex Africa questionnaires, 115 countries + other usual variables	Outcomes of the two standard procedures: eviction of a tenant and check collection	1. Index and subindexes of formalism 2. GDP per capita; legal origins; ethnic fractionalization; average years of schooling; latitude		Formalism does not depend on the level of development. Many developing countries inherited their court system from past colonizers.	The explanatory power of regulation of entry is only 4 to 5 percent, compared with the explanatory power of formalism of 18 to 20 percent.

(Continued)

139

APPENDIX A.3. Examples of Studies Where the Dependent Variable Is Not a Performance Measure (e.g., GDP per capita or TFP) (Continued)

Study	Basic method and aim	Dataset	Dependent variable(s)	1. How is business environment measured? 2. Other key right-hand-side variables	Comments on methodology	1. Main findings 2. Explicit policy conclusions	Comments (quantitative importance)
Djankov, La Porta, López-de-Silanes, and Shleifer (2008)	Focus on shareholders rights protection. OLS (mainly)	Questionnaire completed by attorneys from Lex Mundi law firms.	Stock-market capitalization (percent of GDP); block premium; listed firms per million population; IPOs/GDP; ownership concentration	2. Approval by disinterested shareholders; ex ante disclosure; ex ante private control of self-dealing; disclosure in periodic filings; difficulty in proving wrongdoing; ex post private control of self-dealing; GDP per capita; time required to collect on a bounced check	Construct index of the strength of minority shareholder protection against self-dealing by the controlling shareholder (anti-self-dealing index)	1. To avoid self-dealing, it appears best to rely on extensive disclosure, approval by disinterested shareholders, and private enforcement.	Problems with endogeneity (difficult to find IV). Examples: 2 SD (anti-self-dealing index) raises stock market/GDP ratio by 33 percent. 2 SD (ex ante private control of self-dealing) reduces median block premium by 9 percent.

See note at page 141 for key to abbreviations in Appendix A.3.

| Micco and Pagés (2006) | Panel difference-in-differences approach. Studies effects of employment protection on job flows, employment, economic performance | UNIDO. Industry-level (manufacturing) data for 41 countries + country-level data 1985–90 and 1991–5, 65 countries during the 1980s and 1990s | Job flows. Employment value added; labor productivity, number of plants; employment per plant | 1. Average employment, job reallocation
2. Index of employment protection legislation (EPL): administrative costs, monetary costs, and the sum of the two

GDP per capita; accounting standards; property rights

Rule of law; entry costs; entry rates; dependence on external finance

Intangible intensity

Employment; value added; number of establishments; plant size; interactions with job reallocations | Difference-in-differences estimation approach, → reduces the likelihood of omitted variable bias and lessens endogeneity

Follows Rajan and Zingales (1998); Uses U.S. benchmark for sector characteristics, including sector volatility | 1. Employment protection reduces turnover, employment, and value added by reducing the growth of highly volatile sectors. The decline in employment is mostly accounted for by a decline in net entry of firms, with no discernible changes in average employment or output per firm. | Examples: compare the difference in job reallocation in industries in 10th and 90th percentiles of flexibility requirements → difference is 6.31 percentage points lower in a country with strict EPL (90th) than in one with low EPL. When EPL rises from the 10th to the 90th percentile, employment in the 90th most variable sector relative to the 10th most variable sector decreases by 54 percent. |

Source: Authors' compilation.

Note: EPL, employment protection legislation; GDP, gross domestic product; IMF, International Monetary Fund; IV, instrumental variable; IPO, initial public offering; OLS, ordinary least squares; SD, standard deviation; UNIDO, United Nations Industrial Development Organization.

Notes

1. The consensus is not undisputed For instance, Clark (2007) challenges institutionalist explanations of the industrial revolution, on the grounds that a number of medieval economies (such as England from the thirteenth century on) had institutions such as systems of secure property rights in land that, he asserts, would have earned them high marks in any World Bank policy review. Of course, not all researchers who view good institutions as important for development would claim that they are either necessary or sufficient.

2. The most likely reason for this result would be externalities, but general equilibrium effects might be important as well. For instance, managers of existing firms might be correct in thinking that the reduction of tariffs on imports would be bad for their firms but wrong in thinking that it would be bad for the economy as a whole.

3. Patient samples can sometimes cover entire populations, especially in the fields of epidemiology, nutrition, and preventive medicine.

4. For indivisible private goods such as motor vehicles, this is not correct, but the information revelation problem facing a car manufacturer is nevertheless much less severe than that facing a government supplying most public goods.

5. The outliers here are South Asia and East Asia, where fewer countries have problems with access to finance than with most other constraints; Central and Latin America, where tax administration is less problematic than many other constraints; and the OECD, where policy uncertainty is less frequently problematic than are other constraints. Firms in South Asian countries do not rate anticompetitive practices as problematic, nor is this constraint reported as a major problem in African countries.

6. There is some evidence that the externalities may be large at some stages of development (see Roeller and Waverman 2001).

7. The authors appear to misreport the question asked in the surveys, which refers to "economic policy uncertainty" or "regulatory policy uncertainty," not to "political instability."

8. More detailed analysis confirming the precision of the evaluations of the business environment constraints is provided in Carlin, Schaffer, and Seabright (2007).

9. It is not quite accurate to bracket Young (1995) with the others, since Young's study is not strictly a case history but rather the application of a standard methodology—growth accounting—to a subgroup of countries in a way that affects the view we may wish to take about what there is to explain in the East Asian experience. See Hsieh (1999) and Young (1998) for detailed discussion of this evidence.

10. Noland and Pack (2003) claim that Korea's focus on export performance was a beneficial consequence of the widespread cynicism about official corruption: export figures "were the only statistics that couldn't be faked."

11. An example of taking the insights of case studies to a regression framework is the approach used by Carlin and Mayer (2003), who test the idea that specialization in industries with different characteristics interacts with characteristics of a country's financial structure, using cross-country industry-level data (see Appendix A.1 at the end of this paper).

References

Acemoglu, Daron, and Simon Johnson. 2005. "Unbundling Institutions." *Journal of Political Economy* 113 (5): 949–95.

Acemoglu, Daron, Simon Johnson, and James A. Robinson. 2001. "The Colonial Origins of Comparative Development: An Empirical Investigation." *American Economic Review* 91 (5): 1369–1401.

Aghion Philippe, Peter Howitt, and David Mayer-Foulkes. 2005. "The Effect of Financial Development on Convergence: Theory and Evidence." *Quarterly Journal of Economics* 120 (1, February): 173–222.

Amsden, Alice. 1989. *Asia's Next Giant: South Korea and Late Industrialization.* New York, NY: Oxford University Press.

Ayyagari, Meghana, Asli Demirgüç-Kunt, and Vojislav Maksimovic. 2006. "How Important Are Financing Constraints? The Role of Finance in the Business Environment." Policy Research Working Paper 3820, World Bank, Washington, DC.

Bardhan, Pranab. 2004. *Scarcity, Conflicts, and Cooperation: Essays in the Political and Institutional Economics of Development.* Cambridge, MA: MIT Press.

Barro, Robert J. 1997. *Determinants of Economic Growth: A Cross-Country Empirical Study.* Cambridge, MA: MIT Press.

Bastos, Fabiano, and John Nasir. 2004. "Productivity and the Investment Climate: What Matters Most?" Policy Research Working Paper 3335, World Bank, Washington, DC.

Beck Thorsten, Asli Demirgüç-Kunt, and Vojislav Maksimovic. 2005. "Financial and Legal Constraints to Growth: Does Firm Size Matter?" *Journal of Finance* 60 (1, February): 137–77.

Bockstette, Valerie, Areendam Chanda, and Louis Putterman. 2002. "States and Markets: The Advantage of an Early Start." *Journal of Economic Growth* 7 (4): 347–69.

Calderón, C., and L. Servén. 2004. "The Effects of Infrastructure Development on Growth and Income Distribution." Working Paper 270, Central Bank of Chile, Santiago.

Carlin, Wendy, Jonathan Haskel, and Paul Seabright. 2001. "Understanding 'the Essential Fact about Capitalism': Markets, Competition and Creative Destruction." *National Institute Economic Review* 175 (January): 67–84.

Carlin, Wendy, and Colin Mayer. 2003. "Finance, Investment and Growth." *Journal of Financial Economics* 69 (1): 191–226.

Carlin, Wendy, Mark E. Schaffer, and Paul Seabright. 2007. "Where Are the Real Bottlenecks? Evidence from 20,000 Firms in 60 Countries about the Shadow Costs of Constraints to Firm Performance." IZA Discussion Paper 3059, Institute for the Study of Labor (IZA), Bonn, Germany. ftp://repec.iza.org/RePEc/Discussionpaper/dp3059.pdf.

Chang, Ha-Joon. 2002. *Kicking Away the Ladder: Development Strategy in Historical Perspective.* London: Anthem Press.

Clague, Christopher, Philip Keefer, Stephen Knack, and Mancur Olson. 1999. "Contract-Intensive Money: Contract Enforcement, Property Rights, and Economic Performance." *Journal of Economic Growth* 4 (2): 185–211.

Clark, Gregory. 2007. *A Farewell to Alms: A Brief Economic History of the World.* Princeton, NJ: Princeton University Press.

Collier, Paul. 2007. *The Bottom Billion: Why the Poorest Countries Are Failing and What Can Be Done about It.* Oxford: Oxford University Press.

Commander, Simon, and Jan Svejnar. 2007. "Do Institutions, Ownership, Exporting and Competition Explain Firm Performance? Evidence from 26 Transition Countries." London Business School, London.

Der, G., G. David Batty, and Ian J. Deary. 2006. "Effect of Breast Feeding on Intelligence in Children: Prospective Study, Sibling Pairs Analysis, and Meta-analysis." *British Medical Journal* (October 4).

Dixit, Avinash K. 2006. "Evaluating Recipes for Development Success." World Bank Policy Research Working Paper 3859, World Bank, Washington, DC.

Djankov, Simeon, Caralee McLiesh, and Rita Maria Ramalho. 2006. "Regulation and Growth." *Economics Letters* 92 (3): 395–401.

Djankov, Simeon, Caralee McLiesh, and Andrei Shleifer. 2005. "Private Credit in 129 Countries." NBER Working Paper 11078, National Bureau of Economic Research, Cambridge, MA.

Djankov, Simeon, Oliver Hart, Caralee McLiesh, and Andrei Shleifer. 2006. "Debt Enforcement around the World." Working Paper, Harvard University, Cambridge, MA.

Djankov. Simeon, Rafael La Porta, Florencio López-de-Silanes, and Andrei Shleifer. 2003. "Courts." *Quarterly Journal of Economics* 118 (2): 453–517.

———. 2008. "The Law and Economics of Self-Dealing," *Journal of Financial Economics* 88 (3): 430–65.

Dollar, David, Mary Hallward-Driemeier, and Taye Mengistae. 2005. "Investment Climate and Firm Performance in Developing Economies." *Economic Development and Cultural Change* 54 (1): 1–31.

Dyck, Alexander, and Luigi Zingales. 2004. "Private Benefits of Control: An International Comparison." *Journal of Finance* 49 (2): 537–600.

Easterly, William, and Sergio Rebelo. 1993. "Fiscal Policy and Economic Growth: An Empirical Investigation." *Journal of Monetary Economics* 32: 417–58.

Esfahani, Hadi Salehi, and Maria Teresa Ramirez. 2003. "Institutions, Infrastructure, and Economic Growth." *Journal of Development Economics* 70 (2): 443–77.

Fishlow, Albert, Catherine Gwin, Stephan Haggard, and Dani Rodrik. 1996. *Miracle or Design? Lessons from the East Asian Experience.* Washington, DC: Overseas Development Council.

Giavazzi, Francesco, and Guido Tabellini. 2004. "Economic and Political Liberalizations." NBER Working Paper 10657, National Bureau of Economic Research, Cambridge, MA.

Glaeser, Edward L., Rafael La Porta, Florencio López-de-Silanes, and Andrei Shleifer. 2004. "Do Institutions Cause Growth?" *Journal of Economic Growth* 9 (3): 271–303.

Hall, R. E., and C. I. Jones. 1999. "Why Do Some Countries Produce So Much More Output Per Worker Than Others?" *Quarterly Journal of Economics* 114 (1): 83–116.

Hausmann, Ricardo, Dani Rodrik, and Andrés Velasco. 2006. "Growth Diagnostics." *Finance and Development* 43 (1, March). http://www.imf.org/external/pubs/ft/fandd/2006/03/hausmann.htm.

Hsieh, Chang-Tai. 1999. "Productivity Growth and Factor Prices in East Asia." *American Economic Review, Papers and Proceedings* 89 (2): 133–38.

Kaufmann, Daniel, and Aart Kraay. 2002. "Growth without Governance." *Economia* 3 (1): 169–229.

Khan, Mushtaq H. 1998. "Patron-Client Networks and the Economic Effects of Corruption in Asia." *European Journal of Development Research* 10 (1): 15–39.

Khan, Mushtaq H., and Jomo K. S., eds. 2000. *Rents, Rent-Seeking and Economic Development: Theory and Evidence in Asia.* Cambridge: Cambridge University Press.

Knack, Stephen, and Philip Keefer. 1997. "Does Social Capital Have an Economic Payoff? A Cross-Country Investigation." *Quarterly Journal of Economics* 112 (4): 1251–88.

Ledeneva, Alena. 2006. *How Russia Really Works: The Informal Practices That Shaped Post-Soviet Politics and Business.* Ithaca, NY: Cornell University Press

Masters, W. A., and M. S. McMillan. 2001. "Climate and Scale in Economic Growth." *Journal of Economic Growth* 6 (3): 167–86.

Mauro, Paolo. 1995. "Corruption and Growth." *Quarterly Journal of Economics* 110 (3): 681–712.

Micco, Alejandro, and Carmen Pagés. 2006. "The Economic Effects of Employment Protection: Evidence from International Industry-Level Data." IZA Discussion Paper 2433, Institute for the Study of Labor (IZA), Bonn, Germany.

Noland, Marcus, and Howard Pack. 2003. *Industrial Policy in an Era of Globalization: Lessons from East Asia*. Washington, DC: Institute for International Economics.

Page, John. 1994. "The East Asian Miracle: Four Lessons for Development Policy." *NBER Macroeconomics Annual 1994* 9: 219–69.

Pande, Rohini, and Christopher Udry. 2006. "Institutions and Development: A View from Below." In *Proceedings of the 9th World Congress of the Econometric Society*, ed. R. Blundell, W. Newey, and T. Persson. Cambridge: Cambridge University Press.

Rajan, Raghuram G., and Luigi Zingales. 1998. "Financial Dependence and Growth." *American Economic Review* 88 (3): 559–86.

Rodrik, Dani. 1999. "Democracies Pay Higher Wages." *Quarterly Journal of Economics* 114 (3): 707–38.

———. 2004. "Getting Institutions Right." CESifo DICE Report 2/2004: 10–15. CESifo, Munich, Germany. http://www.ifo.de/pls/guestci/download/CESifo+DICE+Report+2004/CESifo+DICE+Report+2/2004/dicereport204-forum2.pdf.

———. 2005. "Why We Learn Nothing from Regressing Economic Growth on Policies." Kennedy School of Government, Harvard University, Cambridge, MA. http://ksghome.harvard.edu/~drodrik/policy%20regressions.pdf.

Rodrik, Dani, Arvind Subramanian, and Francesco Trebbi. 2004. "Institutions Rule: The Primacy of Institutions over Geography and Integration in Economic Development." *Journal of Economic Growth* 9 (2): 131–65.

Roeller, Lars-Hendrik, and Leonard Waverman. 2001. "Telecommunications Infrastructure and Economic Development: A Simultaneous Approach." *American Economic Review* 91 (4): 909–23.

Rose-Ackerman, Susan. 1999. *Corruption and Government: Causes, Consequences, and Reform*. Cambridge: Cambridge University Press.

Schrank, Andrew, and Marcus J. Kurtz. 2005. "Credit Where Credit Is Due: Open Economy Industrial Policy and Export Diversification in Latin America and the Caribbean." *Politics & Society* 33 (4, December): 671–702. http://pas.sagepub.com/cgi/content/abstract/33/4/671.

Seabright, Paul. 2005. "National and European Champions: Burden or Blessing?" Munich Economic Forum, Munich, Germany.

Stiglitz, Joseph, and Shahid Yusuf. 2001. *Rethinking the East Asian Miracle*. Washington, DC: World Bank.

Wade, Robert. 1990. *Governing the Market: Economic Theory and the Role of Government in East Asian Industrialization*. Princeton, NJ: Princeton University Press.

World Bank. 1993. *The East Asian Miracle: Economic Growth and Public Policy*. Policy Research Report. Washington, DC: World Bank.

Young, Alwyn. 1995. "The Tyranny of Numbers: Confronting the Statistical Realities of the East Asian Growth Experience." *Quarterly Journal of Economics* 110 (3): 641–80.

———. 1998. "Alternative Estimates of Productivity Growth in the NICs: A Comment on the Findings of Chang-Tai Hsieh." NBER Working Paper 6657, National Bureau of Economic Research, Cambridge, MA.

Comment on "Bring Me Sunshine: Which Parts of the Business Climate Should Public Policy Try to Fix?" by Wendy Carlin and Paul Seabright

LOH WAH-SING

In their paper, Carlin and Seabright use statistical (mainly regression) analysis complemented by managerial surveys and case studies to delineate the principal elements of the business climate. It is a sound approach for a study of this nature.

Readers with different backgrounds and different expectations will, however, view the contents from different perspectives. One class of readers consists of prospective investors looking for investment in developing countries. This comment will focus on the perceived needs of these readers.

Statistical surveys invariably entail use of historical data and implicitly embrace the assumptions or background associated with generation of the dataset. It is therefore vital to assess whether these assumptions are still relevant for planning future events such as investments.

Carlin and Seabrook study a range of factors contributing to the business climate, as illustrated by figure 3 in their paper. It is noted that members of the Association of Southeast Asian Nations (ASEAN) were not included in the study—except for Vietnam, which was grouped with China in the East Asia category. It is also noted that some of the current actively pursued issues such as investment in the wider perspectives of information and communications technology (ICT), free trade agreements (FTAs), and synergy arising from regionalization are not covered.

A prospective investor would be interested in looking at regions of current and potential high growth. In this respect, it is appropriate to include ASEAN in the analysis. The following information attempts to augment the contents of the paper.

ASEAN as a Growth Region

Philip Kotler is a champion of the idea that regionalization is an emerging trend that is even more important than globalization (Kotler, Kartajaya, and Huan 2007).

At the time of the Bled Conference, Loh Wah-Sing was the Chief Executive Officer of the International Trade Institute of Singapore. Currently, he is the Senior Advisor in Singapore of Fraunhofer-Gesellschaft.

Annual World Bank Conference on Development Economics 2008, Global

ASEAN has been likened to a squadron of geese flying in formation; it has proved itself by realizing the social and economic advantages of group cooperation and dynamics. Trade (total exports and imports of goods) grew from US$10 billion in 1967 (Kotler, Kartajaya, and Huan 2007), when ASEAN was founded, to more than US$1 trillion in 2005.[1] ASEAN's growth rate of gross domestic product (GDP) was 6.0 percent in 2006, with ASEAN-5 (Indonesia, Malaysia, the Philippines, Singapore, and Thailand) achieving 5.6 percent and the other five members (Brunei, Darussalam, Cambodia, Laos People's Democratic Republic, Myanmar, and Vietnam) registering 8.0 percent.[2]

ASEAN has initiated several FTA negotiations with its trading partners with the aim of establishing further competitive advantages. The current status of such agreements is as follows (Chin 2007):

- The ASEAN Free Trade Area (AFTA) was established in January 1992. More than 99 percent of the products in the common effective preferential tariff (CEPT) inclusion list for ASEAN-6 (ASEAN-5 plus Brunei) have been brought down to a tariff range of 0–5 percent.

- The ASEAN–China FTA for trade in goods entered into force in July 2005, and the trade in services agreement was signed in December 2006.

- The ASEAN–Republic of Korea FTA for trade in goods entered into force in June 2007.

- The ASEAN FTA framework agreement with India and Japan was signed in October 2003.

- Negotiations for the ASEAN–Australia–New Zealand FTA were launched in April 2005.

Recent commitments for major investments by multinational corporations in two ASEAN member countries testify to the resilience of ASEAN economies. Intel will invest US$1 billion in Vietnam and employ 4,000 people in what will be the company's largest assembly and test facility anywhere in the world.[3] In the Philippines, Texas Instruments has committed US$1 billion in investments to build a semiconductor testing and assembly plant that is expected to provide employment for 3,000 people. This will be Texas Instruments' second plant in the country; its existing facility accounts for 40 percent of the semiconductor company's global output of assembled chips.[4]

Nimble Response with Rapid Adaptation

Another important element of the business climate is nimbleness in adapting to the rapid pace of technology development or technology change. This can best be illustrated with an example.

When Kikkoman Japan planned to establish soy sauce manufacturing facilities in Singapore in 1983, it encountered an unexpected hurdle: the company was not allowed to label its product as soy sauce. The Japanese process makes use of a blend of soya bean and wheat, whereas in Singapore, at that time, a product was recognized as soy sauce only if it was fermented from soya bean alone. Further aggravating the difficulties, Kikkoman was asked to disclose the proportions of soybean and wheat in its product, which would obviously raise objections from the company.

The Singapore Economic Development Board, the agency responsible for foreign direct investment, intervened and resolved the deadlock. Singapore extended the definition of soy sauce to include the Japanese variety (Egami 2007).

Concluding Remarks

Anecdotes such as those cited here have not proliferated to an extent and time scale amenable to meaningful statistical analysis. They could serve, however, as examples of best practices for decision makers in public policy in order to inculcate an investor-friendly business climate.

Notes

1. "ASEAN Basic Data," ASEAN Annual Report 2004–05, http://www.aseansec.org/AR05/Basic-Data.pdf.
2. "Macroeconomic Indicators," ASEAN Web site, http://www.aseansec.org/18135.htm.
3. "Intel to Build Its Largest Chip Assembly Plant in Vietnam," *Straits Times,* November 13, 2006.
4. "Chip Plant in Philippines Marks Challenge to China," *Wall Street Journal,* May 4, 2007.

References

Chin, David. 2007. "ASEAN plus FTAs: Implications for Singapore Businesses." Presented at Free Trade Agreement Symposium, International Enterprise Singapore and International Trade Institute of Singapore, March.

Egami, G. 2007. "Kabushikigaisha shingapooru no shoutai [Identity of Singapore Incorporated]," *Bungei Shunjuu* (Tokyo), April.

Kotler, Philip, Hermawan Kartajaya, and Den Huan Hooi. 2007. *Think ASEAN! Rethinking Marketing toward ASEAN Community 2015.* Singapore: McGraw-Hill.

Comment on "Bring Me Sunshine: Which Parts of the Business Climate Should Public Policy Try to Fix?" by Wendy Carlin and Paul Seabright

JAN SVEJNAR

The paper by Carlin and Seabright is a careful methodological and empirical study that addresses an important set of issues. The authors have used both survey and secondary data to carry out their analysis. The study is well conceived and executed; it is innovative, and the conclusions are on the whole plausible. It should be read not only by prime ministers, as suggested by the authors, but by policy makers at all levels.

The paper has two key messages: that the business climate is in many respects a public good, and that cross-country regressions, microanalyses based on managers' surveys, country-level growth diagnoses, and country case studies can together provide valuable policy input—although each alone cannot do so. Both messages are intuitively plausible. The first raises the issue of which aspects of the business climate are key and which constraints in the business climate policy makers should hence try to relax. The second raises the issue of what particular mix of analyses is ideal for policy making.

The authors examine critically the principal analytical approaches. With respect to cross-country regressions, they point out that institutional quality may, for instance, be plausibly expected to determine living standards—but that it is difficult to prove causality and exclude alternative explanations. Surveys of managers' opinions yield direct evidence on the relative importance of different business climate constraints, but different firms may face different constraints, and identical constraints may affect different firms differently. Country-level growth diagnosis is useful because it narrows down the choices for a policy maker, but it is hard to take it below the macroeconomic level. Finally, case studies of countries or regions provide rich information that is good for formulating hypotheses but not for testing them. On the basis of this critical

Jan Svejnar is director of the International Policy Center at the Gerald R. Ford School of Public Policy at the University of Michigan, where he is also a professor of economics and public policy. He is a founder and board member of CERGE-EI, Prague.

Annual World Bank Conference on Development Economics 2008, Global

examination, the authors argue that evidence may be used more effectively if the various approaches are combined. In particular, a combination of approaches can provide clearer policy guidance. On the whole, this argument is credible.

The studies reviewed by Carlin and Seabright are mostly econometric exercises based on cross-country data and cross-firm data of managers' opinions—the Business Environment and Enterprise Performance Survey (BEEPS), and the Productivity and Investment Climate Survey (PICS). The authors also examine country- or regional-level case analyses. They do not do carry out new estimations but report on their earlier research.

Several issues arise in the context of this paper. The first relates to productivity and constraints. The authors' premise is that within a country, more productive firms are more constrained by the business environment; they are ahead of others and "bump against the constraint." Carlin and Seabright then reason that if one does not find this to be the case, there is prima facie evidence that the particular aspect of the environment is not a pure public good. Empirically, they find the premise to be supported for customs but not for electricity or access to finance. The problem with the authors' argument is that if one finds that more productive firms are more constrained by the business environment, there could be other reasons than the fact that the particular aspect of the environment is not a pure public good. For example, less constrained firms could become more productive, or more productive firms might become better at getting around the constraints—for example, by acquiring skills, adapting (pre-saving), or paying bribes. One must therefore be careful to account for alternative explanations of the same phenomenon.

The second issue relates to the presence of contradictory findings. For instance, the econometric estimates of some studies (Dollar, Hallward-Driemeier, and Mengistae 2005; Ayyagari, Demirgüç-Kunt, and Maksimovic 2006) do not accord with the authors' tabulations. The problem may be endogeneity, but there may be other explanations as well. Carlin and Seabright should, for instance, look at both the intensity and the variance of ratings of constraints, not just whether a given constraint is rated as being above or below average. Regression coefficients will, for instance, be low if the given constraints are highly binding for all firms in all countries. So one needs to check whether there is low variation in some ratings across firms.

The third issue stems from the idea that it is useful to combine growth diagnostics with manager information. The authors have a splendid idea here of exploiting complementarity of approaches, and this is excellent when it works—that is, when macroeconomic and manager data yield similar results. The problem arises when the two sets of results differ or are not sufficiently informative. This is observed, for instance, for Brazil (macro) versus El Salvador (micro) in figure 6 in the paper. In particular, corruption in Brazil is rated at about 3.4 and macroeconomic issues at about 3.6, while in El Salvador corruption is rated at about 2.5 and macroeconomic issues at about 2.3 to 2.4. In these cases there is not much within-country difference on which to hinge major policies.

Finally, there is a methodological point that is worth mentioning. The authors emphasize that cross-country analysis can only provide information about the relationship between performance and business environment variables for the average country.

In fact, one can go further. For example, one can split the sample or perform quantile regressions and thereby provide estimates that relate to parts of the distribution other than just averages.

What is to be done next? I think the greatest payoff would come from sharpening the ability of researchers to exploit the aforementioned complementarity of approaches. Two ideas come to mind. First, it would be useful to collect panel (rather than repeated cross-section) data on firms and managers' opinions. The panel data would better enable researchers to handle endogeneity, cross-firm heterogeneity, and country effects. Second, it would be desirable to collect data for duration analysis. For example, one could follow a sample of start-up firms over time to study better the effect of the business environment on their performance and exit. (Exit is rarely studied because surveys usually cover firms that have survived to the date of the survey.) Similarly, one could collect data on college or business school graduates to examine the incidence of entrepreneurship and firm formation (entry), performance, and exit.

Overall, Carlin and Seabright ought to be congratulated on writing an exciting paper that deals with an important topic and provides new and plausible interpretations of observed outcomes.

References

Ayyagari, Meghana, Asli Demirgüç-Kunt, and Vojislav Maksimovic. 2006. "How Important Are Financing Constraints? The Role of Finance in the Business Environment." Policy Research Working Paper 3820, World Bank, Washington, DC.

Dollar, David, Mary Hallward-Driemeier, and Taye Mengistae. 2005. "Investment Climate and Firm Performance in Developing Economies." *Economic Development and Cultural Change* 54 (1): 1–31.

Comment on "Reforming Public Service Delivery," by Timothy Besley and Maitreesh Ghatak

JEAN-PAUL AZAM

Are nongovernmental organizations (NGOs) credible providers of public goods to mitigate the well-known failures of both the market and the state? The NGO sector has emerged over the recent past as a central actor in development policy. In their paper, Besley and Ghatak present most of the arguments brought out in the literature, to which they have contributed the lion's share. Most of their examples are taken from the involvement of NGOs in the provision of education and health services. The NGO sector is perceived as a "third way" between the government and the market. The emphasis is on organizational and motivational issues, and the suggestion is that the main edge of NGOs over both states and for-profit firms comes from their ability to select "better" people to do jobs in that sector. NGOs, it is argued, attract more "principled" people—to use the expression coined by Besley in the title of his recent book on democratic control of politicians (Besley 2006). These people are more devoted than the average person to the provision of public goods for the community, either because they are more altruistic or because of their ideological bent, and this results in cheaper and better delivery of public services. The paper shows the potential advantages of NGOs over the "bureaucratic sphere," resulting mainly from that selection effect.

The main problems in service provision are identified in this paper under three headings: ignorance, resources, and delivery. Ignorance is a key issue in most service industries and even in some goods production, when a wide variety of dimensions exists along which "quality" can be measured. The very concept of "output" is not immediately defined, since what is at stake is really to have some effect on the target

This comment refers to "Reforming Public Service Delivery," by Timothy Besley and Maitreesh Ghatak. That paper, published in 2007 in the *Journal of African Economies* (vol. 16, no. 1, pp. 127–56), was read at the conference by Mr. Ghatak.

Jean-Paul Azam is professor of economics at the Toulouse School of Economics and the Institut Universitaire de France. He is director of the Atelier de Recherche Quantitative Appliquée au Développement Economique (ARQADE), and a research fellow at the Institut d'Économie Industrielle (IDEI), both in Toulouse. The author's helpful discussion with Isabel Günter is gratefully acknowledged.

Annual World Bank Conference on Development Economics 2008, Global

population, such as increased school attendance or improvements in infants' health, rather than to administer this or that intervention. The private sector has resolved this issue by devising clever contracts—for example, in scientific experiments with uncertain outcomes—while the bureaucratic sphere has a clear preference for measuring inputs.

The provision of public services raises special issues that preclude the use of simple contracts. The potential beneficiaries are usually numerous and have neither the opportunity to express their evaluation of the outcome nor a clear incentive to tell the truth; complaining might always be the dominant strategy. Besley and Ghatak side with the current dominant doctrine in the profession, which is to use randomized experiments for evaluating the impact of policy interventions in the field of public service delivery. There are, however, political-economy issues lurking behind the placement of public programs. Politicians might have an incentive to get the spending done for their constituency rather than truly allocated at random, and they might have a vested interest in directing a particular type of spending to some specific area, which might outweigh the long-run benefit of improved knowledge about program effects. Moreover, other types of surveys may be valuable, such as those described by Reinikka and Svensson (2004) that focus on the actual channeling of funds by the administrative sector to the targeted beneficiaries.

The resource issue has a political dimension, as well as an institutional one. Besley and Ghatak report results suggesting that the type of democracy matters, with presidential regimes being associated with less corruption and lower levels of public spending. But beyond the empirical regularities identified in the literature, there are deeper normative issues involved in the determination of the level of public spending for public services. Insofar as political institutions are endogenous in the long run, one might conjecture that some countries want both less spending and more accountability under a directly elected president, while others might prefer looser democratic control, with proportional voting and political parties that play more of a liaison role in getting additional public spending (beyond what the median voter would choose).

At a theoretical level, there is a further issue that is overlooked in the paper: the way in which civil society can influence the outcome by exerting pressure on the government or the civil service. As the discussion of the selection effect mentioned earlier suggests, the people who get involved in NGO activity tend to be more altruistic, more "principled." This is also true at the political level, and these people certainly want more social or development spending than the median voter. NGOs conduct powerful lobbying activities in many developed countries; in the United States, for example, many NGOs with charitable or humanitarian goals have specialized in advocacy and lobbying rather than in service delivery.

When majority rule prevails, however, NGOs are naturally pushed toward providing additional resources to improve the quality and quantity of service delivered, reflecting their above-average level of altruism. For example, in France les restos du coeur (free popular restaurants) provide free meals to the needy in winter on a purely voluntary basis. Numerous other examples could be found in most developed countries and in many other activities such as popular education. This creates a free-rider problem that has been analyzed by Azam (2003); because NGOs have a credible commitment to achieve certain levels of popular well-being, the government has a clear incentive to free ride on them. Spending less money or effort on some social problem is morally and politically less costly when it is known that civil society will step in to fill the gap. The free-riding problem can in fact be mitigated if NGOs become involved in the political game to exert pressure on politicians.

Thus, the discussion of the role of nonstate actors in public service provision cannot be limited to that of improving delivery. NGOs cannot maintain a "hands-off" attitude toward the political game; they necessarily get involved in it in order to provide the right incentives to the government. Otherwise, the fruit of their effort might be offset by the government's free riding. Nevertheless, this does not solve the deeper problem of deciding whether civil society may legitimately impose a higher level of social spending than the median voter wants.

Besley and Ghatak devote considerable attention to the way in which NGOs can substitute for the public sector in service delivery. Nonstate actors can easily be held accountable for their actions by simple contracts, while competition among NGOs pushes them to improve the quality and lower the cost of their services. This gives them a competitive advantage over the civil service, where accountability is much looser and too-powerful incentive schemes could turn out to be counterproductive. In the sphere of service delivery, however, the authors tend to exaggerate the opposition between government and civil society. In fact, NGOs can also influence the quality of service delivery by the government. This is true, in particular, in the environment sector. Many NGOs in Europe and the United States are acting as whistle-blowers, mobilizing people to exert pressure on politicians when environmental issues are ignored by the civil service. This is especially true of localized pollution of rivers or of the countryside by public or private firms—something politicians or civil servants tend to overlook for various reasons. Such complementarities between the quality of public sector service delivery and oversight by civil society are illustrated by Azam and Rinaudo (2004). On the basis of survey work, they show how farmers' associations in Pakistan are exerting political pressure on local politicians to put in place more controls over corruption and the illicit appropriation of irrigation water by powerful people. Reinikka and Svensson (2004) have emphasized how the mere disclosure of information about dysfunctional service delivery by the public sector can bring about improvements and how NGOs can be mobilized to do that. Unfortunately, this role of information disclosure is not foolproof, since it can be manipulated to increase the demand for the services of NGOs by spreading falsified or exaggerated evaluations or, for simple electoral reasons, to embarrass the government.

In the real world, these multiple activities of NGOs are not limited to service delivery, advocacy, and lobbying. Ly (2007b) shows how hybrid NGOs have flourished in many countries, delivering many other things in addition to public services. For example, in Bangladesh, which Ly studies in great detail, the Grameen Bank and the BRAC have built a profitable commercial empire in addition to their highly effective social activity. The resulting flow of privately generated money plays a useful role in public service delivery by providing some insurance against the vagaries of the flow of donations and public contracts. Moreover, pursuing such charitable and humanitarian activities is a good substitute for standard advertisement. These efforts generate a great deal of goodwill from customers, with a positive impact on the outlets for NGOs' commercial activities. Hence, these NGOs might have an incentive to produce even more social services than their "principled-ness" would entail, for the sake of reinforcing their commercial activities. What specialists in competition policy have to say about this, given that NGOs receive some fiscal advantage, remains to be seen.

Moreover, some other hybrid NGOs are producing additional activities whose social value might be more questionable. This is illustrated by Ly (2007a), using the example of the charitable activities of terrorist NGOs. There is no doubt that most of the health and education services delivered in Palestine or in some parts of Lebanon would not have existed had it not been for the actions of such terrorist organizations as Hamas or Hezbollah. Similar comments can be made about other countries, such as Sri Lanka. In all these cases, the complementarity between the charitable and the terrorist activities might not be socially innocuous. Nevertheless, Ly suggests that overall, the main effect of the charitable activities of terrorist organizations is to reduce the incentives for perpetrating terrorist attacks. The latter tend to have negative fallout for the organizations' charitable activities, if only because they trigger intensified police activity and repression, which the hybrid organizations would internalize. Hence, forcing the two types of activities to be run by separate entities—for example, by cutting donations to humanitarian NGOs with direct links to terrorist organizations—would be counterproductive, since it would remove an incentive for moderation.

All these comments show that the discussion presented in the paper by Besley and Ghatak opens many additional avenues that can be fruitfully explored to analyze the issue of the provision of public services by nonstate actors at both the positive and the normative levels. This is to be welcomed, since NGO interventions have become a pervasive phenomenon throughout the developing and the developed worlds, and people tend to adopt highly emotional or ideological views about them. Dispassionate and analytical research is needed to inform donors' attitudes toward NGOs. Besley and Ghatak have established a strong bridgehead in that research area, which is taking development economics far beyond the traditional government–market dichotomy.

References

Azam, Jean-Paul. 2003. "A Theory of Poverty Aversion and Civil Society Development." *Economics and Politics* 15 (1, March): 61–84.

Azam, Jean-Paul, and Jean-Daniel Rinaudo. 2004. "Encroached Entitlements: Corruption and Appropriation of Irrigation Water in Southern Punjab (Pakistan)." IDEI Working Paper 252, Institut d'Économie Industrielle, Toulouse, France. http://idei.fr/doc/wp/2004/encroached_entitlements.pdf.

Besley, Timothy. 2006. *Principled Agents? The Political Economy of Good Governance.* Lindhal Lectures on Monetary and Fiscal Policy. Oxford: Oxford University Press.

Besley, Timothy, and Maitreesh Ghatak. 2007. "Reforming Public Service Delivery." *Journal of African Economies* 16 (1): 127–56.

Ly, Pierre E. 2007a. "The Charitable Activities of Terrorist Organizations." *Public Choice* 131: 177–95.

———. 2007b. "The Commercial Activities of NGOs." University of Toulouse, Toulouse, France.

Reinikka, Ritva, and Jakob Svensson. 2004. "The Power of Information: Evidence from Public Expenditure Tracking Surveys." In *Global Corruption Report 2004.* Berlin: Transparency International.

Comment on "Reforming Public Service Delivery," by Timothy Besley and Maitreesh Ghatak

GÁBOR PÉTERI

Beginning in the late 1970s, the focus of public sector reforms shifted from primarily structural issues toward procedures and capacity development. As a consequence, the organizational and management aspects of public administration and public service provision received greater emphasis in modernization programs. The change in emphasis was reflected in a change in terminology whereby *governance,* as an all-embracing phrase, became a generally used technical term. Since then, good governance has turned into an overall objective of public sector reforms that would increase legitimacy and improve public decision making and policy implementation capacity.

The move from structural issues toward the procedural aspects of reforms also demonstrated improved knowledge about how the public sector works. Better understanding of social and cultural factors in shaping government systems has proved that there is great variety in effective public service provision. Differences in values and norms lead to diversity in management techniques and financing methods. Solutions developed in a country—or, in the case of decentralized services, by a particular local government—might not work in another political-administrative environment (Clark and Hoffmann-Martinot 1998).

This general rule that there are no standardized methods in public service provision is particularly applicable to the use of nonstate actors. Heated professional and political debates have taken place about the role of the private sector in managing public functions. These discussions, however, often ignore the historical differences behind the diverse forms of cooperation between the public and private sectors or neglect the critical regulatory conditions for successful involvement of the nonstate sectors.

This comment refers to "Reforming Public Service Delivery," by Timothy Besley and Maitreesh Ghatak. That paper, published in 2007 in the *Journal of African Economies* (vol. 16, no. 1, pp. 127–56), was read at the conference by Mr. Ghatak.

Gábor Péteri is director of development at LGI Development Ltd. (LGID) (OSI), which is affiliated with the Open Society Network.

Annual World Bank Conference on Development Economics 2008, Global

My comments on the paper by Besley and Ghatak focus on three basic questions:

1. How diverse is the nonstate sector, and who are the nongovernmental organizations (NGOs)?
2. What are the main elements of the regulatory framework for successful contracting with NGOs?
3. How can service beneficiaries' power be increased in public service provision?

Who Are the NGOs (Nonstate Actors)?

The diversity among NGOs is reflected in the great variety of approaches toward defining them. The most typical term, NGO, focuses on the institutional aspects of these organizations, which separate them from the government. This functional approach reflects the special characteristic of NGOs: they are not part of the public sector. But they are not simple business entities, and so, because of the scope of their activities and the voluntary nature of their constituents, they are often called civil society organizations (CSOs).

Another definition highlights the financial side of these organizations' operations. A surplus realized by nonprofit organizations (NPOs) cannot be distributed among the founders, and usually special tax rules apply to these organizations. A subgroup of NGOs is identified by their goals and special government funding schemes. These are the public benefit organizations (PBOs), which provide services desired by the larger community (Koncz 2005).

All these organizations have slightly different agendas and motivations in their daily operations. This is the main reason why the definition of NGO varies greatly by country. It also makes comparison of NGOs' roles in public service provision difficult (Salamon, Sokolowski, and List 2003). Even the basic statistics on the number of CSOs in a country are not always kept up to date. In addition, because of differences in definition (how to categorize churches, religious organizations, chambers with mandatory membership, and so on), internationally comparative data are available only through special research.

Surveys show vast differences in the significance of civil society organizations (Zimmer and Priller 2004). In the United Kingdom, with its traditional, highly developed voluntary sector (charities), the CSO workforce as a percentage of the economically active population is 8.5 percent. The transition countries of Central Europe, with evolving philanthropy and newly (re)established NGOs, have much smaller shares: 2 percent in the Czech Republic, 1.1 percent in Hungary, and 0.8 percent in Poland and in the Slovak Republic.

These survey data do not properly describe the specific role of NGOs in public service provision. As an example, data from Hungary show great diversity of alternative service delivery arrangements on the local government level (table 1). According to these data, in the area of human services, nonstate actors have reached a "critical mass." In public education there are alternative service organizations in 10 percent of the municipalities. As a result of specific privatization rules in basic

TABLE 1. Alternative Service Organizations, Hungary

Municipal service	Percent of municipalities with nonmunicipal service organizations	NGOs as percent of
General practitioner	43.2	2
Dentistry	33.3	3
Primary school	10.6	91
Home for elderly	10.1	78
Kindergarten	9.9	5

Source: Péteri (2007).

health care services, the share of nonstate actors is higher there, with general practitioners in 43 percent of the municipalities and dentists in 33 percent. But these contractors work within rather diverse organizational forms. NGOs are typical only in primary schools and homes for the elderly, while kindergartens, general practitioners, and dentists operate as business entities.

The quality of services provided by these nonstate service organizations in the public sector is determined by several actors and regulations. As summarized in *World Development Report 2004* (World Bank 2003), there are two critical elements of this complex relationship: (a) the "compact" between governments and the service producers, and (b) the forms for expressing client power with respect to service organizations. This triangle of government, clients, and service providers is very much influenced by administrative structures and the scope and forms of decentralization. Use of this explanatory model permits better characterization of the role of NGOs in service provision.

What Are the Conditions for Good Contracting?

Since the 1980s, one of the most important features of New Public Management reforms has been the separation of the functions of service provider and service producer. This is based on the concept of enabling the government, which is not directly responsible for actual service delivery but has to guarantee the necessary conditions for effective services. It has led to a split between client and contractor roles, retaining public authorities' ultimate responsibility but using private or nonstate service organizations for service delivery. Within this framework, customers, as beneficiaries of public services, are able to influence service performance more directly.

The client-contractor split has also made the service provider's role more complex. In the case of human services, when local or national governments are legally responsible for service provision, the actual regulatory and funding decisions might also be separated. Political decisions on public services are made by two entities—for example, in decentralized health care, by local governments and health insurance funds, and in public education, often through municipalities and specific or block grant schemes that target schools.

Learning Policy Development

The more refined roles of the government and the increased influence of beneficiaries transformed politicians' tasks, as well. At the national level the government's policy-making functions became more important than its former direct involvement in public service management. Traditional overall responsibilities of ministers changed, with added new functions such as planning; strategy design; establishment of auditing, supervisory mechanisms, performance measurement, and external control; and launching of sectoral information systems.

The "ignorance" of policy makers mentioned in the paper gradually diminished because of external forces. Regulatory impact assessment became a legal requirement in the legislative process, and governments gained experience in using these new methods. Within the European Union (EU), the open method of coordination (OMC) began to be more widely exercised. OMC is a process for agreeing on common objectives, establishing indicators for comparison, translating EU objectives into action plans, and monitoring their implementation (LGI 2005).

In parallel with improved policy making on the government side, policy research and design capacity has been developed. In transition countries the former state planning organizations and the academic institutions were transformed or were replaced by issue-oriented, flexible, visible, and often more influential think tanks. Emergence of these policy institutes has improved the governments' relationship with the media and with advocacy groups.

Building the Regulatory Framework

Within this new policy-making environment, the compact between governments and nonstate actors is influenced by the overall regulatory framework. In transition and developing countries the first dilemma in establishing the regulatory system for contracting out is sequencing: whether extensive use of nonstate actors can be promoted before the regulatory framework is completed. Examples from developed countries show that privatization and the use of market-based mechanisms were initiated within a highly developed regulatory system, unlike the situation in developing countries, where often the public monopolies are replaced with private ones. Lack of proper regulation of tendering, contracting, and financing mechanisms will decrease the efficiency of contracted services (Horváth and Péteri 2001).

Another external factor influencing the use of nonstate actors is the scope of devolution in the public sector. In general, accountability is greater in the case of decentralized services. Services are more often contracted out in decentralized systems, and forms of cooperation with private service producers are more diverse. Local governments, working under fiscal pressure, are often more successful in finding new, innovative forms of service delivery.

The regulatory framework for using nonstate actors in public service provision depends on the diversity of organizational forms. The traditional budgetary organizations, operating under strict financial rules and with limited incentives, have to be supplemented by more business-oriented entities. Usually, the classical forms of companies are legislated in emerging market economies, but the more refined forms of nonprofit organization have to be introduced in practice.

When these diverse alternative service organizations and forms of cooperation (for example, concessions) are in place and widely known, the next step is the establishment of tendering and contracting regulations. Purchase of public services should be adjusted to the general public procurement system. This would require special procedures for services of general public interest and some complementary regulations—for example, on the compulsory use of services.

Financing schemes should be adjusted to the market-based mechanisms of service provision. As user charges assume a greater role in funding contracted municipal services, the lower tiers of government should enjoy greater autonomy in setting fees and charges. Obviously, this will affect subsidies and methods of managing problems of arrears and nonpayment. Capital investment financing schemes are also important tools for regulating client-contractor relations, since they are based on shared funding responsibilities through matching grants, subsidized loans, and so on.

How Can Clients' Power Be Increased?

The other critical dimension of involving nonstate actors in public service provision is the direct linkage between the service organizations and the beneficiaries. The role of customers as beneficiaries of the contracted services depends greatly on the funding scheme. Incentives within government units or in service organizations are much influenced by intergovernmental fiscal relations. In the case of decentralized public services, local governments are interested in using alternative forms of service delivery if the transfer system supports diversity and leaves sufficient autonomy in municipal spending.

Per capita grants allocated by users of public service organizations and the gap-filling method of national budget grant allocation do not provide incentives for lower-level governments to search for efficient forms of service provision. Block grants allocated through needs-based formulas and standardized expenditure and revenue capacity-based allocation schemes make local governments more interested in finding alternative service organizations.

The direct influence of users on service providers can be influenced by greater neutrality in funding public services. Voucher schemes are based on the concept that public or private service organizations are eligible for similar grant amounts based on units of service (assuming that the performed services are standardized, as well).

The general trend in financing CSOs is that they have a balanced revenue structure. Sample-based statistical data on financing CSOs shows that in developed countries government grants, user charges, and revenues from philanthropy (donations) account for more or less equal shares. In the developing and transition countries CSOs are predominantly funded through charges and voluntary contributions; government financial input is minimal. This is an important factor explaining country differences in the use of nonstate actors. In developing countries classical public functions are less often contracted to NGOs, and NGOs are limited to activities directly financed through charges.

Beyond improving service users' direct influence, client power can be increased by eliminating the main obstacles to cooperation in NGOs and in governments. The paper and the plenary presentation listed some impediments in nonprofit organizations. The often-cited argument against NGOs is lack of accountability, which could lead to elitism or political capture. Issue-oriented civil society organizations sometimes lack sufficient professional capacity. This amateurism might narrow their focus when only a specific group of beneficiaries is served, but governments need broader service coverage. Grant dependency could lead to insufficiency in funding, which makes NGOs financially weak and unstable. Usually, there are geographic differences in the location of registered NGOs. They are more frequently available in urban areas, and often CSO capacity in villages does not match municipal demand.

There are several obstacles on the government's side, as well. NGOs' functions often go beyond pure service provision; they promote certain agendas and carry out advocacy. This mixed characteristic of CSOs exposes them politically, and consequently local elected officials establish selective partnerships with them. NGOs may be differentially informed, resulting in unequal positions in tendering and contracting public services.

At the same time, reputable NGOs are able to promote politicians or specific political programs, which also increases differences in access to public contracts. Chances of individual deals between NGOs and the government are greater if the contracting procedures are not regulated or if conflict of interest regulations are absent or are not followed.

Depending on the mission and management style of local governments, there might be fears of losing control over service performance on the clients' side. This is a result of insufficient information on NGOs and lack of monitoring capacity on the part of the local administration.

References

Besley, Timothy, and Maitreesh Ghatak. 2007. "Reforming Public Service Delivery." *Journal of African Economies* 16 (1): 127–56.

Clark, Terry Nichols, and Vincent Hoffmann-Martinot, eds. 1998. *The New Political Culture.* Boulder, CO: Westview Press.

Horváth, M. T., and Gábor Péteri, eds. 2001. "Navigation to the Market: Regulation and Competition in the Local Utility Sector in CEE." Open Society Institute (OSI)/Local Governance and Public Service Reform Initiative (LGI), Budapest.

Koncz, Katalin E., ed. 2005. "NGO Sustainability in Central Europe: Helping Civil Society Survive." Open Society Institute (OSI)/Local Governance and Public Service Reform Initiative (LGI), Budapest.

LGI (Local Governance and Public Service Reform Initiative). 2005: "Doing while Learning: How Governments Use Policy Advice?" *Local Governance Brief* (Budapest), Spring–Summer.

Péteri, Gábor. 2007. "Greater Responsibilities, Modified Tasks, New Roles: Changes in Local Services and Municipal Decision Making, according to the Mayors (1991–2006)." Hungarian Institute of Public Administration, Budapest.

Salamon, Lester M., S. Wojciech Sokolowski, and Regina List. 2003. *Global Civil Society: An Overview.* Baltimore, MD: Johns Hopkins University Institute for Policy Studies.

World Bank. 2003. *World Development Report 2004: Making Services Work for Poor People.* Washington, DC: World Bank.

Zimmer, Annette, and Eckhard Priller, eds. 2004. *Future of Civil Society: Making Central European Nonprofit Organizations Work.* Wiesbaden, Germany: Robert Bosch Foundation.

Themes and Participants for the

ANNUAL WORLD BANK CONFERENCE ON

DEVELOPMENT ECONOMICS—GLOBAL

Cape Town, South Africa

"PEOPLE, POLITICS, AND GLOBALIZATION"

June 9-11, 2008

Trade and Investment
Migration, Remittances, and Transition from Foreign Aid
Higher Education and High-tech Industries
Human Development
Political Economy

Justin Lin • Melvin Ayogu • Jean-Paul Azam • Boubakar Barry • Rakesh
Basant • Ruxanda Berlinschi • Pankaj Chandra • Nazmul Chaudhury •
Jean-Luc Demonsant • Anil Deolalikar • Lawrence Edwards • Alan Gelb •
Stephen Gelb • Flore Gubert • Lakshmi Iyer • Beata Javorcik • Bassma
Kodmani • Trevor Manuel • Thabo Mbeki • Partha Mukhopadhyay • Sunil
Kant Munjal • Caglar Ozden • Francisco Rodriguez • Erik Sander •
Akilagpa Sawyerr • Paul Schultz • Michael Spence • John Strauss •
Arvind Subramanian • Harsha Thirumurthy • Duncan Thomas •
Ashutosh Varshney • Tony Venables • Shahid Yusuf

Look for publication of the proceedings from this conference in the December 2009
under the title *Annual World Bank Conference on Development Economis 2009,
Global: People, Politics, and Globalization* (ISBN 978-0-8213-7722-2).